Educating Teachers
for Leadership
and Change

Teacher Education Yearbook

Volume 3   *Founded 1991*

Editors

Mary John O'Hair, *University of Oklahoma*
Sandra J. Odell, *Western Michigan University*

Assistant Editor

Angela McNabb Spaulding, *Texas Tech University*

Educating Teachers for Leadership and Change

Teacher Education Yearbook III

Editors

Mary John O'Hair
Sandra J. Odell

Association of Teacher Educators

CORWIN PRESS, INC.
A Sage Publications Company
Thousand Oaks, California

For information address:

Corwin Press, Inc.
A Sage Publications Company
2455 Teller Road
Thousand Oaks, California 91320

SAGE Publications Ltd.
6 Bonhill Street
London EC2A 4PU
United Kingdom

SAGE Publications India Pvt. Ltd.
M-32 Market
Greater Kailash I
New Delhi 110 048 India

Printed in the United States of America

Teacher Education Yearbook ISSN 1078-2265

ISBN 0-8039-6216-9 (cl). — ISBN 0-8039-6217-7 (pb).

The paper in this book meets the specifications for permanence of the American National Standards Institute and the National Association of State Textbook Administrators

95 96 97 98 99 10 9 8 7 6 5 4 3 2 1

Corwin Press Project Editor: Susan McElroy

This book is dedicated to all teacher leaders in democratic schools who listen to the needs of their local communities, who constantly ask "Is this the best decision for students?," who debate the big issues affecting teaching and learning, and who act on their beliefs and convictions.

M.J.O.

This book is dedicated to Douglas P. Ferraro, who has helped me understand many of the complex dimensions of effective leadership and who has been my courageous partner in facing the challenges of personal and professional change.

S.J.O.

Contents

Foreword

Thomas J. Sergiovanni is Lillian Radford Professor of Education and Administration at Trinity University, San Antonio. Prior to joining the Trinity faculty he was for 18 years Professor of Educational Administration and Supervision at the University of Illinois (UC). A former associate editor of *Educational Administration Quarterly*, Dr. Sergiovanni serves on the editorial boards of *The Journal of Educational Research*, *The Journal of Curriculum and Supervision*, and *The Journal of Personnel Evaluation in Education*. He has broad interests in the areas of school leadership and the supervision and evaluation of teaching. Among his recent publications are *Value-Added Leadership: How to Get Extraordinary Performance in Schools* (1990); *The Principalship: A Reflective Practice Perspective* (2nd edition, 1991); and *Moral Leadership: Getting to the Heart of School Improvement* (1992), all based on his extensive studies of leadership in successful enterprises and his collection of "memorable leadership incidents" from school leaders. His most recent book is *Building Community in Schools* (1994).

Dare we redefine the profession of teaching? Dare we challenge the basic theories that drive today's schools? Dare we think and act differently in schools of education? Yes, we dare—if we dare educate teachers for leadership and change, the theme of this fertile and empowering yearbook.

New ground is broken in every section of this book as the authors struggle to provide a theory for the work that lies ahead, discuss complex issues, and share glimpses of practice through the eyes of research. Preparing teachers for new leadership and change roles involves issues of process and substance woven together with issues of virtue. New habits must be cultivated. New competencies must be developed. And new moral commitments must be made. Process, substance, and virtue are recurring themes throughout the book.

Particularly noteworthy is that the chapters are crafted by authors who represent both teacher education and educational administration. Included in this latter group are change theorists and experts on school reform. This combination works very well. I hope the idea catches on.

With all of these pluses, finding the book to be an easy read was a pleasant surprise. In part the easy reading results from the use of "respondents" who introduce each of the book's sections, and then summarize by providing a critique of each chapter and drawing conclusions about all of the section's chapters. The respondents are brilliant. Unlike the typical edited book, in which introductory sections tend toward the perfunctory, some of the yearbook's best thinking appears in these sections.

Professionalism is often viewed narrowly and often gets bogged down in technical-rationality and themes of expertness. This view is reminiscent of Mr. Lewis's soliloquy on professionalism that appears in Kazuo Ishiguro's *The Remains of the Day*:

> Now we're all being so frank, I'll be frank too. You gentlemen here, forgive me, but you are just a bunch of naive dreamers. And if you didn't insist on meddling in large affairs that affect the globe, you would actually be charming. Let's take our good host here. . . . Decent, honest, well-meaning. But His Lordship here is an amateur. . . . The days when you could act out of your noble instincts are over. . . . You here in Europe need professionals to run your affairs. If you don't realize that soon, you're headed for disaster. A toast, gentlemen. Let me make a toast to professionalism. (p. 102)

This yearbook makes a different kind of toast to professionalism. Virtue, moral purpose, democratic principles, and goodness are considered to be important to both the quest for educating teachers for leadership and change, and the substance of that education. The editors and authors, it appears, seek a return to "the days when you could act out of your noble instincts." Sixty-one years have passed since George Counts gave his famous speech, "Dare the Schools Build a New Social Order?" This yearbook's call to educate teachers for leadership and change is much more modest in purpose and scope than the social reconstructionism proposed by Counts. But I think he would have liked this book nonetheless.

Thomas J. Sergiovanni
Radford Professor of Education and Administration

Reference

Ishiguro, K. (1989). *The remains of the day*. London: Faber and Faber.

Message From the President of the Association of Teacher Educators: The Study of Change

Thomas J. Buttery is a professor in the Department of Elementary and Middle Grades Education at East Carolina University. He is the 1994-1995 President of the Association of Teacher Educators (ATE). As a researcher, he has twice been the recipient of ATE's Distinguished Research Award. He is a two-time recipient of the University of Alabama's Academic Excellence Award for Faculty and was named a Distinguished Alumnus of Kean College.

Reform and restructure seem to be the key words of the 1990s. The goals and aspiration of education are fraught with perplexing challenges that have produced a barrage of professional and media critical commentary, some accurate and some misleading. How do we know the difference? The problems of education in general and the concerns of teacher education in particular must be examined with a sense of intellectual curiosity. We must learn to pose the right questions if we hope to uncover the right answers. Philosophically we must learn to question our own questions; however, it is imperative we understand that rarely can we fully answer all our questions. Even if we could, the answers are not guaranteed to make the solutions more palatable.

Alvin Toffler (1970) helped to shape our perceptions about change in *Future Shock*. This was followed a little more than a decade later by John Naisbitt's (1982) *Megatrends*. In his treatise, "The New America for the Third Millennium," Bill Georgiades (1988) observed that the past 2000 years have been ones of dynamic and unbelievable human change. However, nearly three fourths of that period transpired without European culture even knowing of the Americas, and an additional 300 years lay between this time and the Industrial Revolution. The postindustrial era, the period of most rapid change, comprises only 2% of this total time period. He stipulates that the process of rapid change continues to accelerate on a daily basis with virtually no slowdown in sight.

Georgiades (1988) goes on to observe that the rapid-fire change affecting our society at large also has a direct impact on the schools and the education of teachers. Among the changes most relevant to education are the shifting ethnicity of the United States; the changing nature and structure of the family; different ways of viewing those with handicaps; and forces such as technology, a shrinking world, and changing values.

Stephen Covey, in his books *The 7 Habits of Highly Effective People* (1989) and *Principle Centered Leadership* (1991) calls for a paradigm shift in how individuals and organizations handle problems if we are to survive and thrive amid tremendous change. Additionally, Robert Kriegel and Louis Patler (1991) posit in *If It Ain't Broke . . . Break It!* that outmoded ideas can lead to obsolescence and failure. Conventional wisdom can no longer help us to keep pace with the rapidly changing times.

Robert Schuller (1973) advocates that we should become "possibility thinkers": Do not look for perfection, for we know something is wrong with nearly every idea, plan, tradition, or organization. Read professional material with the following question in mind: "What positive value is there in this suggestion?" The "possibility thinker" discovers ways to activate, cultivate, and harvest positive values. You may fulfill this sense of achievement through leadership. By thinking of possible ways to improve the educational system, leaders are looking ahead. They are attempting to spot problems in ideas, plans, and directions. They help to carefully think out potential answers to possible questions that may be raised, they anticipate and meet problems before they arise, and they find and cultivate solutions. Possibility thinkers understand that problems represent opportunities for creative thinkers and those who choose to provide leadership.

Consider *Teacher Education Yearbook III* as a source of information to help stimulate your thinking and to help you clarify and provide direction to your ongoing projects targeted at educating teachers for leadership and change. Carefully consider the constituent elements of the rationales, arguments, and suggestions that are offered in these chapters. Also consider potential distortions and faults to the authors' logic, viewpoints, and calls to action. Consider the underlying assumptions that provide the foundations for these positions. Ponder these ideas like diamonds, searching for new facets. When you discover intriguing points and positions that beg for further elaboration, develop alternative viewpoints. After you have honed your thoughts, perceptions, and ideas, develop them and then share them with us as new articles and chapters to appear in forthcoming publications of ATE.

Thomas J. Buttery
ATE President, 1994-1995

References

Covey, S. (1989). *The 7 habits of highly effective people.* New York: Fireside.

Covey, S. (1991). *Principle centered leadership.* New York: Fireside.

Georgiades, W. (1988). The new American for the third millennium. In D. E. Oriosky (Ed.), *Society, schools, and teacher preparation* (pp. 25-30). Washington, DC: Association of Teacher Educators and Clearinghouse on Teacher Education.

Kriegel, R. J., & Patler, L. (1991). *If it ain't broke . . . break it!* New York: Warner.

Naisbitt, J. (1982). *Megatrends.* New York: Avon.

Schuller, R. H. (1973). *You can become the person you want to be.* Old Tappan, NJ: Spire.

Toffler, A. (1970). *Future shock.* New York: Bantam.

Acknowledgments

Many people have played critical roles in the development of this yearbook. We particularly wish to thank Thomas Buttery, President of the Association of Teacher Educators. Also, the ATE Executive Board and Gloria Chernay, Executive Director, are appreciated for their continual support of the yearbook. We appreciate the involved and talented efforts of our editorial advisory board members and the ATE Communications Committee for their insightful reviews. A special heartfelt thanks goes to Angela Spaulding, assistant editor, for her enthusiasm and long hours devoted to helping us produce a book that is truly different.

Few editors could hope for a more involved and talented publishing team. At Corwin Press, Gracia Alkema, Ann McMartin, Susan McElroy, and Stephanie Hoppe have made valuable contributions to the final product.

Lastly, we thank Dan, Douglas, Erica, and Jonathan, if for no other reason than they are special to us.

M.J.O
S.J.O

For generous contributions to this volume of *Teacher Education Yearbook*, The Association of Teacher Educators wishes to thank

Texas Tech University
College of Education
Lubbock, Texas

Introduction:
Weaving Leadership and
Change Into Teacher Education

Mary John O'Hair

Sandra J. Odell

Mary John O'Hair is Associate Professor in the Department of Educational Leadership and Policy Studies at the University of Oklahoma. Her research interests include preparing teachers and administrators for changing roles in restructured schools, and cooperative interdisciplinary studies on interpersonal and organizational communication in schools.

Sandra J. Odell is Professor of Education and Professional Development and Director of Undergraduate Studies at Western Michigan University. She has published articles on teacher induction, mentoring, and teacher development. She maintains a career-long research interest in teacher development in the context of collaborative university/school district programs.

A noiseless patient spider,
I mark'd where on a little promontory it stood isolated,
Mark'd how to explore the vacant vast surrounding,
It launch's forth filament, filament, filament, out of itself,
Ever unreeling them, ever tirelessly speeding them.

And you O my soul where you stand,
Surrounded, detached, in measureless oceans of space,

Ceaselessly musing, venturing, throwing, seeking the spheres to connect them,
Till the bridge you will need be form'd, till the ductile anchor hold,
Till the gossamer thread you fling catch somewhere, O my soul.

Walt Whitman, 1862-1863

Just as the spider works diligently to spin a web, educational reformers and reform movements have spun school reforms designed to enhance public education. Most reforms, however, have enjoyed but one brief moment of glory before being labeled trendy, becoming outdated, and being replaced by another. Unfortunately, most threads of school change have failed to reticulate change with the overall goal of public education, which is to prepare productive citizens for a democratic society—citizens who have learned how to identify, analyze, and solve problems that face their immediate and local communities (Glickman, 1993). Rather, change efforts have focused mainly on subgoals of education (i.e., cooperative learning versus individualized learning, return to the basics versus the arts, among others) rather than the primary goal of education. Thus, the intricate lacework of school change has appeared often a lopsided, tangled mesh—serving to incite public outcry and increasing educators' professional insecurities.

As guidance for school improvement is sought, frequent questions include: Can school reforms ever really improve schools? Will isolated efforts of school reform ever become consolidated, meaningful, collective efforts? Can even collective efforts web the foundation necessary to positively impact over 100,000 schools? And if so, what role must teacher education assume in all of this? Michael Fullan asserts that successful educational improvement is most often a result of simultaneous bottom-up and top-down initiatives that converge into a clear, moral center (Fullan, 1991).

Although the "clear, moral center" may appear murky at times, *Teacher Education Yearbook III: Educating Teachers for Leadership and Change* takes a stab at clarifying critical issues by unraveling the relationship among teacher education, leadership, and school change. Authors from teacher education, educational administration, and communication, along with educational change theorists, discard the comfort of their disciplinary boundaries and collaboratively weave themes on how better to prepare teachers for leadership and change.

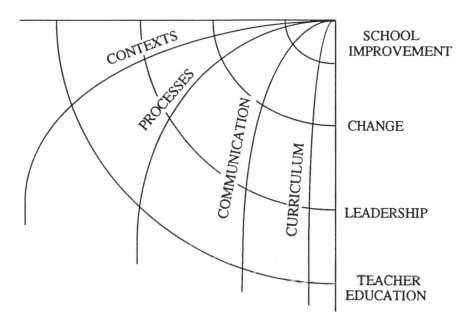

Figure I.1. Weaving Leadership and Change Into Teacher Education

The organization of the book spins individual threads of leadership and change, provided by chapter authors in four divisions (context, processes, communication, and curriculum). Respondents—recognized experts in education—cross-weave a pattern of careful analysis, synthesis, and implications for reflective practice. A concluding chapter strengthens the connections by focusing on two themes: Change is on the agenda for schools, and teachers need to be key actors in helping define and shape that change. Last, teacher educators are challenged to renew and broaden teacher education programs to include a strong emphasis on proactive teacher leadership roles in schools.

Where to Begin?

In Figure I.1, the genesis or center of the web is school improvement anchored tightly to the overall goal of public education. Next, contexts for leadership and change are enmeshed. The respondent Michael Fullan along with the chapter authors Carl Glickman, Barbara Lunsford, Kathleen

Szuminski, Paul Bredeson, Walter Gmelch, and Forrest Parkay outline changing teacher and principal roles, co-reform efforts, and occupational stress. A compelling argument is made for guided action in school change to advance a more comprehensive framework of teacher development.

The web is expanded with a focus on processes for leadership and change. The respondents Kenneth Zeichner and Bernadette Baker deftly weave the preparation of teachers for urban schools into the web by discussing research conducted by Norvella Carter, Patricia Larke, Judith Ponticell, George Olson, Patricia Charlier, and Diane Holt-Reynolds.

Communication is often cited as the most-needed skill for school success as educators move from traditional, isolated schools to shared-vision, collegial schools. Communicating leadership and change is developed by the respondent Cassandra Book, who connects the research of the chapter authors Richard Jacobs, Gretchen Hess, Robert Short, Ann Darling, and Martha Dewey into a conceptual framework highlighting the importance of communication and teacher leadership development.

The respondent Kenneth Sirotnik critiques the curriculum for leadership and change, offering insightful commentary on implications given by the chapter authors Theodore Kowalski, Richard Ponzio, Charles Fisher, Robert Alley, and Burga Jung.

A final chapter, authored by Joseph Murphy, examines the changing role of the teacher with an examination of the forces reshaping education, reactions to forces by the education industry, and how the changing nature of schooling is redefining the role of teachers.

Teacher Education Yearbook III concludes with a challenge for teacher educators. Teacher educators are encouraged to expand teacher education to include teacher leadership development. Traditionally, teachers have been responsible for individual classroom decisions only. Now they must begin making schoolwide decisions and accepting responsibility for school successes and failures. Teacher education programs must work collaboratively with educational administration programs to better prepare teacher leaders who not only demonstrate leadership skills but also consider their involvement in the decision-making process crucial for school improvement.

Teacher Education Yearbook III demonstrates that collaboration among educational disciplines strengthens and improves schools by preparing those people closest to students—teachers—to take leadership along with responsibility to truly improve schools. Teacher education, leadership, and change are critical threads to fling. We hope that the threads flung collectively with guided action will catch somewhere and decrease the ceaselessly musing, venturing, throwing, and seeking of meaningless school change.

References

Fullan, M. G. (1991). *The new meaning of school change.* New York: Teachers College Press.

Glickman, C. D. (1993). *Renewing America's schools.* San Francisco: Jossey-Bass.

DIVISION I

Contexts for Leadership and Change

CONTEXTS:
OVERVIEW AND FRAMEWORK

Michael Fullan

Michael Fullan is Dean of the Faculty of Education, University of Toronto, and Professor in Sociology of Education. An innovator and leader in teacher education, he has developed a number of partnerships designed to bring about major school improvement and educational reform. He participates as researcher, consultant, trainer, and policy adviser on a wide range of educational change projects with school systems, teachers' federations, research and development institutes, and government agencies in Canada and internationally. He has published widely on the topic of educational change. His most recent books include *Change Forces: Probing the Depths of Educational Reform* (1993) and *The New Meaning of Educational Change* (1991).

For almost a decade, teacher development has received increasing attention as a strategy for reform. The argument that quality teachers produce quality learning is compelling. One of the two new goals added to the six national educational goals for the United States highlights this argument: "By the year 2000, the Nation's teaching force will have access to programs for the continued improvement of their professional skills and the opportunity to acquire the knowledge and skills needed to instruct and prepare all American students for the next century" (U.S. Department of Education, 1993).

Despite a greater emphasis on teacher development, the results to date are not promising. A large part of the reason is a failure to conceptualize what the new role of teacher should be for the 1990s and beyond. I shall briefly critique existing efforts and then offer a framework to guide future teacher developments (see Fullan, in press).

A Critique of Existing Efforts in Teacher Development

My intent is not to put down current attempts at teacher leadership. On the contrary, many of these attempts contain elements that will be essential for success. But it is necessary to understand some of the basic flaws of the status quo if one is to achieve breakthroughs in future developments.

The following paragraphs do not constitute a formal review of research, although virtually all the criticisms raised have empirical backing (see Fullan, 1991, 1993; Goodlad, 1990, 1994; Sarason, 1993a, 1993b). Rather, I shall use a variety of teacher development and teacher leadership strategies to illustrate the range and consistency of current problems. These include field-based teacher education initiatives; university-school partnerships, including professional development schools; and various teacher leadership and teacher development strategies, such as formal teacher leadership roles, narratives, and autobiographies, site-based management, and state or national efforts to raise standards.

Field-Based Initiatives

Field-based teacher education and teacher leadership (e.g., mentors) programs are on the rise for both push and pull reasons. The push comes from the historical inadequacy of university-based teacher education. Long criticized for theoretical irrelevance, lack of coherence, and superficiality, university-based teacher education programs have increasingly fallen into disrepute.

The pull factor relates to the common finding that student teachers consistently report that time in schools is the most valuable component of their teacher education experience. On the surface both ideas are true enough—the college of education component is often irrelevant, and practice teaching is frequently beneficial. The error comes in launching a whole new direction in the absence of critical analysis of what is needed. For example, England established a national policy that funds schools and school authorities directly as agents of initial teacher education with up to 80% of time spent in schools (United Kingdom, 1993). If critical analysis is lacking, alternative certification programs that are largely school-based begin to flourish.

The point is not that these directions are without merit, but rather that they are partial solutions, superficially conceived. There is, for example, overwhelming evidence that schools and school districts are conservative rather than innovative *as systems,* and that schools are frequently not particularly healthy organizations for the growth and development of their members. Why then would one think that increasing the amount of time in a conservative and less than healthy system would produce the innovative teachers we need for the future? Schools as learning organizations are basically nonintellectual in the way they are organized, structurally and normatively. They are not amenable to experimentation, critical reflection, continuous learning, assessment, rethinking, and the like. This is not a criticism of teachers per se. But it is a fact that schools by and large are not places of reflection and learning when it comes to their own continuing development. It would be a mistake, then, to expect school-based teacher development to provide fundamental answers to generating teacher leadership on a large scale.

University-School Partnerships

Countering the one-sided solution of school-based programs has been the nominally balanced strategy of establishing university-school partnerships, often with professional development schools as a major platform. These exhibit several levels of problems. As with most bandwagons, the rhetoric outstrips the reality. Such partnerships are frequently narrowly conceived, affecting only a handful of schools and only a small part of the college of education. They are frequently confined "projects" rather than wider institutional reform strategies. The professional development schools (PDS) experience considerable internal developmental difficulties, not to mention the gaps created between PDS project schools and other schools in the district (Duffy, 1994). In almost all cases, despite the language of equal partnership, the focus is on the school side of the equation, not the changes needed in the university as an institution.

University-school partnerships, touted as a powerful vehicle for educational reform, become yet another project. As my colleague Andy Hargreaves (in press) puts it:

> Innovative university-generated schemes of school-based teacher preparation often conspire to reduce the reflective component in teacher education still further. Schemes are concocted which lodge much of the day-to-day work of teacher preparation in schools, supervised by school-based mentors who also have regular teaching roles and who meet periodically with their students and each other in the university. In principle, such schemes integrate initial teacher preparation with inservice teacher development and even ongoing school improvement. In practice, however, reflection tends to be confined to classroom-based issues of improving individual instruction and rarely extends to critical, contextual reflection on schoolwide issues that impede individual and collective improvement efforts in the long term.

Teacher Leadership and Teacher Development Strategies

The expansion and growth of various teacher leadership roles has been an enormous benefit to the individuals who hold these positions, but not to the profession as a whole. In some cases the effect has been contrary to the intention. Many teacher-leader roles end up distancing those who assume the roles from other teachers. Little (1990) found that lack of clarity and ambivalence on the part of teachers in "mentor" roles tended to produce a lower rate of direct teacher-to-teacher involvement of the very sort needed to make the role credible and effective. Smylie and Denny (1989) report the same finding—lower incidence of direct classroom and instructional exchanges—for the teacher leadership roles they studied.

Induction programs for beginning teachers under conditions of supervised mentoring also hold out great promise, but aside from the fact that they are not widely available, they can become formalized and stultified without a compelling conceptualization. Even at their best, induction programs represent only one small piece of the solution.

Narratives, autobiographies, and other methods of teacher reflection have been a great boon to personal introspection, but they suffer major limitations. As Hargreaves (n.d.) has pointed out, "research on teachers' voice and teachers' knowledge is replete with studies of teachers who are caring, committed and child-centered" (p. 13). Such studies fail to connect with other realities on the job or "voices" of a range of teachers, not to mention of students, parents, and administrators.

Site-based management is yet another strategy aimed at broadening and increasing leadership at the school level among teachers, parents, and students. I recently reviewed the research on site-based or school-based decision making, and the findings are quite clear. In the majority of cases the research shows that although there have been some changes in the participation in governance matters at the school level, there is no evidence that changes in the teaching-learning core of the school has been impacted, nor even the development of collaborative leadership norms among teachers (Fullan, 1993).

Finally, at the state and national levels, a number of jurisdictions are attempting to advance teaching and reform by codifying the knowledge base of teachers and establishing corresponding assessment methodologies to determine "what teachers should know and be able to do" (National Board for Professional Teaching Standards, 1993). It is not sufficient to identify the knowledge base without a more basic understanding of the role of teachers and teaching.

In conclusion, although many of the above initiatives are aimed in the right direction, they lack the broader conceptualization needed to guide future teacher development and hence are unlikely to achieve the necessary breakthroughs.

Toward a More Comprehensive Framework of Teacher Development

The first and foremost point in teacher development is that a wholesale transformation is required for *all* teachers. This is not a matter only for administrative and teacher leaders. It represents a sea change in the teaching profession as a whole.

Quality learning for all students depends on quality learning for all teachers. Quality learning for teachers in turn depends on the development of the six interrelated domains of teaching and learning, collegiality,

Figure DI.1. Teacher Development Domains
SOURCE: Adapted from Fullan (in press).

context expertise, continuous learning, change process, and moral purpose (see Figure DI.1).

Teaching and Learning

First, the knowledge base for being an effective teacher, focusing (for the moment) directly on the learning situation, has increased dramatically over the past decade. Teachers need to understand how diverse, multi-ethnic students learn and develop, and must draw on a repertoire of teaching strategies to meet a wide range of individual needs. Teachers must be skilled in the world of technology and international telecommunications. They must know subject areas and how to teach these subjects both individually and in relation to other disciplines. Teachers must master assessment and monitoring techniques for identifying and exhibiting a range of learning outcomes, and they must take corresponding action to alter curriculum and instruction.

Collegiality

Second, and this widens the knowledge base for teachers of the future compared to teachers of the past, teachers must become committed to, skilled at, and involved in the creation of collaborative work cultures inside and outside of the school while working closely with colleagues. Domain 1 involves doing a better job in the direct learning situation, whereas Domain 2 stresses that this will never happen unless teachers (and others) assume direct responsibility for changing the norms and practices of the entire school (and for that matter the profession). The learning agenda and the learning conditions are two sides of the same coin. It is easy to specialize in one or the other by closing the classroom door or by becoming a professional committee member. Reforming pedagogy and reforming the norms of the profession are intimately interrelated, but one must *conceptualize* them in this way if reform is to happen. Failure to do so produces much "restructuring" but little "reculturing" in teaching and learning and professional collegiality (Fullan, 1993).

Context Expertise

Third, teacher leadership and development also means becoming experts in context. This does not mean expertise in the foundations courses of history, philosophy, and sociology, but refers to specific knowledge, understanding, and skills needed for relating to and taking into account parents, communities, business, and social agencies. Further, context expertise is needed to grapple with the questions of where one's community, state/province, and country are heading—all within the givens of increasingly multicultural, multiracial, multilingual existence. Becoming experts in context is mind expanding on the one hand but quite specific in application on the other hand (see Zeichner, 1993). It includes specific strategies for connecting parents to learning, for learning to teach for cultural diversity, and for partnering with other educative agencies and institutions (early childhood programs, social agencies, businesses, colleges of education, etc.).

Continuous Learning

Fourth, the combination of teacher skills depicted in Figure DI.1 brings to life the oft-stated exhortation that teachers must lead the way in being *continuous learners* throughout their careers. There is much to learn and it keeps changing. Improvement is a never-ending proposition. The intellectual and emotional habits of critical reflection and action about one's "calling and daily work are the mark of a professional continuously engaged in self-improvement" (Goodlad, 1994, p. 38).

Sarason (1993b) states the case more forcefully: "Unless you [as a teacher] take active responsibility for your professional development, unless you protect yourself against the insidious consequences of intellectual-professional loneliness, you reduce the satisfactions you will derive from your career" (p. 68). Time and again he has underscored the vital link between teacher continuous learning and student learning. For example, "Yes, we expect teachers to give their all to the growth and development of students. *But a teacher cannot sustain such giving unless the conditions exist for the continued growth and development of the teacher*" (1993b, p. 62).

Change Process and Moral Purpose

The fifth and sixth domains of Figure DI.1 permeate and override the four previous domains. They concern what I call *teachers as moral change agents.* This concept has two interlocking aspects: (a) the knowledge and skills of the dynamics of the change process and (b) the moral purpose of making a difference in the lives of students. Teachers as experts in the change process represent a major transformation because (a) change is complex and extremely difficult and (b) teachers and educational systems are known more for their capacity to resist change than for their roles as agents of reform. Yet, it is clear that teachers are de facto in the midst of change all the time. There is a great deal of knowledge about the change process now available. Much of this knowledge runs counter to traditionally held rational models of planned change. Teachers must know how to initiate change despite the system, how to understand and manage the "implementation dip" (see Fullan, 1993), how shared visions are created over time through action, how to plug into networks of ideas and resources, and how to hold their own by practicing positive politics.

In other words, the teacher development curriculum of the future must contain *explicit* education in the management of change, because without it, it is not possible to make any sustained progress in the other five domains of development in Figure DI.1.

Lastly, moral purpose—a front-and-center commitment to making a difference in the lives of all students, especially the disadvantaged—must be part and parcel of the conceptualization of teacher leadership. Good teachers have always been driven by moral purpose, but the image is one of lonely martyrs soldiering on against all odds. I wish to make three additional observations. First, those few teachers who believe that their high ideals and commitment are sufficient inevitably burn out, leaving no institutional residue for their efforts. Second, steps can and should be taken to articulate and develop the moral purpose of *all* teachers. Third, pursuing moral purpose is a change, both in content (the substance of achieving moral purpose means making substantive changes) and in terms of process (what you would have to do to create the conditions to accomplish the changes).

Teachers are in the business of helping to improve society. There is little danger that teachers will be smug about this lofty role, but they may be daunted. However, there is no need for them to be. As a practical matter, it requires teachers to think about what their role in society means and to take it seriously. Sarason (1993b) devotes an entire book to advising prospective teachers to think and to prepare carefully for what they are getting into, and urges those who have a conventional image of an isolated teacher in an isolated classroom not to pursue teaching: "Teaching is not and should not be for those unwilling or unable to be active agents of educational-institutional change. From the standpoint of the larger society, there is too much at stake to allow teachers to be passive participants in the dynamics and processes of change" (p. 19).

In summary, good intentions and even strong efforts fail in the absence of a strong conceptualization that informs and is informed by actions taken. So far, teacher leadership strategies are not being guided by strong conceptualizations. The following chapters provide some insight into developing conceptualizations for changing teaching and teacher education. In Chapter 1, Glickman, Lunsford, and Szuminski provide a framework for university teacher educators and public school teachers to join together in co-reform initiatives. In Chapter 2, Bredeson focuses on the changing role of principals in restructured schools. In Chapter 3, Gmelch and Parkay address the increased level of stress among teachers as they adjust to their roles in restructured schools.

References

Duffy, G. (1994). Professional development schools and the disempowerment of teacher and professors. *Phi Delta Kappan, 75*(8), 596-601.

Fullan, M., with Stiegelbauer, S. (1991). *The new meaning of educational change.* New York: Teachers College Press.

Fullan, M. (1993). *Change forces: Probing the depths of educational reform.* Bristol, PA: Falmer.

Fullan, M. (in press). *Teacher leadership: A failure to conceptualize teachers as leaders.* Bloomington, IN: Phi Delta Kappan.

Goodlad, J. (1990). *Teachers for our nation's schools.* San Francisco: Jossey-Bass.

Goodlad, J. (1994). *Educational renewal.* San Francisco: Jossey-Bass.

Hargreaves, A. (in press). Towards a social geography of teacher education. In N. Shimahara & I. Z. Holowinzky (Eds.), *Teacher education in industrialized nations.* New York: Garland.

Hargreaves, A. (n.d.). *Dissonant voices: Teachers and the multiple realities of restructuring.* Unpublished manuscript, Ontario Institute for Studies in Education.

Little, J. W. (1990). The "mentor" phenomenon and the social organization of teaching. In C. Cazden (Ed.), *Review of Research in Education, 16,* 297-351.

National Board for Professional Teaching Standards. (1993). *What teachers should know and be able to do.* Detroit, MI: Author.

Sarason, S. (1993a). *The case for change: Rethinking the preparation of educators.* San Francisco: Jossey-Bass.

Sarason, S. (1993b). *You are thinking of teaching.* San Francisco: Jossey-Bass.

Smylie, M. A., & Denny, J. W. (1989). *Teacher leadership: Tensions and ambiguities in organizational perspective.* Paper presented at the annual meeting of the American Educational Research Association, San Francisco.

United Kingdom. (1993). *The government's proposals for the reform of initial teacher training.* London: Department of Education.

U.S. Department of Education. (1993). *Goals 2000.* Washington, DC: Author.

Zeichner, K. (1993). *Educating teachers for diversity.* East Lansing: Michigan State University, National Center for Research on Teacher Learning.

1 Co-Reform as an Approach to Change in Education: The Origin of Revolution

Carl D. Glickman

Barbara F. Lunsford

Kathleen A. Szuminski

Carl D. Glickman is Professor of Teacher Education and Educational Leadership and Chair of the Program for School Improvement at the University of Georgia. Most recently, he has been the founder and head of various university-public school collaborations. The collaborations have involved more than 80 elementary, middle, and secondary schools representing 37 school districts focused on school renewal through democratic governance.

Barbara F. Lunsford is Director of the League of Professional Schools and Assistant Professor, Department of Educational Leadership, University of Georgia. As the League Director, she works with League schools, conducts staff development, organizes conferences, and oversees the governance body of the League.

Kathleen A. Szuminski is Assistant Professor in the Department of Education at Oglethorpe University, Atlanta, Georgia. Her interests include teacher education curriculum reform and school-university partnerships for educational change.

ABSTRACT

Debates about educational change have failed to recognize the original mission of public education—preparation of educated citizens to participate in a democratic society. Education for a democratic society suggests the need for public school educators and teacher educators to work in unison to create and achieve a common agenda for long-standing educational change. Co-reform, an approach to educational change that brings together educators for the mutual benefit of both public schools and teacher education programs, holds promise for achieving and sustaining educational changes for all students.

In this chapter, we outline a moral framework for making decisions about symbiotic programs and discuss the issues that emerge as the co-reform process begins. Constraints common to public school educators and teacher educators during the co-reform efforts and suggestions for increased understanding are discussed.

The word *revolution* was originally an astronomical term meaning revolving back to some preestablished point. The English civil wars and the French and American revolutions were not about creating new ideas, but about revolving back to or returning to fundamental, old ideas about "the rights of man." These struggles were about restoring the liberties and freedom that should have been the conditions of a natural state. Thomas Jefferson wrote about creating a society that would foster a revolution by the people every 20 years. He was referring to decisions by the people to break the accumulation of cumbersome, undemocratic structures and replace them with structures that moved back to the original intent of the Declaration of Independence and Bill of Rights. Thus, the revolution was to be an ongoing, cleansing process to keep government rooted in its beginning aspirations.

Unfortunately, in discussions about the reform of public education and teacher education, this original intent has been lost. The clamor for change is couched in terms of student academic achievement, international competition, and economic or workforce preparations (see *America 2000*, 1991) and has resulted in pedagogical and school innovations of teaching methods, learning assessments, scheduling and placement of students, decentralization, and site-based management. Although these innovative changes are well intentioned toward improving student academic achievement, they are changes based on political or personal agendas and are made without the original intent of public education as a priority. Because these changes are not focused on the original mission of public education, they are haphazard, unrelated activities that do little to improve education (Goodlad, 1992). In this chapter, we discuss democracy and public education, including the central goal of public education in a democracy and one means of achieving that goal. It is our belief that uniting teacher educators with public school teachers in a co-reform process may be the means to achieve the goal of public education in a democratic society.

The changes many of us in public education have experienced have been seen as political and ideological agendas supporting innovations as a response to a crisis. The poor success rate of innovations in public and teacher education is depressing. Innovations are often viewed by many experienced educators with skepticism, and justifiably so. Over their careers, too many public school teachers have seen too many innovations implemented with few background preparations, minimal staff development, and a weak rationale for making the change. These innovations are generally brought to the classroom from an external source such as university professors, outside consultants, district offices, state departments, and legislatures. Examples of innovations that have come and gone and return again are open education, competency-based education, performance contracting, core curriculum, individualized instruction, direct instruction, mastery learning, cooperative learning, and higher-order thinking. The lack of success or any long-term change in schools is not the fault of any specific innovation, but rather failure in the process used to make the changes, and the fact that the change was not clearly driven by a commonly acknowledged mission of education.

Change in public education is void of the revolutionary process driven by the original intent for democratic public education. If educators don't center their work on the intent of education in our democracy, then pedagogical and structural reforms will continue in the pattern of passing on after a few years, replaced by the next generation of hot innovations that have the political backing and media attention of the time. We will continue to educate on shifting sands and pendulum swings without firmness of direction (see Barber, 1993).

The inadequacies and failures of prior public educational reforms result from a lack of attention to both the goal of public education and the process that should be followed for successful implementation of the goal. The common goal of teacher education and the public schools has been fuzzy to many outside the field of education and unclear to many within the educational arena. The problems that exist for both teacher education and public schools often have been dealt with by blaming the other for lacking understanding. This constant debate about faults has done little to push the dialogue toward a common agenda for teacher education and public schools. Further, constant debating has kept both teacher educators and public schools from seeing why they have to work together to accomplish the same goal.

Perhaps the only way that teacher education and public school educators get past throwing criticisms and collaborate is to engage in a common revolution that weeds out those practices inconsistent with education and democracy. This bonding of teacher educators and public school teachers for the mutual benefit of public schools and teacher education programs is defined as co-reform.

Common Goal of Education

Education in a democracy is established as an instrument of the society to promote the healthy participation of its future citizens. This is why public school educators and teacher educators are contracted employees of the state. They share the obligation to prepare students to contribute to the public good.

The U.S. Supreme Court in *Board of Education v. Pico* (1982) concluded that:

> The Constitution presupposes the existence of an informed citizenry prepared to participate in governmental affairs, and these democratic principles obviously are constitutionally incorporated into the structure of our government. It therefore seems entirely appropriate that the State use "public schools to . . . inculcate fundamental values necessary to the maintenance of a democratic political system." (p. 876)

According to Jefferson, public education has two corollary purposes: to provide for an educated citizenry to participate in decisions about promoting the future good of our democratic society, and to allow for leadership in a democratic society to develop from the merits, abilities, and talents of the individual. Leadership in a democratic society should not be based on family privilege, economic wealth, religion, race, or group privilege (see Lee, 1961). Following this line of thought, we can quickly articulate the basis toward which all efforts in public education reform should be directed. With the insertion of a few words, we have the central goal:

> All Students are created equal; that they are endowed by their Creator with Certain inalienable Rights; that among these are an education that will accord them Life, Liberty, and the pursuit of Happiness; that whenever any Public School becomes destructive of preparing Students for these ends, it is the Right of the People to alter or abolish it.

Teacher education programs are responsible for preparing future teachers to make appropriate decisions (with their colleagues and students) to realize this central goal. At the same time, public school educators have the responsibility of refining their current practice to help all students become true participatory citizens. Public school educators and teacher educators in conceiving, designing, and implementing their educational programs need to be morally consistent with their common goal.

What Is a Good Education for Students in Public Schools and Teacher Education Programs?

Research on effective teaching will never answer the question of what is a good education. "Effective" connotes the efficient accomplishment of intended learning results. "Good" connotes a determination first of what are worthy learning results, and second, what methods are appropriate to achieving those ends. Effective teaching can be good and good education must be based on effective teaching, but the terms are not synonymous (see Glickman, 1993). Therefore, debates about the use of particular instructional strategies cannot be resolved by research data. Both sides can always find evidence to support their own preferences and to refute other points of view. This is why there are endless debates about what research says about phonics versus whole language, cooperative learning versus individualized instruction, or homogeneous versus heterogeneous grouping. The only way to decide upon these research debates is to answer them in accord with the higher question: What should students be taught and how should they be taught so that the methods of teaching are consistent with an education for a democratic life?

Such good education would ensure that all students:

- Enjoy and exercise freedom of speech and accept the obligation to show respect for the rights of others
- Understand the key importance of separation of church and state in governmental affairs
- Know and be committed to the steps of due process prior to the deprivation of life, liberty, property, and the pursuit of happiness
- Be knowledgeable and conversant about the issues of our society
- Know how to reason well, consider various perspectives, test ideas, and form informed opinions
- Practice and communicate the acceptance of the equality of all humans

When it is clear what is meant by a good education, appropriate teaching practices become more apparent. The research line that runs from the developmental research of Piaget, Bruner, Inhelder, Kammi, Vygotsky, and Kohlberg to the constructivist research of Gardner, Slavin, Joyce, Resnick, and others provides the strategies and techniques that engage, challenge, and involve students in active, participatory learning, consistent with democratic principles. In the same manner, the structural school reform debates about grade levels versus multiage grouping, authentic assessment versus standardized testing, and tracking versus nontracking of students can also be screened according to the concept of democratic education (see Gutmann, 1987). Grouping students in ways to label and limit their aspirations is wrong. Allocating more money to privileged students at the expense of underprivileged students is wrong. Keeping students from advancing beyond their peers is wrong. Restructuring teaching to a daily routine of compliance and passivity is wrong. Not allowing students to develop their abilities to think, reason, and solve problems is wrong. Teaching teachers to apply these strategies to public school children is equally inconsistent with the common goal of educating for a democracy. Therefore, the problems of current educational solutions and reforms are problems of public educators and teacher educators alike.

Of course, there will be thoughtful disagreements about the degree of activity, participation, and involvement of students, but the direction is set. Our schools must reflect the democratic principles of our society if students' experience in school is to have relevance and meaning to their lives outside of school. We must purge our schools of practices that are in direct contradiction to the democratic principles that guide our society. Changing our schools means changing our university teacher education programs as well. In doing so, we will create the Jeffersonian concept of revolution as a continual recentering to provide for long-term substantive changes in education.

So far we have made no mention about subject matter or academic content achievement as part of a democratic education. One might incorrectly interpret good education as being process. Students need to master reading, writing, mathematics, history, art, music, science, economics, and technology. Without substantive knowledge, understandings, and skills, a student has little chance to become an independent, proactive, and valued citizen. The focus on education for a democracy, however, assists students to learn academics in the context of choice, activity, application, relevance, and extension to one's life in immediate and future communities. To teach content without visible connection to how it is applied to individual power and influence in a larger democratic society is to relegate at least half of our students to not learning content; performing poorly on achievement measures; and continuing generational cycles of disengagement, cynicism, illiteracy, and hopelessness. To put it succinctly, students who do well in schools know how school learning will help them (even if this is conveyed more by their parents than the school). Those who do not perform well in school will never perform better until learning is connected to a viable and real democratic future (Glickman, 1993).

A Common Agenda for Co-Reform

Teacher education and public education have the same ultimate purpose. Faculties in both are contracted agents, commissioned to serve the higher purpose of education for democratic citizenship. If public schools are to reflect democratic principles and provide the student with opportunities to experience firsthand the acquisition of knowledge, an understanding of democracy, the opportunity to be actively engaged in one's own learning, and the application of those learning experiences to the society at large, then teachers in public schools must possess certain qualities. They must have a clear understanding of the mission of schools, have firsthand experiences in being engaged in their own learning, have a broad base of knowledge and content, possess appropriate pedagogical strategies, and have the ability to assess their own work and the needs of their students.

This type of teacher will not exist unless teacher educators understand the goal of public education and create learning environments for future educators that enable them to graduate from a teacher education program with the attributes just listed. Historically, rather than working together toward this common goal, the public school and teacher educators have attacked and kept each other at a distance. Restructuring too often has become what one party sees as the need of the other to correct, not a joint responsibility for both to assess and change. For example, many public school educators deplore the practices of teacher education programs at colleges and universities. They criticize the programs for being too easy, too boring, and too detached from the real world of schools. Tit for tat, teacher educators launch criticisms at public education as being too convention bound, too focused on control, and too atheoretical. Both groups see educational improvement as lying in rectifying the decaying operations of the other. Ignoring the obvious relationship (public educators were prepared by teacher educators and most teacher educators were public educators), they each take comfort in the other's lack of responsiveness.

On the other hand, collaborative and simultaneous reform of public schools and teacher education programs based on understanding reinvigorates the natural symbiotic relationship. As a public school improves, it provides better preparation sites for teacher education students and provides insights into future changes in teacher education programs. As teacher education programs improve, they provide future teachers with the skills for further changes in public education. For a teacher education program to change in isolation and without compatible educational changes in the public school means inadequate preparation for future teachers and therefore an inadequate educator of future citizens.

For a substantive co-reform revolution to occur, both institutions need to develop a moral framework for decisions about symbiotic programs. Co-reformers need to develop:

- A covenant of learning based on the democratic goal of education (i.e., mission, vision, and principles of learning) that serves as the core values of education at both the public school and the teacher education institution
- A democratic charter for decision making that ensures the equal representation of both parties in developing the covenant and subsequent implementation decisions

- A critical study process that includes a data collection process (i.e., action research) to assess the effects of programmatic changes on public school students, future teachers, and current teachers

In other words, to prepare students for the goal of democratic citizenship, the co-reform collaboration among teacher educators and their students, and teachers currently teaching, must include the same beliefs of democratic principles and procedures for decisions about structure, activities, and resources of the joint effort.

Co-Reform Dimension

The programmatic linkages can now be illustrated using the following program elements as illustrations:

- Interdisciplinary curriculum
- Team teaching
- Portfolio and performance assessments
- Peer coaching
- Extended communities of learners
- Technology integration
- Project-centered learning
- Student choice and involvement
- Cooperative learning

If both institutions are to assist each other toward a common, moral goal, then "what is good for the goose is good for the gander" becomes apparent. For example, if one party (teacher education or public school) is moving toward greater implementation of integrated and interdisciplinary teaching, so should the other. If one party (teacher education or public school) is moving toward peer coaching, so should the other. When a joint decision is made for one institution to move toward greater implementation of a specific strategy based on action research and the close examination of the goal and the current results, the other institution should support this strategy as well.

A common vision for education based on democratic principles should result in similar program components and educational practices. It is a contradiction for a teacher education program to exhort authentic assessment, team teaching, and heterogeneous learning for public schools if its own program is based on standardized examination, individually led teacher classrooms, and homogeneous grouping. In the same way, it is a contradiction for a teacher education program to use constructivist, student-oriented, and technologically infused learning methods if the public school uses regimented, teacher-centered, textbook-driven learning methods.

When professionals across settings have a common goal or direction, they can then check for compatible activities that allow both institutions to gain greater insights and power for educating their students. With some notable exceptions, the vast array of teacher education programs and public schools are unlinked—both groups tolerating the other, taking up space in each other's facility and classrooms, and going about education in their own separate ways and with no clear common purpose. A clear understanding about the original intent of public education and the priority of democratic principles is not articulated. Without this common understanding, the two groups proceed with their own agendas and without a common link.

To begin the co-reform process, awareness and understanding of each other are necessary. For many classroom teachers in public schools, knowledge of what is happening in teacher education is limited to what was taught or current when they were in college. There is little opportunity for teachers within a public school to meet teachers recently out of college to find out what is being taught or how field experiences are being implemented. Likewise, many teacher educators have little or no experience with practitioners and what is currently happening in public schools. To understand and prepare teachers, teacher educators need to be current about issues facing public schools. This can be achieved by visiting schools and talking with teachers, students, administrators, and parents.

This initial awareness is not enough to put the two groups on a common course. Opportunities for working with each other, exploring the issues, problem solving, and accepting joint responsibility for programmatic and symbiotic changes is essential. Such collaboration requires drastic changes in the way the two faculties think of each other and how they respond to the idiosyncratic context of their respective work.

Different Constraints, Same Issues

All three authors of this chapter work at a large teacher education institution and have been involved for many years with university and public school reform. We coordinate two networks of public schools, involving more than 80 schools in 37 districts. The focus of that work has been assisting the schools to make internal educational improvement consistent with democratic principles and procedures. At the same time, we are involved as participants or researchers in the internal reforms of our own university preparation programs, including new undergraduate programs in elementary, middle, and secondary teacher education and new graduate programs in educational leadership. Some of our university faculty collaborate with a few of our network public schools (as professional development sites) for simultaneous, co-reform programs.

In our dual roles with both public school reform and higher education reform, we have been struck by the similar difficulties experienced by both. For example, university faculties have the same problems as school faculties in developing clearly articulated programs; in creating a covenant of mission, goals, purpose, core values, and guiding learning principles; in creating a charter for democratic decision making; and in developing a critical study process.

Among ourselves, we have found the same problems of miscommunication, conflicting ideologies, apathy, lack of sufficient time and money, and discomfort with change. In both settings, faculties tend to see their work as individual with allegiance more for their department or grade level than for their school or college. In both settings, faculties are more concerned about their immediate, day-to-day work and less concerned about interdepartmental or interdisciplinary planning. Organizational structures make it difficult for even those most eager to achieve broad-based, long-term change. In both institutions one finds faculty eager and change oriented, willing to challenge existing structures. Yet, they tend to become isolated from the rest of the faculty, who are content with existing practices. In both, the vast majorities of faculty are caring, well intentioned, and committed to their students; they simply have learned how to work within the existing framework of autonomy and isolation and see no reason to change (see Cuban, 1992; McNeil, 1988).

There are intra-institutional differences that can impede change in some significant ways. Many university faculty members have difficulty accepting public school educators as their peers. Higher education means to many that public schools are "lower" education and of lower status, esteem, and expertise. Democracies are based on *equal* rights and power, but the norms of the two institutions have not been equal. Even when higher education faculty members are open to the idea of equality, the institution can impede equality in many ways, such as:

1. Lack of recognition for such planning (i.e., doesn't count for tenure or promotion)
2. Lack of released time for such planning (i.e., other research, writing, teaching, and service obligations in one's department receive higher priority)
3. Lack of a previous history of peers within the same institution knowing of each other's work (i.e., beginning meetings spent in wheel spinning and finding out the who, what, and how of each faculty member and department)
4. Lack of a mutual time for planning with public school colleagues who have less flexibility as to when meetings can be arranged

These factors can create an inertia among university faculty in moving beyond the planning-to-plan stage to program purpose, features, and implementation. The institution of public schools exerts its own difficulties about co-reform activities, such as public school teachers and administrators:

1. Not having the academic freedom to make changes in their own schools (i.e., control from the district or state)
2. Not being able to respond quickly to school planning and implementation due to the day-to-day incessant demands of students, parents, unpredictable crises, and community resistance
3. Harboring traditional skepticism toward university people about whether they will roll up their sleeves and work and understand a public school setting

University faculty members do have greater flexibility in the use of their time, but they feel greater constraints on how to use such time. Public school faculties have less flexibility in scheduling time for planning but have institutional pressure to be involved in schoolwide efforts (i.e., site-based management, strategic plans). The ultimate result is that members of neither group can truly understand the life of the other until they work in each other's setting.

How these understandings can be developed is for:

1. Teacher education programs to hire clinical practitioners from schools to be part of the university setting
2. Public schools to invite university faculty to teach in their settings for extended periods
3. Educators in different settings to trade places with one another for short periods of time
4. Teacher education classes to take place in the public schools
5. Parties of both to shadow each other during parts of each other's normal work
6. Both parties to sponsor jointly extra-educational activities (i.e., summer school programs, after-school programs, tutorial programs)

Ultimately, the best way for people to understand one another is through active participation in mutually important work. Unfortunately, because of different institutional constraints, it is hard to identify the mutually important work (co-reforms) until other cross-collaborations have occurred.

Messy Work for a Clear and Common Goal

There is no algorithm for the specifics of how co-reform programs should be developed or how they should look. Clarity about common goals and purpose is the beginning. Programs that mutually reinforce educational activities across teacher education and public education programs are the means. The end is a continual quest—the ongoing revolution to educate future generations of democratic citizens. This is no small task by any means, but the task that gives meaning to our professional lives.

References

America 2000. (1991, September 1). Washington, DC: U.S. Department of Education.

Barber, B. R. (1993). America skips school. *Harpers, 287*(1722), 39-46.

Board of Education v. Pico. (1982). 457 U.S. 853.

Cuban, L. (1992). What happens to reforms that last? The case of the junior high school. *American Educational Research Journal, 29*(2), 227-251.

Glickman, C. D. (1993). *Renewing America's schools.* San Francisco: Jossey-Bass.

Goodlad, J. I. (1992). On taking school reform seriously. *Phi Delta Kappan, 74*(2), 232-238.

Gutmann. A. (1987). *Democratic education.* Princeton, NJ: Princeton University Press.

Lee, G. C. (1961). The precious blessings of liberty. In G. Lee (Ed.), *Crusade against ignorance: Thomas Jefferson on education* (pp. 27-28). New York: Columbia University Press.

McNeil, L. N. (1988). Contradictions of control. Part 2: Teachers, students, and curriculum. *Phi Delta Kappan, 69*(6), 432-438.

2 Role Change for Principals in Restructured Schools: Implications for Teacher Preparation and Teacher Work

Paul V. Bredeson

Paul V. Bredeson is Associate Professor of Educational Administration at the University of Wisconsin-Madison. His research interests include role transition in restructured schools and instructional leadership in educational organizations. He taught high school Spanish and was a high school principal prior to becoming a professor. He received the Jack A. Culbertson Award (1990) for outstanding contributions to research and leadership in educational administration and has been very active in professional organizations. He is a past President of the National Council of Professors of Educational Administration (NCPEA) 1990-1991, serves on the National Policy Board for Educational Administration, and is President of the University Council for Educational Administration (UCEA).

ABSTRACT

Within the context of school reform, it is important to examine the effects of specific reform initiatives on the work of principals and teachers. In this chapter, using findings from a study of the effects of empowerment and restructuring initiatives on the role of school principals, I examine how changes in the principal's leadership role in schools have had concomitant effects on teachers and their professional work. As new understandings of the roles, rules, relationships, and responsibilities

25

that govern the daily work of educational professionals are forged, it is critical that we understand the implications of these changes for teachers.

In the first section, I report findings from a study of principals' perceptions of restructuring and empowerment in their schools. In the next section, I describe readjustments in personal, position, and political power for teachers and principals in schools. These readjustments have affected the traditional leadership role of school principals. The data indicate that principals are moving toward group-centered leadership. Key group-centered leadership behaviors include (a) recognizing and attending to individual and group needs; (b) acting as consultant, adviser, resource person, and teacher; (c) modeling of desired behaviors; (d) establishing supportive climates; (e) encouraging teachers to be self-monitoring; and (f) relinquishing control. Changes in the traditional leadership role(s) of school principals have affected teachers' roles and have implications for teacher preparation, socialization, and work in schools. At least five areas warrant attention: (a) an expanded professional role for teachers, (b) enhanced professional skills, (c) awareness of and ability to deal with role transitions, (d) capacity and training to work effectively in collaborative teaching and learning settings; and (e) acquisition and demonstrated ability in group-centered leader behaviors. In the final section, I discuss the implications of changes in sources of power and in the principal's leadership role for teachers' work in schools and for teacher preparation.

Unprecedented attention and energy have been focused on public education over the past decade in the United States. Each successive wave of school reform has highlighted changes in the various dimensions of education from curriculum content, teacher preparation, and qualifications to fiscal equity, organizational structure, and governance. More recently empowerment and restructuring provide the current metaphors for persistent, yet no less ambitious and wide-ranging, reform efforts of the 1990s. Within the context of school reform, it is important to examine the effects of specific reform initiatives on the work of principals and teachers. In this chapter, using findings from a study of the effects of empowerment and restructuring initiatives on the role of school principals, I examine how changes in the principal's leadership role in schools affect teachers and their professional work. As new understandings of the roles, rules, relationships, and responsibilities that govern the daily work of educational professionals are forged, it is critical that we understand the implications of these changes for teachers and for teacher preparation.

In the first section, I report findings from a study of principals' perceptions of restructuring and empowerment in their schools. In the next section, I describe readjustments in sources of power for teachers and principals in schools. Next, I examine how changes in sources of power affect the traditional leadership role of the principal. In the final two sections, I discuss the implications of changes in sources of power and in the principal's leadership role for teachers' work in schools and for teacher preparation.

Background and Context for School Reform

Current literature on reform in schools provides us with various descriptions of empowerment and restructuring. Restructuring and empowerment encompass many ideas and represent a variety of change processes. Although a single and commonly accepted definition of restructuring is lacking, Newmann (1993) identified four common themes in schools where empowerment and restructuring initiatives were under way. These include "major changes in students' learning experiences, in the professional lives of teachers, in the governance and management of schools, and in the ways in which schools are held accountable" (p. 4). Such changes dramatically alter existing roles, rules, relationships, and responsibilities of teachers, principals, students, and other stakeholders in schools. Timar (1989) noted that empowerment and school restructuring are fundamentally changing "the rules of behavior that define both the roles of individuals and their actions " (p. 266). Fullan (1993) described the relationship between restructuring and reculturing, that is, the establishment of a culture supportive of change:

> Clearly there must be a reciprocal relationship between the two; but restructuring might be more effective if the attempted conceptual and normative changes were to accumulate to drive structural changes conducive to new ways of working. When teachers and administrators begin working in new ways and in the process, discover that school structures must be altered, reform and restructuring are much more powerful and meaningful than when the reverse happens. (p. 131)

Brandt (1993) equated restructuring with systemic reform: "Restructuring is changing the system of rules, roles, and relationships that govern the way time, people, space, knowledge, and technology are used and deployed. That's what systemic reform is too" (p. 8). A common theme across these descriptions of school change is role change. Whether described as empowerment, restructuring, systemic change, or reculturing, changes in rules, relationships, values, norms, beliefs, and responsibilities for teachers and principals alter organizational roles.

In formal organizations, rules, roles, relationships, and responsibilities are tied to sources of power. Individual power resides in an individual's potential to influence the attitudes and behaviors of others. Yukl (1989) describes three major sources of power for individuals in formal organizations—position power, personal power, and political power. Examining changes in sources of power for teachers and principals in restructured schools, Bredeson (in press) reported,

> Readjustments in sources of power and in power relationships among principals and teachers have occurred in these schools. Changes in allocations of power based on formal position, personal attributes and political strategies have changed the day-to-day working relationships of these teachers and principals. The changes in sources are not described in "win-lose" terms. Rather than being seen as a threat to the principals, empowerment offers many more advantages for enhancing leadership in the school, not threatening its foundations. As leadership responsibilities and control are shared among teachers and principals, the traditional role of the building principal continues to be redefined.

Principals' Perceptions of Empowerment and Restructuring in Their Schools

In earlier reports of these interview data, I described the impact of teacher empowerment and school restructuring on the traditional roles of teachers and principals, examined role transition and role strain for principals, and described readjustments in sources of power and in power relationships among principals and teachers (Bredeson, 1989, 1993a, 1994).[1] In interviews with 20 school principals (11 elementary, 4 high school, and 5 middle school), I asked building administrators for their perceptions about how empowerment and restructuring initiatives in their schools had affected them as principals.

Each principal could quickly describe what empowerment and restructuring meant in their buildings: "Teachers are invited to participate in the way the school is managed"; "This is a systematic way to improve the educational climate . . . and this is connected to our district's goals and priorities for the products of learning, work environment, and the relationships between people"; "The idea is for teachers and administrators to share in the ownership on matters that affect us both. The focus is on daily work life issues. It is the sands of daily operations where things happen."

Individual experiences with restructuring and teacher empowerment initiatives were contextually unique. Nevertheless, the responses of these principals suggested similarities and patterns in changes in roles, rules, relationships, and responsibilities for teachers and principals as the result of changes in decision making, governance, and management. Participative decision making, shared governance, and site-based management were replacing traditional hierarchies of decision authority, top-down governance, and rigid organizational structures.

Significant changes in rules, roles, relationships, and responsibilities occurred locally and were products of unique community and organizational cultures, moderated by various opportunities and constraints. Leadership from superintendents was important, but the empowerment of teachers had not been a top-down, hierarchically imposed reality accomplished with blitzkrieg administrative strategies. Successes with authentic empowerment and restructuring in each of these buildings and districts had been built upon the foundations of readiness, volunteerism, incrementalism, legitimacy, and ownership. One respondent described what he meant by authentic empowerment: "To me shared governance is involving professional staff in things that are related to their job and that impact instruction and quality of the work place. I don't involve teachers in petty things. That doesn't make them feel professional."

One definition of "empower" is to enable. In these four districts, superintendents enabled principals, and principals in turn enabled teachers to assume greater responsibility for critical issues in their schools. Those who became empowered needed to be ready to internalize the meaning of change in their daily work and in their professional responsibilities. Not all teachers were ready, nor did they enthusiastically volunteer to participate in restructuring activities. After years of administrator dependency, often characterized by unauthentic experiences in shared decision making, principals reported that many of their teachers had adopted a wait-and-see attitude. Some teachers were so uncomfortable with empowerment and changes in role expectations that they preferred to be left alone in their classrooms: "I teach. Let me teach. You're the principal. Just tell me what you want me to do."

These principals also noted that systemic change was a process that evolved slowly. In these schools, change was more incremental than radical. Changes in decision structures and processes, daily work, and relationships among staff relied on collegial trust and positive staff morale built up gradually over time. School climate was a powerful antecedent condition and moderating factor in role transitions for teachers and principals. "School environments soured by poor relations between teachers and the principal were likely to be non-supportive of, and possibly resistant to, restructuring and empowerment initiatives" (Bredeson, 1993a, p. 35).

Legitimacy, ownership, time, and money were also important to work role transitions for teachers and principals. Authentic empowerment did not mean teachers chose to involve themselves in every aspect of school affairs. Clearly, teachers had preferences based on the amount of time required away from their students and on personal and professional expertise. As principals and teachers assessed the costs and benefits of greater professional empowerment in their schools, they cited repeatedly the importance of money and time. Given the current structure of the teacher's work day, it was not surprising that time for planning, interacting, and carrying out program efforts was greatly constrained. One elementary principal stated, "If it [empowerment] fails, it will be because of a lack of time. I want it to succeed but time is lacking. Buying time in the teacher's work day or during the summer translates into significant budget allocations" (Bredeson, 1994, p. 207). Two major changes characterized empowerment and restructuring in these schools: readjustments in sources of power for teachers and principals, and changes in the traditional leadership role of principals.

Changes in Sources of Power

What evidence is there that restructuring and empowerment in these schools resulted in significant readjustments in sources of position, personal, and political power and in power relationships among teachers and principals? If one were to visit these schools, changes in the sources of power and in power relationships among teachers and principals might at first be invisible. No radical changes in formal position titles and structures existed. Principals were still located in the main office, the school day was still the traditional one, and teachers and students were in their classrooms. Closer examination, however, revealed important changes in the ways these educational professionals worked together.

Readjustments in Position Power

Traditionally, the position power of a building principal was based on an ability to exert control over resources, rewards, sanctions, information, work routines, and the physical environment itself. A principal's ability to influence these elements made her or him "the boss." In the schools examined in this study, control over many of these factors was being shared among the professional staff. The degree to which teachers had assumed control over particular aspects of their professional work was a function of local context, school climate, and traditions of trust.

In one middle school, for example, teachers had complete control over the staff development budget. They also determined the agenda, time, and day for faculty meetings. Extensive building and renovation projects in the district had provided teachers with significant roles in assessing, planning, and allocating physical spaces for one new school and several remodeled ones. In another middle school, teachers exercised control over the curriculum and the daily class schedule. They controlled a 5-hour block of time during their day and made decisions about the frequency and use of parent-teacher conference days. Teachers' roles had been greatly enhanced in this middle school. In a city district, teachers had begun to replace traditional supervision practices with peer evaluations. In building-level committees, teacher and principals shared problems and ideas much more than had been done in the past. One long-time veteran of the district described an environment in which traditional adversarial postures between teachers and administrators were replaced by greater professional trust in collegial dialogues, in peer evaluations, and in building-level committees. As a result of greater trust among teachers and principals, principals were no longer doing "punitive write-ups" if people had problems. In fact, the entire professional evaluation process was undergoing major changes that required significant modifications of existing language in local union contracts and in state education department requirements. Perhaps the most convincing evidence of new levels of professional trust among teachers and principals in this district related to collective bargaining. Problems related to contract language or procedures were not left until the next round of bargaining between the school board and the teachers' union. Both sides agreed to reopen the contract if problems arose, regardless of where they were in the negotiation cycle.

As to the process of gaining control over resources and rewards, the principals indicated that teachers were still in transition. Teachers wanted recognition and support for their decisions from their principals. "We're in transition in professional development. Now they're seeking approval from the administrators." However, as teachers began to assume greater responsibility and were encouraged to empower one another, they began to rely more on each other and less on their principals. One principal remarked, "Teachers don't run in here for every little thing. This building operates on its own." Another principal added, "With any kind of a problem, they [teachers] feel comfortable in making those decisions themselves."

To facilitate and nurture the sharing of control over decision processes and their outcomes, principals indicated that it was important to create and maintain a nonthreatening and supportive environment. In each school, problems did arise as teachers assumed control over a variety of decisions in their work lives: "Occasionally, a teacher's decision may negatively affect another staff member. We're trying to get people to tolerate these types of mistakes. We need to be careful not to create negativism."

Finally, control over information is an important source of power for any role incumbent. In these schools, teachers "read the literature and the research." In areas of curriculum and instruction, for example, control over the selection of textbooks and other materials, over the assignment and grouping of children, and over professional development programs remained in teachers' hands. One principal described how relinquishing control over many of these traditionally guarded resources helped blur customary lines of authority in his school. However, at the same time the blurring of lines of authority created problems for principals. When board members, parents, or other community members wanted to know something about what was going on in the school they naturally called the principal. One principal recalled, "I might get a call from outside. A parent wants to know what's going on. I'll say I need to talk with the teachers about what they're doing. They think 'why the hell don't you know what's going on in your school?' " As control over resources, rewards, information, and work design becomes a shared responsibility among teachers and principals, communication to stakeholders outside of the school about these changes and their implications is critical. Relinquishing control for these principals meant they no longer had to sustain the myth that principals controlled, knew about, and were responsible for everything under the schoolhouse roof.

Readjustments in Personal Power

Readjustments in sources of personal power also occurred in these schools. Generally, personal power emanated from individual expertise, personal loyalty, and charisma. One principal reflected, "Teachers here have a mindset to empower themselves." As teachers shared in decision making that affected their students and their own work lives, they gained confidence in their own abilities and in the choices they made: "Teachers feel the effects of their efforts that they are making and come to believe their input and participation are appreciated." As teachers worked together to solve problems, they gained respect and began to motivate one another. In one school, after the teachers and principal had worked through a number of important building-level concerns in an extended faculty meeting, the principal recalled with great satisfaction, "At the end of our last faculty meeting everyone applauded everyone else." Teachers' recognition of their successes in planning, problem solving, decision making, and governance reinforced feelings of professional and personal efficacy.

Another source of personal power for teachers was subject matter expertise. Principals deferred to teacher expertise in curriculum and instruction so long as the decisions were within legal and district policy boundaries and the outcomes of their choices were not harmful to children. These principals no longer were the sole intermediaries to the superintendent, school board, or community groups. When academic programs were the subject of school board deliberation, when special activities needed to be presented, or when commendations were given for program successes, teachers were there to advise the board, make the presentations, or receive the praise.

Faculty meetings at one middle school became occasions for celebrating the individual successes of teachers, such as completing a graduate degree program or receiving outside recognition for their work. Each of these examples contributed to what these respondents described as real professional growth and professional efficacy. The perceptions of these principals also suggested that as teachers learned to accept more responsibility for decision areas beyond their classrooms, they defined their professional role differently. They were no longer "just classroom teachers."

Changes in teachers' sense of professional efficacy affected what principals did. A few principals, for example, no longer perfunctorily carried out classroom observations and evaluations. They spent less time monitoring compliance and more time in activities supporting the work and decisions of their professional staff.

Readjustments in Political Power

In terms of political power, both teachers and principals exerted a great deal of influence over building-level decisions. Previously guarded decisions over budget management, long-range plans, curriculum design and reform, and program evaluation became legitimate arenas for teacher input and shared responsibility. Long-range curriculum review processes and the design of a new school provided the catalyst in two districts for meaningfully involving teachers in critical decision making at district and building levels. From experiences gained in these projects, districtwide committees for textbook and instructional materials selection, staff development teams, and new project implementation teams emerged. As teachers assumed leadership in these areas, they were asked to take the lead in other areas. As their skills for group process and consensus building matured, teachers in three schools assumed responsibility for faculty meetings. Principals in these buildings became resource people and facilitators to the faculty. As one respondent stated, "Once teachers get the ball rolling with positive and energetic people, critics are ignored or addressed by positive leaders in the teacher group. Teachers go to teachers on resolving problems." Principals no longer had to be the Mintzbergian problem solver, disturbance handler, information officer, and decision maker.

Political power and professional prerogatives varied in the four districts. In one city district, problem-solving teams became the locus for building-level and district-level decision processes, but only within tightly controlled parameters of what the central administration defined as allowable issues. Inside these boundaries there was great freedom to identify and resolve important work life and professional concerns. In another city district the building-level committees (BLC) and the districtwide governance body (PIC) provided new organizational structures and processes for addressing critical issues and for institutionalizing the voice of teachers. In part, this institutionalization provided teachers with more direct and quicker channels to the school board and to district policy making.

In each of these districts, teachers learned early on that shared governance and decision making did not always mean that issues and problems were resolved to their complete satisfaction. When unsatisfactory outcomes happened, principals said that some teachers believed this demonstrated that shared governance was only a management ruse, not a new work place reality. "They need to understand the notion of mutually accepted decisions." As teachers participated actively in decision making, they began to gain a clearer understanding of shared governance processes and of the effects and limitations of their own professional empowerment. Although still in their infancy, empowerment and restructuring in these districts had resulted in fundamental shifts in sources of position, personal, and political power. How had changes in sources of power affected the leadership role of the principal?

Changes in Principals' Leadership Role

Yukl (1989), summarizing Bradford's research, provides a useful analytical framework for assessing changes in what principals do in schools where teachers are sharing in decision-making and leadership functions. The traditional view of leaders is that they should retain "The initiative and power to direct, drive, instruct and control those who follow" (Bradford, 1976, p. 8). In contrast, Bradford (1976) described the group-centered leader who shares responsibility and control with the group. Is there evidence that these principals were reexamining their role and moving from traditional leader behaviors to group-centered leader behaviors?

Given the source of these interview data, it is important to recognize that corroborating data from teachers within these schools would strengthen the assertions about actual changes in these 20 principals' behaviors in their formal leadership role. With this limitation acknowledged, I will review the principals' insights into how their roles had been affected by readjustments in sources of power. The data revealed that these 20 administrators were moving, some more easily than others, from more traditionally defined leader behaviors to more group-centered ones. These included: (a) recognizing and attending to individual and group needs; (b) acting as consultant, adviser, resource person, and teacher; (c) modeling of desired behaviors; (d) establishing supportive climates; (e) encouraging teachers to be self-monitoring (group maintenance); and (f) relinquishing control. This is not to say that principals had relinquished all control; nor had they removed all of their controlling and managerial behaviors from their daily routines.

Attention to Group Needs. Listening and attending to teacher needs, feelings, interactions, and conflicts was the most frequently cited behavior. From the principals' perspectives, teachers expected them to listen, be supportive, and provide feedback on their initiatives. Because teachers and principals were experiencing role anxiety and strain from changes in their schools, both needed reassurance and support as they responded to new role expectations, developed new relationships, and established new norms of professional behavior.

Principals described certain areas where teachers remained reluctant to take on new responsibilities. For example, in the selection of teachers they preferred access and input to selection processes more than the final say on who was hired. Readiness to assume responsibility in new decision arenas could not be taken for granted. According to a principal, some teachers "Still expect me to be in charge of everything, every discussion." Weaning professional staff from habits of principal dependency became a primary staff development objective for these leaders: "There are teachers who would rather be told what to do. There are a few unhappy teachers because they are uncomfortable with empowerment."

Principals as Consultants and Advisers. Some principals described themselves as consultants, facilitators, and teachers of teachers, not the directors/managers/controllers of everything going on in the school. In response to the question, "Can you see ways in which your role as principal is changing because of greater involvement of teachers in your school's governance?" one principal stated, "I think initially I viewed things as 'we-they' not necessarily adversarial, but differently. I'm not sure how much I've changed as a principal versus how much schools have changed. I'm much more process-oriented than 6 years ago." Another principal remarked, "Some teachers would still like the principal to be the administrator and be the person in charge. However, the principal here is not the boss."

Modeling Leadership. Modeling of group-centered behaviors by principals was also reported. Referring to his superintendent, one principal said, "He models what he expects us to do." Another principal added, "My superintendent models these skills. We talk, we don't always agree. But he models, he listens. He does the stuff he expects of me." Each of these principals was convinced that through modeling of specific leadership behaviors they could pass on strategies and styles that would support teacher leadership. One said that teachers "expect me to model a leadership style that's effective." Another principal described how he encouraged and nurtured empowerment by "modeling and showing them that

I'm going to work hard and in the best interest of kids." Modeling of tolerance and patience was also important. Individual or group missteps became opportunities to learn from mistakes and approach the problem in a different way. Finally, in their work, principals modeled group process skills and consensus-building strategies.

Providing a Supportive Climate for Empowerment. By modeling their own acceptance of diverse views from others, principals worked to establish and nurture affirming school climates where empowered teachers could safely express diverse ideas and opinions. When asked what were the three most important things they did as principals to encourage and nurture teacher empowerment, they responded that they listened, provided support, and remained open to the ideas and feelings of their professional staffs (Bredeson, 1989). Lastly, the climate of acceptance is further supported by one principal's stated belief, "We need to let them make mistakes. Support is provided even when things that were tried did not turn out the way they had been planned" (Bredeson, 1994, p. 215).

Group Maintenance. The data suggested that these principals encouraged teacher-led groups to deal with internal group maintenance and process problems. Though it was difficult for principals to ever be "just another member of the professional work group," these principals worked to encourage teachers to assume responsibilities for group effectiveness. Principals used group or team projects as opportunities for deliberate modeling of behaviors encouraging group members to assume responsibility for task completion, internal group maintenance issues, and self-evaluation. Through active listening and feedback to groups and to individuals, these principals suggested strategies for addressing group maintenance concerns. When teachers came to principals with problems, their first inclination was to fix it. Though not easy for some principals, they exercised restraint, provided support, and helped generate alternatives but did not assume responsibility for the group. As teacher work teams organized tasks, principals were sounding boards for ideas, provided insights from their own experiences, and encouraged teachers to select and frame problems that could realistically be addressed given the constraints of time, energy, and money.

Relinquishing Control. Relinquishing control over decisions was a liberating experience for the principals, but not one that was risk free or easy. One middle school principal reflected on his own experience: "Initially that was the most frightening thing for me as a principal. It was a growth process for me. They're smarter than I thought they were or than I trusted they would be." Teachers are "bound to make decisions that you wouldn't make yourself." The principals reported that they needed to translate their controlling behaviors into supportive behaviors that helped teachers, individually and in groups, achieve desired outcomes. Supervisory conferences were another occasion for relinquishing control. "The conference I have with teachers is a 50/50 dialogue. They're expected to contribute equally in terms of their perceptions, goals, and outcomes of the class."

With program initiatives sprouting up like mushrooms around the school and teachers taking on new roles and responsibilities, principals described their personal discomfort with not being able to stay on top of everything that was going on in their school. A middle school principal described his anxieties about relinquishing control to teachers: "Initially everyone has a messianic complex that comes from a compulsion to do everything. One grows out of that because of necessity one can't do everything. One's success depends on the success of others. The only way to be successful is to help others be successful. I'm becoming more and more trusting of groups. Groups don't make the same mistakes individuals do." In discussing the principal's role strain, Bredeson (1993b) stated, "The empowerment of others relieved some of the strain caused by role overload and helped to dispel the myth of principal omniscience while at the same time it resulted in other sources of strain" (p. 47).

Shifts in positional, personal, and political power as well as changes in principals' formal leadership role reflecting group-centered leader behaviors have profound implications for teachers and for the preparation of teachers. Next, I discuss how each affects the preparation, socialization, and professional work of teachers.

Implications for Teachers

In the interview study described above, the focus was on the changing role of school principals in teacher-empowered, restructured schools. Significant shifts in traditional sources of positional, personal, and political power in schools, however, affected teachers and their work as profoundly as they did principals.

Role Changes for Teachers

Changes in power and in the principal's leadership role greatly affected the role of teachers in these schools. New understandings of leadership, professional responsibility, power, and formal roles had an impact on teachers in their classrooms and beyond. As principals relinquished control in particular decision arenas, teachers were beginning to assume responsibility in those areas. This expanded the traditional role of the classroom teacher. Curriculum design; student assessment; professional development; and the allocation of time, money, space, and facilities were areas where many teachers were making substantive contributions. Expanding teacher responsibility beyond the classroom resulted in significant reallocations in positional, personal, and political power in each school.

Role Strain

Changes in traditional roles engendered anxiety and, in some cases, active resistance. The principals reported that expanded roles for teachers, new role expectations, role overload, and role conflict became sources of stress for teachers, and that role strain for themselves and for teachers was beginning to be a problem (Bredeson, 1993a). Lack of time was identified as the factor that created the most stress in these schools. New role expectations, new leadership responsibilities, committee work, and collaboration with other teachers required time. In a few schools, teachers and principals had been creative in blocking out time within the school day for teachers to work outside of their classrooms. In one district, the budget included substitute pay for 15 days for teachers who worked on the school curriculum development committee. However, even when money was available to free teachers up to work on important school- or district-level issues during the school day, teachers felt conflict over their new responsibilities and time away from "their kids." Limited time forced teachers to make choices between competing professional responsibilities. Forced choices added to their sense of role strain.

Need for Staff Development

New roles and responsibilities often required new sets of personal and technical skills for teachers. Principals recognized that teachers were eager to take on important tasks but often lacked knowledge, technical expertise, and group process skills necessary to be successful. Principals did not simply hand over new roles and responsibilities to teachers and wish them luck. Staff readiness was crucial to successful transitions. Staff development was critical in providing the training and experiences teachers needed to meet requirements of expanded professional roles. Examples of staff development were training in budgeting, the organization of meetings, conflict resolution, collaboration with others, and facilities planning.

Capacity Building

Changes in the roles of principals and teachers required what Fullan (1993) referred to as "reculturing" in the schools. Each school culture was defined by values, beliefs, and norms of professional behavior. Shifts in power and new work relationships among teachers fostered new norms for teacher work and thus contributed to changes in existing school cultures. Teacher successes in team projects, collaborative work, and shared decision making were changing their beliefs about their roles, responsibilities, and sense of professional efficacy. Similar to what Little (1982) described as behaviors reflecting norms of professional collegiality, principals reported that their teachers were talking about their work, observing each other, planning and designing the curriculum together, and teaching one another. Collaborative cultures did not emerge quickly, however, and were dependent on the level of trust in each school. "In schools where trust levels were high, traditions of trust were products of on-going professional dialogues among principals and their staffs. Trust helped to build confidence in evolving processes, to suspend premature judgments, and to sustain enthusiasm for change, even when things went wrong" (Bredeson, 1993a, p. 52).

Modeling Collaborative Behavior

By definition and by example, principals' group-centered leadership behaviors had a rippling effect throughout the school. Schein (1985) described primary mechanisms leaders use to create and nurture cultures in organizations. To find out what's valued and what's important in any culture, watch what the leaders do. As restructuring unfolded, teachers watched their principals for clues as to what was really important. They looked for congruence between principals' "talk" about empowerment and their "walk" with empowerment. Teachers expected their principals to embody what was valued by modeling effective communications, group process, and interpersonal skills. In turn, teachers emulated these behaviors as they worked in classrooms and on school and district-level committees.

Authentic Empowerment and Restructuring

The pressure for schools to demonstrate that they are dynamic organizations attuned to the latest educational innovations can result in a frenzy of activities that create the illusion of change but marginalize the effects of those changes on teaching and learning. Teachers struggled to balance professional work beyond the classroom with their responsibility to students. For teachers in these schools, there was a positive relationship between levels of involvement on school and district committees and work teams and the focus of those activities. When teachers could see that the decisions and outcomes of their work directly affected teaching and learning, they were more willing to spend time away from their classrooms. Activities peripheral to their students were much less likely to engender enthusiasm or participation. Clearly, empowerment and restructuring did not mean that teachers wanted to be involved in every decision and all issues in their schools.

Implications for Teacher Preparation

So what do all of these changes in roles for teachers and for principals mean for the preparation and socialization of teachers? The following, in particular, need specific attention in teacher preparation programs: (a) an expanded professional role for teachers, (b) enhanced professional skills, (c) awareness of and ability to deal with role transitions, (d) capacity and training to work effectively in collaborative teaching and learning settings, and (e) acquisition and demonstrated ability in group-centered leader behaviors.

Expanded Professional Role for Teachers

The first implication for teacher education is expanding the definition of teachers' professional work in schools. The notion of teacher as "sage on the stage" in a self-contained classroom fails to recognize important changes in teachers' roles. Teachers wear many professional hats. They are facilitators, coaches, and models of lifelong learning in classrooms; planners, designers, decision makers, and educational leaders outside the classroom. The role of a teacher has always been a complex one requiring at least four levels of professional competence—technical, clinical, personal, and critical (Zimpher & Howey, 1987). Rather than adding yet another level of competence to teacher professional expertise, which often means adding more credits to professional licensure, it seems more helpful to think about how requisite professional knowledge for meeting the expectations of an expanded role for teachers in restructured schools can be integrated with these four levels of professional competence.

Enhanced Professional Skills

Expanded roles for teachers require enhanced professional skills. Subject matter expertise and specific teaching and learning strategies for effective instruction are crucial components of any teacher preparation program. Expanded professional roles for teachers require more than content knowledge, effective instructional strategies, and understanding and caring for children. Experiences and training in collaboration and teamwork with adults, new technical and interpersonal skills for facilitating group processes, dealing with conflict, and the development of leadership skills are needed by novice teachers moving into restructured, teacher-empowered schools.

Work Role Transitions

By definition, restructuring means changes in roles for principals, teachers, and students. For teachers, substantial changes in the rules, roles, relationships, and responsibilities that define their work require periods of personal and professional adjustment. Accordingly, new and experienced teachers will need to be aware of work role transitions and develop strategies for dealing with the anxiety and strain that accompany them. Nicholson's (1984) theory of work role transition suggests that teachers can deal effectively with role changes through personal development (altering their personal frames of reference, values, and relationships) and through role development (actively attempting to personalize new roles and role demands) to meet their own needs, values, abilities, and sense of professional identity.

Collaborative Work:
Norms of Professional Collegiality

In my research methods and instructional supervision classes, collaborative work teams are an important teaching and learning strategy. Most of my students are experienced teachers who have relied on their individual intellect and skills and on personal tenacity to complete a graduate program while working full-time. A typical reaction from some students when I first assign the team projects is, "Can I work alone on this project?" The amount of work to complete the project is far less intimidating to my students than is the thought of having to coordinate schedules, to deal with the limitations of others, to agree on a division of labor and work routines, and to deliver a team research report, presentation, or other product that represents their best work as students. I would argue that most aspiring teachers have similar discomfort and apprehensions about collaborative work. Teamwork requires particular skills that need to be developed throughout teacher preparation programs. To assume that teachers will be collaborative simply because we restructure time in their school day to meet is naive. Successful collaboration requires skill, trust, and patience. The norms of professional collegiality described by Little (1982) are good organizers for incorporating training and development of these behaviors in teacher preparation. Throughout their professional preparation, aspiring teachers need to learn to *talk* about their professional work in meaningful, concrete, and precise ways; to *observe* and critique each other; to *collaborate* on curriculum work—researching, evaluating, designing, planning, and implementing; and to *teach* each other what they know and thereby share professional expertise and craft knowledge.

Group-Centered Leader Behaviors

Collaborative work in schools and norms of professional collegiality require leadership that is responsive to the group and its shared purposes. As traditional views of leadership give way to group-empowering leader behaviors in restructured schools, preparation programs need to provide opportunities for novice teachers to acquire important group-centered leadership skills. Again these behaviors and skills ought not be add-ons to the teacher preparation curricula but integral components and processes of the entire preparation program. The ability to recognize and attend to group and individual needs; to act as consultants, advisers, and facilitators in groups; to establish safe and affirming climates for group members; to model appropriate group behavior to others; to be self-monitoring and responsible for group maintenance; and to relinquish control are important teacher behaviors for working with students, other teachers, administrators, and community members.

Beyond the rhetoric of teacher empowerment and school restructuring, there is evidence that significant changes in the roles, rules, relationships, and responsibilities of principals and teachers are occurring. In response to these changes, teachers and those who prepare teachers might take the advice of Lee Iacocca, former CEO of Chrysler Corporation: "Lead! Follow! Or get out of the way!"

Note

1. This chapter draws heavily on previous works by the author, Bredeson, 1989, 1993a, 1993b, and a chapter in press.

References

Bradford, L. P. (1976). *Making meetings work.* La Jolla, CA: University Associates.

Brandt, R. (1993). On restructuring roles and relationships: A conversation with Phil Schlechty. *Educational Leadership, 51*(2), 8-11.

Bredeson, P. V. (1989). Redefining leadership and the roles of school principals: Responses to changes in the professional work life of teachers. *High School Journal, 73*(1), 9-20.

Bredeson, P. V. (1993a). Letting go of outlived professional identities: A study of role transition and role strain for principals in restructured schools. *Educational Administration Quarterly, 29*(1), 34-68.

Bredeson, P. V. (1993b). Responses to restructuring and empowerment initiatives: A study of teachers' and principals' perceptions of organizational leadership, decision making and climate. In J. R. Hoyle & D. M. Estes (Eds.), *NCPEA: In a new voice* (p. 297). Lancaster, PA: Technomic.

Bredeson, P. V. (1994). Empowered teachers—empowered principals: Principals' perception of leadership in schools. In P. Thurston & N. Prestine (Eds.), *Advances in educational administration* (Vol. 3). Greenwich, CT: JAI.

Fullan, M. (1993). Innovation, reform, and restructuring strategies. In G. Cawelti (Ed.), *Challenges and achievements of American education* (pp. 116-133). Alexandria, VA: Association for Supervision and Curriculum Development.

Little, J. W. (1982). Norms of collegiality and experimentation: Workplace conditions of school success. *American Educational Research Journal, 19*(3), 325-340.

Newmann, F. M. (1993). Beyond common sense in educational restructuring: The issues of content and linkage. *Educational Researcher, 22*(2), 4-13, 22.

Nicholson, N. (1984). A theory of work role transitions. *Administrative Science Quarterly, 29,* 1972-1991.

Schein, E. H. (1985). *Organizational culture and leadership.* San Francisco: Jossey-Bass.

Timar, T. (1989). The politics of school restructuring. *Phi Delta Kappan, 71*(4), 264-275.

Yukl, G. A. (1989). *Leadership in organizations.* Englewood Cliffs, NJ: Prentice-Hall.

Zimpher, W. L., & Howey, K. R. (1987). Adapting supervisory practices to different orientations of teaching competence. *Journal of Curriculum and Supervision, 2*(2), 101-127.

3 Changing Roles and Occupational Stress in the Teaching Profession

Walter H. Gmelch

Forrest W. Parkay

Walter H. Gmelch is Professor and Chair of the Department of Educational Leadership and Counseling Psychology at Washington State University as well as Director of the UCEA Center for the Study of the Department Chair. His research focuses on leadership development with special emphasis on stress, conflict, and team building.

Forrest W. Parkay is Professor and former Chair, Department of Teaching and Learning, and Professor, Department of Educational Leadership and Counseling Psychology, at Washington State University. His research interests focus on inquiry-oriented teacher education programs, curriculum development, beginning principals, the case method in teacher training, and school restructuring.

ABSTRACT

Changing roles are resulting in increased levels of occupational stress and burnout among today's teachers. Seven of these changes are discussed in this chapter: new leadership roles, increased diversity, disruptive behavior and violence, accountability for addressing social problems, inadequate resources, lack of parental support, and expanding partnerships. To clarify the concept of stress, the authors examine six myths: (a) stress is harmful; (b) stress should be avoided; (c) administrators experience greater stress than teachers; (d) the more control teachers have, the more stress they will experience; (e) stress is largely a male phenomenon; and (f) there is one right way to cope with stress. To enable teachers to manage stress and use it to their advantage, the authors also describe a four-stage stress cycle and examine three dimensions of burnout. Then, drawing from a survey of 1,800 educators, the authors describe seven coping strategies that teachers have found useful in managing stress and avoiding burnout.

Are teachers becoming role prisoners of our changing society? Most would agree that teaching has always been a challenging occupation. Day in and day out, teachers spend much of their lives "on stage" before audiences that are not always receptive. As every teacher knows, the outcomes of teaching can be unpredictable and inconsistent; in spite of carefully crafted lesson plans and good intentions, students do not always respond as their teachers desire. In the classroom, teachers must orchestrate a daunting array of interpersonal interactions and build a cohesive, positive climate for learning.

For most teachers, responding to the complex, shifting ambiguities of the classroom is exciting, energizing, and rewarding; for others, however, it can be stressful, even debilitating. Fortunately, most teachers master the challenges of the profession and learn to savor the joys and satisfactions of helping young people grow and develop; other teachers, however, experience acute levels of occupational stress that may lead to job dissatisfaction, emotional and physical exhaustion, and a general inability to cope effectively—all classic symptoms of burnout. In this chapter, we first review the changing roles and new challenges that currently face teachers and then assess the stress of teaching by exploring the myths of teacher stress and methods for coping with the teacher stress cycle.

New Challenges for Today's Teachers

As we approach the 21st century, the roles of teachers are changing. An ever-widening circle of interest groups is placing new, higher expectations on teachers, and the job is becoming even more complex and challenging. As a result, we may expect that increasing numbers of teachers will report acute levels of occupational stress and burnout.

Many school reform efforts initiated in the 1980s continue to be implemented today, creating more complex, demanding roles for teachers. Shared decision making, teacher empowerment, the professionalization of teaching, mentor teacher programs, merit pay plans—these and scores of other reform efforts continue to place new demands on teachers. In addition, teaching is becoming more conflict ridden than it has been in the past. Frequently, teachers must deal with disgruntled students, parents, community members, legislators, and members of the public at large.

Many factors add significantly to the stress with which today's teachers must cope. It is beyond the scope of this chapter to examine these stressors in detail, but in the following sections we briefly address seven factors that currently pose significant challenges to teachers: new leadership roles, increased diversity, disruptive behavior and violence, accountability for addressing social problems, inadequate resources, lack of parental support, and expanding partnerships.

New Leadership Roles. Efforts to empower teachers and to "professionalize" teaching are leading to unprecedented opportunities for today's teachers to extend their leadership roles beyond the classroom. As Livingston (1992) points out: "Recently, there have been calls for expanded, and qualitatively different leadership opportunities for teachers . . . the nation is coming to realize a need for more authentic forms of school reform or restructuring to meet the needs of an increasingly diverse student population and our rapidly changing society" (p. 10).

Under the banner of the movement to restructure schools, countless districts have implemented changes such as shared governance, bottom-up policy making, school-based planning, school-based management, and shared decision making. What these policies have in common is providing those who know students best—their teachers—greater opportunities to exercise their leadership at the school site.

Increased Diversity. Clearly, the demographic profile of the United States is changing dramatically. Projections indicate that by the middle of the next century almost half of the population will be members of minority groups (Hodgkinson, 1992). In addition, many students will come from homes where English is not spoken. In 1993, for example, one in seven U.S. residents spoke a language other than English at home. According to a 1993 estimate by the National Clearinghouse on Bilingual Education, the number of people from non-English-speaking backgrounds is expected to reach almost 40 million by the year 2000.

The increase in minority-group populations is having a profound effect on enrollments in our nation's schools. In 1992, the District of

Columbia had a minority-group enrollment of 96%; Hawaii, 77%; New Mexico, 58%; California, 54%; Mississippi, 52%; and Texas, 50% (National Center for Education Statistics, 1992). Hodgkinson (1992) estimates that by the year 2000 the majority of students in most urban school districts will be from groups traditionally thought of as minority. In 1992, Anglo-European American students numbered less than 20% in Atlanta, Baltimore, Chicago, Detroit, Los Angeles, New Orleans, Oakland, Richmond, and San Antonio (National Center for Education Statistics, 1992).

Even as our nation's student population is becoming more diverse, the teaching force continues to be primarily Anglo-European American. In short, there is an alarming "discontinuity" between our nation's student and teacher populations (Education Commission on the States, 1990; Grant & Secada, 1990; Southern Education Foundation, 1990). At one time, 18% of teachers were minorities (Haberman, 1989); in 1991, however, this percentage had dropped to just over 13% (National Education Association, 1991). Further, it is estimated that by the year 2000 only 5% of teachers will be minorities, although minorities will make up about one third of the total school enrollment (Education Commission on the States, 1990). A reality of teaching today, then, is that some teachers may experience the free-floating anxiety known as *culture shock* as they address the diverse needs of students who come from cultural backgrounds different from theirs (Parkay, 1983).

Disruptive Behavior and Violence. Crime statistics indicate that U.S. society is becoming increasingly violent, and not surprising, schools reflect this trend. At an alarming rate, teachers at urban, suburban, and rural schools report having to cope with disruptive behavior and violence. For example, the National Education Goals Panel reported in 1993 that 50% of 10th graders felt unsafe at school, and 10% brought a weapon to school during the last month. Similarly, a survey of almost 2,500 youth indicated that 60% said they could get a handgun if they wanted one, and more than one in three said they knew someone who had been killed or hurt by gunfire (ALH Research, 1993). According to the *Metropolitan Life Survey of the American Teacher 1992* (Louis Harris & Associates, 1992) only 77% of teachers and 50% of students report that they feel very safe in and around their schools. The survey also indicated that 11% of public school teachers have been victims of violence that occurred in or around school.

Accountability for Addressing Social Problems. A complex array of social issues impacts today's schools, and these problems often create stressful working conditions for teachers. Teachers are often charged with the difficult (if not impossible) task of providing a frontline defense against such problems. Increasingly, the public looks to teachers to provide leadership for addressing social problems such as drug abuse, poverty, crime and violence, child abuse, teen suicide, sex education, and dropout prevention. For example, the 1990 Gallup Poll of the Public's Attitudes Toward the Public Schools indicated that more people would require drug abuse education in high schools than would require education in any subjects other than mathematics and English.

Inadequate Resources. Many of today's teachers experience unnecessarily high levels of stress from working in schools that are poorly equipped and underfunded. Moreover, the fact that scarce resources are not equitably distributed among schools may cause additional frustration and dissatisfaction. For example, Kozol (1991) points out that some affluent suburban districts spend more than twice as much per pupil as schools in the nearby inner city. For teachers who find themselves in settings such as the following, the potential for high levels of stress is significant: "In some of our most disadvantaged school districts in and around larger urban centers, the specter of a dual society suggests political conflict and potential social upheaval in the years ahead. Needs will outstrip resources and push may well come to shove" (Borich, 1993, p. 20).

Lack of Parental Support. Although evidence indicates that there is a direct relationship between grades and parental involvement (National Center for Education Statistics, 1985), teachers experience frustration because parents are not as involved in their children's education as teachers would like them to be. According to the *Metropolitan Life Survey of the American Teacher 1992* (Louis Harris & Associates, 1992), lack of parental support was a major source of dissatisfaction among second-year teachers—a concern greater than drug abuse or violence. Among teachers who planned to leave teaching, "lack of support or help for students from their parents" was identified most often as the major factor in their decision (Louis Harris & Associates, 1992).

Expanding Partnerships. In their new leadership roles, teachers are being called upon to form new partnerships with business and industry; institutions of higher education; social service agencies; professional associations; and local, state, and federal governmental agencies. In this new role, teachers will be the key to promoting widespread improvement of our educational system. Until levels of trust are developed among these new partners, some teachers will no doubt experience higher levels of stress. They will need to learn new skills as they begin to work collaboratively on common concerns with agencies and individuals in the public and private sectors.

The Incidence of Occupational Stress Among Teachers

Within the last two decades, there has been an exponential proliferation of articles about stress in schools (6,843 citations in educational journals and documents alone). The incidence of occupational stress and burnout among teachers has been well documented (Blase, 1986; Coates & Thoresen, 1976; Dedrick & Raschke, 1990; Dunham, 1992; Dworkin, 1987; Farber, 1991; Humphrey & Humphrey, 1986). However, varying definitions of *stress* and *burnout*, and difficulties related to measuring these factors, have resulted in widely varying reports of the incidence of stress and burnout among teachers. Holt, Fine, and Tollefson (1987) report that surveys conducted by the National Education Association (NEA) show that the percentage of teachers reporting "considerable stress" in their work has climbed steadily from 37.5% in 1938 to 43% in 1951 to 78% in 1967 and 1976. Feitler and Tokar (1981) reported that 16.5% of the teachers in 60 school districts found their work very or extremely stressful, and Brown (1983) found that 53% of a sample of elementary teachers in Missouri believed their work was very or extremely stressful.

Common Myths About Stress

Stress intrigues and plagues the teacher and administrator alike. Internationally, scholars and professionals have authored over 100,000 books, journals, and articles dedicated to the phenomena of stress, with an additional 6,000 publications catalogued each year (Gmelch, 1988b). The word *stress* is familiar to the teacher and scholar alike. Typically, one associates stress with change, anxiety, frustration, strain, conflict, and tension. Although children, teachers, administrators, and researchers all can recognize the feeling of stress, the exact understanding of the concept remains vague. An examination of several myths about stress may clarify some of the misconceptions and misuses surrounding the concept of stress over the past few decades (Gmelch & Chan, 1994):

Myth #1: *Stress is harmful.* Although the popular connotation is that stress is unpleasant or negative, it can be positive as well. The Chinese, for example, represent stress with two characters, one signaling *danger* and the other *opportunity.* Like the Chinese representation, stress today actually encompasses both distress (bad or unpleasant events) and eustress (good or pleasant events). Through slurring, the old French and Middle English word *distress* came into common English usage as stress, with only a negative connotation in the Western world. Teacher failure is stressful, but so is success.

Myth #2: *Stress should be avoided.* Stress is a natural part of life and helps teachers respond to threat or rise to challenge. In essence, it cannot and should not be avoided, for without stress you could not be an effective educator. What "under stress" actually means is that educators are under "excessive" stress, or distress. An analogous condition is that of "running a temperature," meaning above normal. Body temperature itself is essential to life, just as is stress. Stress cannot be avoided, other than by death. Therefore, teachers should not always seek to avoid stress: *It can be the spice of life, when handled right.*

Myth #3: *Administrators experience greater stress than teachers.* It is popularly believed that high-level executives lead the list of heart disease patients. However, a Metropolitan Life Insurance Company study challenged this assumption with the finding that presidents and vice presidents of the 500 largest industrial corporations suffered 40% fewer heart attack deaths than middle managers of the same companies. Similar data support the conclusion that middle managers have a higher rate of peptic ulcers than chief executive officers. Results in education are mixed on who suffers the most from stress; several studies found that superintendents reported greater stress than all other administrators, but only in the area of boundary-spanning stress. In fact, superintendents experienced less stress than other educators in the areas of conflict mediation and time or task constraints (Gmelch & Swent, 1984; Torelli & Gmelch, 1993). In a comparative study of 23 occupations, higher education administrators ranked first, ahead of faculty (ranked sixth) in reported stresses and strains (Caplan, Cobb, French, Van Harrison, & Pinneau, 1980). In addition, faculty reported more satisfaction with their jobs than administrators.

Myth #4: *The more control teachers have the more stress they will experience.* The search for the most stressful position in education may not lead to meaningful conclusions—a more productive line of inquiry might be to focus on the fit between the person and the job (see Person-Environment Fit theory). For example, University of Michigan researchers have generally concluded that jobs are particularly stressful when employees do not have clear objectives, are torn between conflicting demands, have limited control over decisions affecting them, or are responsible for other people's development (Caplan et al., 1980). A NASA study also revealed that employees responsible for *people* have higher stress (measured by higher blood pressure and nervous habits like smoking) than employees responsible for *things*. What is most fascinating in times of site-based management and employee empowerment is the effect a "sense of control" can have on teachers' stress. Studies using the Teacher Events Stress Inventory (adapted from Homes and Rahe's Life Events Inventory) discovered that the most stressful event teachers perceived was "being involuntarily transferred." Ironically, it was not the "transfer" that caused the stress as much as the "involuntary" nature of the event, as the least stressful item on the Teacher Events Inventory was "voluntary" transfer (Young, 1980).

Myth #5: *Stress is largely a male phenomenon.* Until the 1980s, the literature commonly referred to "men under stress." This misguided reference no longer prevails, but it is well known that men suffer higher rates of alcoholism, ulcers, lung cancer, suicide, and heart disease than do women. A study of school administrators found that women principals reported less stress than their male counterparts in all areas except task-based stress (Koch, Tung, Gmelch, & Swent, 1982). With respect to classroom teaching, a national study of professorial stress reported women experienced more stress than men, and married women experienced even more stress than single men or women professors (Gmelch, Lovrich, & Wilke, 1984). Overall, the evidence that either men or women experience more stress is inconclusive and has not proven to be a productive or functional line of inquiry for applied research.

Myth #6: *There is one right way to cope with stress.* Although researchers have addressed popular and academic concerns as well as conceptual, theoretical, and empirical investigations on coping, a definition of effective coping processes remains elusive. Given the recent interest in educator stress, it is surprising to find little attention is given to the precise ways educators cope with stress. Hans Selye (1976), the father of stress research, pointed out that despite everything that has been written and said about stress and coping, there is no ready-made formula that suits everyone.

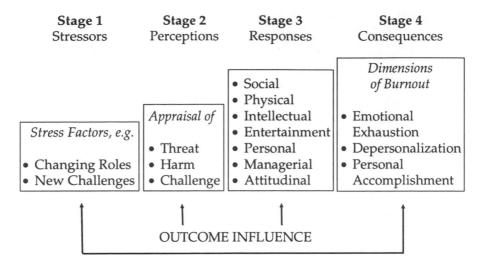

Figure 3.1. Stress Cycle

The Stress Cycle

Rather than avoid stress, teachers need to control it and use it to their advantage. Behind many achievements of both students and educators lies stress. A moderate amount of stress helps individuals reach their peak performance. However, when stress mounts, teachers sometimes enter the danger zone where counterproductive attitudes and behaviors surface. Psychologically, teachers can become confused, disoriented, irritable, irrational, apathetic, and emotionally withdrawn. After all, a teacher can only deal with so much change and put out so many brush fires before eventually burning out. In the remainder of the chapter, we focus on how to maintain effective performance.

The four-stage stress cycle portrayed in Figure 3.1 provides a broad perspective clarifying stress and introducing a framework for action. The process begins with Stage 1, *stressors*, or a set of specific demands. Excessive meetings, paperwork, and confrontations represent some of common teacher stressors. How much stress is produced by these stressors depends on Stage 2, the teacher's *perception* of these demands. If you do not have the physical or mental resources to meet the demand, you perceive the demand as a stress trap. Stress created by this discrepancy between *demand* and *personal resources* results in a specific stress *response*—Stage 3. The fourth and final stage, *consequences,* pertains to the intensity and long-range negative effects of stress, such as teacher burnout.

Stress, as defined by the cycle, is *The anticipation of inability to respond adequately to a perceived demand, accompanied by the anticipation of negative consequences for an inadequate response* (Gmelch, 1982, p. 3). Note the negative connotation of this definition—distress or negative stress resulting from harm or threats. However, stress can be positive if resulting from challenge or excitement, transforming this negative definition into a positive response by changing the perception from *inability* to *ability:* The anticipation of *ability* to respond adequately to a perceived demand, accompanied by anticipation of a *positive* consequence for an *adequate* response.

Stress reduction programs for teachers should focus on all four stages of the stress cycle: identify stressors in Stage 1; investigate their relation to stressed personality types and behaviors in Stage 2; broaden the repertoire of effective coping responses in Stage 3; and convert the possible negative consequences in Stage 4 from illness to wellness. If the stressors can be identified, negative perceptions turned into positive ones, and a variety of responses utilized in numerous ways, then the consequence will be a healthy and productive teacher.

Stress Traps: Stage 1. Before looking at the stressors that impact teachers, it should be pointed out that these factors are not equally stressful to all teachers, and they do not necessarily lead to burnout. On the contrary, the ability to cope with these stressors can lead to feelings of efficacy—the satisfaction that comes with the knowledge that one can master difficult situations.

Specific sources of stress that teachers experience have been well cataloged. These include the changing roles and new challenges identified earlier in this chapter:

- New leadership roles
- Increased diversity
- Disruptive behavior and violence
- Accountability for addressing social problems
- Inadequate resources
- Lack of parental support
- Expanding partnerships

Here we present several additional, more specific, sets of working conditions that have been found to contribute to stress and burnout among teachers. Major stressors in teaching identified in published research findings and unpublished surveys can be clustered in the following categories:

- Student behavior
- Employee/administrator relations
- Teacher/teacher relations
- Parent/teacher relations
- Time management
- Intrapersonal conflicts

A factor analysis of stressful teaching events discloses three similar themes: *communications within building and district management, classroom management,* and *personal safety and welfare* (Young, 1980).

Turning to a recent nationwide sample, the 1989 Gallup Poll of the Public's Attitudes Toward the Public Schools (Gallup & Elam, 1989) revealed the following conditions, in rank order, that contribute to teacher stress:

- Lack of parent interest/support
- Lack of financial support
- Lack of student interest
- Lack of discipline
- Lack of public support
- Use of drugs
- One-parent households
- Lack of respect for teachers/other students
- Large schools/overcrowding
- Problems with administration
- Low teacher salaries

Last, in his comprehensive review of stress and burnout among teachers, Blase (1986) cites the following stressors:

- Administrative insensitivity

- Bureaucratic incompetence
- Unreasonable or unconcerned parents
- Public criticism
- Involuntary transfers
- Overcrowded classrooms
- Mainstreaming
- Excessive paperwork
- Loss of autonomy and sense of professionalism
- Inadequate salaries/lack of promotional opportunities
- Isolation from other adults/lack of a psychological community
- Inadequate preparation

Teachers begin to control the four stages of stress by examining these potential stressors. A single conflict, for example, may not cause a great deal of difficulty, but couple the conflict with unexpected and unwanted drop-in parents, irate faculty members, or a backlog of paperwork, and teachers are likely to find some prime, personal stress traps. The key to stress reduction rests with identifying stress traps.

The Perception of Stress: Stage 2. Demands surrounding teaching cannot always be diminished, but teachers' perception, attitude, and approach toward their expanding roles can represent the deciding factor in whether or not these demands become stress traps. We usually attribute nervous, tense, and uptight feelings to outside conditions rather than looking within ourselves. Teachers typically blame the upper administration or state and national regulations for pressures to perform beyond one's capabilities. In actuality, much of the stress experienced by teachers is self-imposed. Individual personalities play an important role in determining how stressful academic conditions are. Stressors, by themselves, represent objective demands that only become stress traps when subjectively perceived to be troublesome.

Consider again the definition of stress: The anticipation of inability to respond adequately to a *perceived demand,* accompanied by anticipation of negative consequences for an inadequate response. This definition is based on teachers' *perception* of their ability to meet the challenges of the teaching profession. Thus, it is how they approach their job and life that causes most of their stress. Perception plays the major role in their resilience to, or acceptance of, stress. Of particular importance and deserving of attention is the coronary heart disease personality (Type A behavior) (Friedman & Rosenman, 1974). Type A teachers approach their jobs with intensity and impatience, so much so that they are attacked by heart disease at triple the rate of more relaxed and easygoing Type Bs. But what exactly is Type A behavior and to what extent do teachers exhibit it? A Type A teacher can be characterized as an overly competitive achiever, aggressive, fast working, impatient, restless, hyperalert, explosive in speech, tense, always feeling under pressure, insecure, and unaware of his or her own limitations. In contrast, Type B behavior is the mirror opposite: relaxed, easygoing, seldom impatient, takes more time to enjoy things in life besides work, not easily irritated, works steadily, seldom lacks time, not preoccupied with social achievement, and moves and speaks more slowly.

But who are the Type As? Are administrators more prone than faculty members? A major study entitled *Job Demands and Worker Health* investigated the extent of Type A personality characteristics in 23 occupations, including higher education faculty and administrators (Caplan et al., 1980). Two occupations had by far the highest scores on the Type A index, academic administrators and family physicians. Academic administrators ranked first in Type A behavior, and faculty ranked sixth. In addition, 12% of the academic administrators in this study suffered from coronary heart disease—three times the heart disease rate of faculty (4%).

The stress of being a teacher is what the teacher makes of it—that can be the difference between coping and collapsing. The secret of success is not avoiding stressors in Stage 1 but challenging them with a more positive perceptual response in Stage 2. Whether teachers are exhausted or relaxed under constant pressure depends on how they approach the stress of crisis.

The Coping Response: Stage 3. The literature on coping is significant in volume and diverse in attention, but the exact coping process remains elusive. Researchers from the disciplines of medicine, psychiatry, clinical psychology, behavior science, and education have undertaken studies to understand the phenomenon of stress and the coping responses.

The foremost authority on stress, Hans Selye (1976), pointed out that despite everything that has been written and said about stress and coping, there is no ready-made formula that will suit everyone. As no one technique will suit everyone, how can teachers positively respond to the stress traps identified in Stage 1 of the stress cycle? The first step, of course, is to develop a more positive perceptual awareness to drive the search for effective coping techniques. When faced with a dilemma, teachers might attempt to conceive a technology to control it. Once enough information about a stressor is generated, the tendency is to transform the information into a prescription and control it. However, a prescriptive approach may not be an appropriate technology for coping. Blueprints for exact techniques are not available to teachers. One could even assert that coping is an art, not a science, and therefore should be personalized.

Some researchers have attempted to specify effective and ineffective techniques, which has resulted in misleading conclusions and advice. Others approach coping with a single technique such as relaxation, aerobics, biofeedback, or other such stress interventions. When developing a coping strategy, consider the following propositions as a basis for teachers' response to stress:

1. The teacher is the most important variable; no one coping technique is effective for all teachers in all schools. Therefore, coping techniques must be sensitive to cultural, social, psychological, and environmental differences in teachers.
2. Teachers cannot change the world around them, and they cannot change all the barriers in schools, but they can change how they relate to them.
3. Teachers who cope best develop a repertoire of techniques to counteract different stressors in different situations. Their repertoire of techniques, hence, should represent a holistic approach toward coping.

From Illness to Wellness—Consequences: Stage 4. Behind the achievements of many great academics lies the factor of stress. A study of 1,200 faculty members shows how stress interacted with their productivity (Wilke, Gmelch, & Lovrich, 1985). A moderate amount of stress helped them reach peak performance; however, when stress reached "excessive" proportions (burnout), their performance significantly declined. Note also that without sufficient stress (lack of motivation or challenge—rustout), their performance also declined.

Teachers do experience excessive stress. After all, they can only put out so many brush fires before they run out of resources. It is at this point that stress becomes a most powerful and elusive enemy, playing a major role in a variety of illnesses. By proper management of the stress cycle, the end result of stress should not be illness but wellness. The stress cycle can be a positive, upward spiral toward wellness if teachers are able to manage their stressors in Stage 1, reinforce their resilient personality in Stage 2, and develop a repertoire of positive coping techniques in Stage 3. They can then step up to wellness—they become free of the signs, symptoms, and disabilities of illness—and go beyond, into the preventive, holistic medicine and build up strength through a variety of stress-reduction practices.

Teacher Burnout

The fourth stage of the stress cycle, consequences, takes into account the long-range effects of stress. The consequences of excessive stress are long-range effects on teachers' health and performance. In addition to the physiological ailments of headaches, ulcers, illnesses, or disabilities, some researchers have separated the psychological consequences of stress into three dimensions of burnout: *emotional exhaustion, depersonalization,* and feelings of *low personal accomplishments* (Maslach & Jackson, 1981).

Emotional Exhaustion. Emotional exhaustion occurs when teachers' emotional resources are depleted and they feel they are no longer able to give of themselves at a psychological level. At this stage they feel fatigued, frustrated with their job, and emotionally drained from working at school.

Depersonalization. The second symptom of burnout, depersonalization, occurs when teachers feel negative and cynical attitudes about students, staff, and administration. A depersonalized teacher treats students like objects and may label them with distancing adjectives or pronouns rather than using their names. Teachers at the depersonalization stage may not care what happens to students. They may exhibit signs of detachment and feel callous and cynical toward their colleagues.

Personal Accomplishment. Teachers with low personal accomplishment evaluate themselves negatively and become dissatisfied with their accomplishments in the classroom. Teachers who repeatedly fail to produce desired results develop symptoms of stress and depression. Eventually they believe their actions no longer make a difference and give up trying.

In a recent study of principal burnout and levels of school administration, elementary, middle school, and high school principals experienced significantly higher levels of emotional exhaustion and had lower levels of personal accomplishment than superintendents (Torelli & Gmelch, 1993). This is the bad news, but the good news is that teachers in other studies showed lower levels of burnout than other professionals in the human services area (Iwanicki & Schwab, 1981).

How Teachers Cope With Stress

The general literature on coping is significant in volume and diverse in attention, but the exact coping process remains elusive. Researchers from the disciplines of medicine, psychiatry, clinical psychology, behavior science, and education have undertaken studies to understand the phenomenon of stress and the coping responses. As no one technique will suit everyone, how can teachers maintain their peak performance?

Categories of coping have been identified that if used holistically can help teachers systematically address the stress of teaching. To find out how educators cope with stress we asked over 1,800 of them: "Recognizing that being an educator is demanding, what ways have you found useful in handling the pressures of your job?" (Gmelch & Swent, 1984). The majority of educators cited more than one response. In all, they identified over 3,000 coping responses. Content analysis of these responses enabled grouping in seven categories: social support, physical activities, intellectual stimulation, entertainment, personal interests (e.g., hobbies), self-management, and supportive attitudes (Gmelch, 1988a).

Because coping with stress is a holistic and polytechnic proposition, it is much like weight loss in that if one exercises more, but eats more too, the results may not be as beneficial as exercising more while cutting back or stabilizing one's diet. In much the same way, effective coping consists of building a repertoire of techniques equally balanced in the social, physical, intellectual, entertainment, managerial, personal, and attitudinal categories. The teacher's goal is to reduce stress by adding some of these techniques to his or her present repertoire of stress response. It is not the teacher who masters one technique that copes most effectively and creatively, but the one who possesses the flexibility to call upon any number of techniques from various sources—physical activity, managerial skills, social support, and so on.

1. Teachers indicated *social support* activities helped them break out of stress traps. These included having lunch with colleagues; talking it

out with a trusted friend; developing companionship with friends outside the school; and developing a good working relationship with faculty, staff, and students.

2. Teachers reported that the following *physical activities* helped break the stress attack: individual sports such as jogging, swimming, walking, hiking, horseback riding, martial arts, golf, skiing, and sailing, as well as the team sports of tennis, racquetball, and basketball.

3. Within the third category, *intellectual stimulation*, teachers cited attending professional conferences and experiencing cultural outlets such as theaters and museums.

4. *Entertainment* encompassed the fourth category and included watching television; going to a movie or out to dinner; and taking a vacation, mini vacations, or weekend vacation.

5. The fifth category consisted of *personal interest* techniques such as playing a musical instrument, gardening, gourmet cooking, taking a nature hike, working on arts or crafts, creative writing, taking avocational classes, and other personal hobbies unrelated to work. Some cited just plain "dropping out of sight."

6. Teachers identified a proliferation of *self-management* techniques they used to cope with the pressures, including planning strategically; effectively and efficiently using time; dealing with conflict constructively; and having an excellent, dedicated principal and staff.

7. Finally, teachers identified numerous coping techniques that could be categorized simply as supportive *attitudes*. The majority of all the coping responses fell into this important category.

Each teacher has his or her own tastes, time schedules, and preferences. Teachers must discover for themselves the activities most agreeable to them in each of the coping categories—but remember, the answer is in the holistic approach to stress reduction. No one response taken separately presents *the* answer to coping, but taken collectively teachers can view these categories as a coping taxonomy from which to seek their own stress reduction.

Conclusion

As teachers develop new partnerships and learn new ways of integrating theory and practice to improve schooling for diverse populations, they will continue to experience stress. However, as Selye (1976) suggests and our examination of six common myths about stress affirms, stress can be both positive and negative—positive to the extent that it energizes teachers and leads to feelings of accomplishment and mastery, and negative to the extent that it results in failure to properly manage the stress cycle discussed in this chapter.

In helping teachers develop the sense of personal efficacy needed to manage stress and avoid burnout (Parkay, Greenwood, Olejnik, & Proller, 1988), teacher educators and staff developers play a key role. They are in a position to help pre- and inservice teachers dispel the common myths about stress, understand the four stages of the stress cycle, and develop effective coping strategies. To the extent that pre- and inservice teachers gain insight into unique dynamics of their stress cycles, they will be able to develop more effective coping strategies and thereby increase both their effectiveness and their professional satisfaction.

References

ALH Research, Inc. (1993). Poll for Harvard School of Public Health.

Blase, J. J. (1986). A qualitative analysis of sources of teacher stress: Consequences for performance. *American Educational Research Journal, 23*(1), 13-40.

Borich, G. D. (1993). *Clearly outstanding: Making each day count in your classroom.* Boston: Allyn & Bacon.

Brown, N. J. (1983). *An analysis of stress factors as perceived by elementary teachers.* Unpublished doctoral dissertation, University of Arkansas.

Caplan, R. D., Cobb, S., French, J.R.P., Van Harrison, R., & Pinneau, S. R. (1980). *Job demands and worker health: Main effects and occupational differences.* Washington, DC: U.S. Government Printing Office.

Coates, T. J., & Thoresen, C.E. (1976). Teacher anxiety: A review with recommendations. *Review of Educational Research, 46,* 59-184.

Dedrick, C.V.L., & Raschke, D. B. (1990). *The special educator and job stress.* Washington, DC: National Education Association.

Dunham, J. (1992). *Stress in teaching* (2nd ed.). London: Routledge.

Dworkin, A. G. (1987). *Teacher burnout in the public schools: Structural causes and consequences for children.* Albany: State University of New York Press.

Education Commission on the States. (1990). *New strategies for producing minority teachers.* Denver, CO: Author.

Farber, B. A. (1991). *Crisis in education: Stress and burnout in the American teacher.* San Francisco: Jossey-Bass.

Feitler, F. C., & Tokar, E. B. (1981, April). *Teacher stress: Sources, symptoms and job satisfaction.* Paper presented at the annual meeting of the American Educational Research Association, Los Angeles.

Friedman, M., & Rosenman, R. H. (1974). *Type A behavior and your heart.* New York: Knopf.

Gallup, A. M., & Elam, S. M. (1989). The 21st annual Gallup poll of the public's attitudes toward the public schools. *Phi Delta Kappan, 71*(1), 41-54.

Gmelch, W. H. (1982). *Beyond stress to effective management.* New York: John Wiley.

Gmelch, W. H. (1988a). Educators' response to stress: Towards a coping taxonomy. *Journal of Educational Administration, 26*(2), 134-140.

Gmelch, W. H. (1988b). Research perspectives on administrative stress: Causes, reactions, responses and consequences. *Journal of Educational Administration, 26*(2), 1-9.

Gmelch, W. H., & Chan, W. (1994). *Thriving on stress for success.* Thousand Oaks, CA: Corwin.

Gmelch, W. H., Lovrich, N. P., & Wilke, P. K. (1984). Stress in academe: A national perspective. *Research in Higher Education, 20*(4), 477-490.

Gmelch, W. H., & Swent, B. (1984). Management team stressors and their impact on administrators' health. *Journal of Educational Administration, 22*(2), 192-205.

Grant, C. A., & Secada, W. G. (1990). Preparing teachers for diversity. In W. R. Houston (Ed.), *Handbook of research on teacher education* (pp. 403-422). New York: Macmillan.

Haberman, M. (1989). More minority teachers. *Phi Delta Kappan, 70*(10), 771-776.

Hodgkinson, H. L. (1992). *A demographic look at tomorrow.* Washington, DC: Institute for Educational Leadership, Inc./Center for Demographic Policy.

Holt, P., Fine, M. J., & Tollefson, N. (1987). Mediating stress: Survival of the hardy. *Psychology in the Schools, 24,* 51-58.

Humphrey, J. N., & Humphrey, J. H. (1986). *Coping with stress in teaching.* New York: AMS.

Iwanicki, F. E., & Schwab, R. L. (1981). A cross validation study of the Maslach Burnout Inventory. *Educational and Psychological Measurement, 41,* 1167-1174.

Koch, J. L., Tung, R., Gmelch, W. H., & Swent, B. (1982). Job stress among school administrators: Factorial dimensions and differential effects. *Journal of Applied Psychology, 67*(4), 493-499.

Kozol, J. (1991). *Savage inequalities: Children in America's schools.* New York: Crown.

Livingston, C. (1992). Introduction: Teacher leadership for restructured schools. In C. Livingston (Ed.), *Teachers as leaders: Evolving roles* (pp. 1-15). Washington, DC: National Education Association.

Louis Harris & Associates. (1992). *Metropolitan Life Survey of the American Teacher 1992.* New York: Author.

Maslach, C., & Jackson, S. E. (1981). The measurement of experienced burnout. *Journal of Occupational Behavior, 2,* 99-113.

National Center for Education Statistics. (1985). The relationship of parental involvement to high-school grades. *Bulletin.* Washington, DC: U.S. Department of Education.

National Center for Education Statistics. (1992). *Digest of education statistics, 1992* (Vol. 60). Washington, DC: Office of Educational Research and Improvement, U.S. Department of Education.

National Education Association. (1991). *Status of the American public school teacher, 1990-91.* Washington, DC: Author.

Parkay, F. W. (1983). *White teacher, black school: The professional growth of a ghetto teacher.* New York: Praeger.

Parkay, F. W., Greenwood, G., Olejnik, R., & Proller, N. (1988). A study of the relationships among teacher efficacy, locus of control, and stress. *Journal of Research and Development in Education, 21*(4), 13-22.

Selye, H. (1976). *The stress of life.* New York: McGraw-Hill.

Southern Education Foundation. (1990). *Desperately seeking teachers.* Atlanta: Author.

Torelli, J. A., & Gmelch, W. H. (1993). Occupational stress and burnout in educational administration. *People and Education, 1*(4), 363-381.

Wilke, P. K., Gmelch, W. H., & Lovrich, N. P. (1985). Stress and productivity: Evidence of the inverted U-function. *Public Productivity Review, 9*(4), 342-356.

Young, T. (1980). Teacher stress: One school district's approach. *Action in Teacher Education, 2*(4), 39.

Contexts:
Reflections and Implications

Michael Fullan

In the overview to this division, I stated that a more comprehensive framework was needed to guide teacher development efforts. Here I will build on this argument by emphasizing that guided *action* is essential. We need to become preoccupied by working on how to "get there from here."

Chapter 1:
University-School Partnerships in Co-Reform

Glickman, Lunsford, and Szuminski in Chapter 1 provide a powerful framework for action. The authors rightly stress that although there exist different normative and logistical issues embedded in their respective histories, teacher educators and public school teachers must join together in co-reform initiatives. The authors elaborate on what I called the moral purpose of teaching by addressing the higher order question: What should students be taught, and how should they be taught so that the methods of teaching are consistent with an education for a democratic life?

The action for Glickman et al. consists of deliberate co-reform projects that attempt to change the university and the school conjointly. These authors propose many more "crossovers" of involvement between the two cultures while working on common themes of reform.

Goodlad (1994) has gone some distance in mapping out what this means for university-school partnerships. Similarly, at the University of Toronto we are moving toward a new way of life with school districts and school partners that have the following characteristics:

- Cohorts of student teachers

- Teams of faculty and school-based staff
- Small clusters of schools in which subgroups of students spend considerable time as part of the staff of the whole school (not just in a classroom)
- College of education development that emphasizes, for example, continuous improvement of teaching and greater collaboration for teacher educators
- Additional alliances with other postsecondary faculties and institutions, businesses, and social agencies
- Teacher development curriculum focused on the educational reform issues of the day (e.g., authentic assessment, parent involvement, technology, etc.)

These elements are not new, but their deep and comprehensive implementation is new. These developments do not consist of identifying only a few professional development sites, but rather in establishing a new culture and way of life for *schools as a whole*. Student teacher development, teacher development for school staff, and college of education professional development all become interrelated with educational reform being the substance of action as we work toward developing new cultures and new structures in education. Glickman et al. set the stage in that such co-reform represents our greatest need and greatest challenge for the future.

Chapter 2:
School Principals and Changing Roles

Bredeson, in Chapter 2 on role changes for principals in restructured schools, describes some of the early dilemmas for principals and teachers as schools move toward greater school-based reform. He takes up the various dimensions of changes in power relationships entailed in restructured schools. In my view, there are several key elements involved in changing educational roles, not all of which are clear. First, the research shows that most examples of site-based empowerment result in some changes in governance participation (on the part of teachers and parents), but not necessarily any changes in the *teaching-learning culture* of the school (Fullan, 1993). Thus, it is easy to get lost in the "empowerment triangle" without moving ahead.

Second, and the inverse of the first point, it is becoming increasingly clear that the new work of the school principal is to lead the development of collaborative work cultures in what we call "reculturing" (Fullan, 1993). Clark and Astuto (1994) describe the new role well:

> Viewing teachers as members of a professional community focuses attention on norms of collegiality and on the ethics of professional practice. This shift has implications for the work of principals. Sources of control are built into the processes of professional work and collaboration, not into the hierarchy of authority. Principals' actions that focus on stability, goal setting, regularity, accountability, intervention, control, and efficiency are either redundant, destructive of cooperation and a sense of community, or both. Alternative actions that support the professional community and the stakeholder community require more complex, professional expertise on the part of principals. Facilitating the working communities of a school requires actions that foster activity, the development of a professional community that incorporates diversity and difference, and the creation of a sense of individual efficacy and empowerment among students and staff members. (p. 513)

Third, it is not at all clear where the changing roles of principals and teachers will end up. One could entertain the provocative hypothesis that one of the reasons that the "principal as key" theme stands out in the literature is that teachers are too dependent on the strong principal (and too vulnerable when the principal is weak). The more basic goal of teacher development is the development of *all* teachers, as I argued earlier. If and when this occurs, the role of the principal may not turn out to be so prominent, or in the long run the role may disappear. Be that as it may, the role of the principal for the immediate future is to help develop collaborative work cultures.

Chapter 3:
Changing Teacher Roles and Occupational Stress

Gmelch and Parkay in Chapter 3 provide us with another broad perspective on the social-psychological conditions of teaching, in particular, how societal changes have dramatically increased the complexity and stressfulness of teaching. They document the nature and extent of stress but unpack the concept in an insightful way by identifying several myths about stress, such as "stress is harmful." With this more balanced perspective they offer a model by which we can analyze the pros and cons of stress and begin to act more effectively to control its consequences. Bredeson in Chapter 2 also discussed role strains and called for support for the new role of the teacher.

I should like to put the problem another way in the form of an illustration. Organized groups of critics of schools are becoming effective, I believe, because they are increasingly using clear language and specific examples, to which educators respond with philosophical rationales ("we are using active learning to teach the whole child"). Generalized responses to specific charges lack credibility and add to the stress and fortress mentality of teachers. One (not the only) answer is for teacher development to be addressed more broadly as in Figure DI.1 in the overview.

In other words, teachers must develop the knowledge base and interactive skills to be able to "explain themselves" in the face of criticism. This is not to say that the critics are right or that they will be satisfied, but rather that one of the most fundamental ways to alleviate stress and role strain is to develop the expertise and confidence to respond to critics by participating in forums and by establishing alliances. Stress, as Gmelch and Parkay emphasize, is not just "objective"—that is, people with certain capacities are able not only to manage stress more effectively, but also to turn it in many situations to opportunities for growth and improvement.

On Getting There From Here

The external pressures for reform will continue to mount. What is absolutely crucial is that reformers internal to the educational system begin to establish more comprehensive initiatives, in the first instance, in spite of the system. Breakthroughs will occur when internal and external forces for change connect.

There has never been a more compelling time for the teaching profession to come to the fore. As Sarason (1993) explains: "No profession more than education provides as exciting an opportunity to understand the society in which we live: how it has changed, will change, should change" (p. 138).

The implications of this new role for education are enormous, and they apply equally to teacher educators in universities as to school- and district-based educators. It will take a quantum increase in the co-reform activities of universities and schools working together to achieve any serious impact. Fortunately, there are many small-scale initiatives moving in this direction. It is not at all clear that they will reach a critical mass in time to make a difference, but the direction is more and more compelling as we realize that failure to move rapidly is going to result in a deterioration of the status quo.

References

Clark, D., & Astuto, T. (1994). Redirecting reform: Challenges to popular assumptions about teachers and students. *Phi Delta Kappan, 75*(7), 513-520.

Fullan, M. (1993). *Change forces: Probing the depths of educational reform.* Bristol, PA: Falmer.

Goodlad, J. (1994). *Educational renewal.* San Francisco: Jossey-Bass.

Sarason, S. (1993). *You are thinking of teaching.* San Francisco: Jossey-Bass.

DIVISION II

Processes for Leadership and Change: Teacher Leadership for Urban Schools

PROCESSES: OVERVIEW AND FRAMEWORK

Kenneth Zeichner

Bernadette Baker

Kenneth Zeichner is Hoefs-Bascom Professor of Teacher Education, University of Wisconsin-Madison, and Senior Researcher with the National Center for Research on Teacher Learning, Michigan State University. His recent publications include *Educating Teachers for Cultural Diversity*, "Personal Renewal and Social Reconstruction Through Teacher Research," and *Issues and Practices in Inquiry-Oriented Teacher Education*.

Bernadette Baker is a Ph.D. student in the Department of Curriculum and Instruction, University of Wisconsin-Madison. She has an undergraduate degree in human movement studies from the University of Queensland and a master's degree in education from Deakin University. Her research interests include teacher education, curriculum studies, and feminism and history.

Teacher Education for Urban Schools: The Status Quo

Much has been written in recent years about the poor track record of college- and university-based teacher education in preparing teachers who are willing and capable of teaching in the urban school systems of the United States (e.g., Haberman, 1987). For the most part, teacher education students who are white and monolingual come to their teacher education programs with very little direct experience with people from backgrounds different from their own, even in states with a lot of cultural diversity, such as California (Gomez, in press). In addition, they tend to view diversity as a problem rather than a resource and have little knowledge about different ethnic and racial groups in the United States, their cultures, their histories, and their contributions to the making of our nation (Paine, 1989; Zimpher & Ashburn, 1992). Finally, most teacher education students want to teach students like themselves, in settings they are familiar with, and are often uncomfortable with personal contact with parents from ethnic and language minorities (Larke, 1990). According to Howey (1992), the majority of teacher education students nationally report that they are not well prepared to teach students from ethnic and language minorities. According to Goodlad (1990), the majority of teacher education students do not even believe that all students are capable of learning within schools.

The fact that the urban schools of the United States are increasingly populated by the very students that teacher education students do not want to teach is one aspect of the current crisis in urban teacher preparation. Students from ethnic and language minorities already comprise the majority of students in many urban districts (Quality Education for Minorities Project, 1990) and will increasingly do so in the future. These students are more likely to be poor, hungry, and in poor health, and to drop out of school, than their middle-class counterparts. College- and university-based teacher education programs for the most part have continued as Carter and Larke's chapter states to prepare teachers for middle- and upper-class students who do not attend urban public schools.

The Task of Preparing Teachers for Urban Schools

Recent research has identified the scope of the task that lies ahead if college- and university-based teacher education is to make a contribution to the preparation of teachers for urban schools. Unless colleges and universities make a concerted effort to recruit and prepare teachers specifically for urban schools, it is likely that the alternate-route programs (e.g., Stoddart, 1990) that have increasingly assumed responsibility for urban teacher preparation in the United States will become the major provider of teachers to urban school districts.

There are three dimensions involved in the preparation of teachers for cultural diversity in urban schools: (a) selection, (b) socialization, and (c) institutional change. First, given the description provided above of the culturally encapsulated nature of prospective teachers across the United States and their generally negative attitudes toward cultural diversity and low expectations for learning by students of ethnic and language minorities, it seems questionable that conventional teacher education programs with their fragmented curricula and low status in the institutions that house them (Liston & Zeichner, 1991; Schneider, 1987) can remedy these cultural deficits of candidates within the scope of time available to work with them. The literature on teacher learning indicates that even under the best of circumstances, teacher education programs are weak interventions (Zeichner & Gore, 1990). If all that were involved were "training" prospective teachers to use certain teaching strategies, that would be one thing, but when the task involves, as it does here, the transformation of attitudes, assumptions, and practices developed over a lifetime (Nieto, 1992), the issue of selection becomes crucial.

It is becoming increasingly clear that some selection criteria, such as the interviews developed by Haberman (1987) to screen candidates for urban teaching, must be used to determine potential abilities for successful teaching in urban schools. It is clear that instead of depending solely on grade point averages, test scores, and the glowing testimony of young college students wanting to be teachers because they "love kids," we have to focus more on picking the right people rather than on changing the wrong ones because, as so much research on teacher learning has shown—including two of the chapters in this section—teacher education often reinforces and strengthens the attitudes and orientations that prospective teachers bring to it (see National Center for Research on Teacher Education, 1991).

A second dimension of the task of preparing teachers for urban schools involves what is done within teacher education programs to develop the cultural sensitivity and intercultural teaching competence of teachers. Here research has shown that certain practices, such as the integration of a concern for cultural diversity throughout a teacher education program and community field experiences that use community people as teacher educators, contribute toward the preparation of teachers who can engage in the kind of culturally congruent, interactive, and meaning-oriented teaching that we already know is needed if we hope to be able to teach all students to achieve high academic standards (Au & Kawakami, 1994; Ladson-Billings, 1990; Villegas, 1991; Zeichner, 1994).

The institutional context of teacher education is critical in determining the success of socialization efforts within teacher education programs to develop the intercultural teaching competence needed for success in urban schools (Villegas, 1993). The lack of diversity and the cultural insularity among teacher education faculty (Howey & Zimpher, 1990) and the lack of broad institutional commitments to diversity in colleges and universities (Grant, 1993) raise serious questions about the capacity of teacher education institutions to support and sustain the kind of teacher education programs needed to prepare teachers for urban schools. Research has identified several promising strategies for enhancing the institutional capacity of teacher education programs to prepare teachers to teach all students successfully, including consortium arrangements that provide faculty expertise to programs in multicultural education and staff development for teacher educators (Melnick & Zeichner, 1994; Zeichner, in press).

Three Research Reports

What follows is a set of three chapters that, in different ways, address the task of preparing teachers for urban schools. In Chapter 4, Carter and Larke present a case study of 45 prospective teachers who had initially expressed a preference for teaching in suburban schools. After volunteering over a three-semester period to participate in urban field experiences and seminars, 9 of the 45 (20%) applied for teaching positions in urban areas and were hired. Ponticell, Olson, and Charlier, in Chapter 5, focus on the important task of inservice teacher education and the teacher's work context in urban schools. Finally, in Chapter 6, Holt-Reynolds examines how prospective teachers construct meaning from a course, the importance of beliefs based on personal history in how prospective teachers interpret course material, and prospective teachers' support for teaching practices advocated in the course for reasons different from those held by the instructor.

References

Au, K., & Kawakami, A. (1994). Cultural congruence in instruction. In E. Hollins, J. King, & W. Hayman (Eds.), *Teaching diverse populations* (pp. 5-23). Albany: State University of New York Press.

Gomez, M. L. (in press). Teacher education reform and prospective teachers' perspectives on teaching "other people's children." In K. Zeichner, S. Melnick, & M. Gomez (Eds.), *Complexities of reform in teacher education.* New York: Teachers College Press.

Goodlad, J. (1990). *Teachers for our nation's schools.* San Francisco: Jossey-Bass.

Grant, C. (1993). The multicultural preparation of U. S. teachers: Some hard truths. In G. Verma (Ed.), *Inequality and teacher education* (pp. 82-106). London: Falmer.

Haberman, M. (1987). *Recruiting and selecting teachers for urban schools.* New York: ERIC Clearinghouse on Urban Education, Institute for Urban and Minority Education.

Howey, K. (1992). Teacher education in the U.S.: Trends and issues. *Teacher Educator, 27*(4), 3-11.

Howey, K., & Zimpher, N. (1990). Professors and deans of education. In W. R. Houston (Ed.), *Handbook of research on teacher education* (pp. 349-370). New York: Macmillan.

Ladson-Billings, G. (1990). Culturally relevant teaching. *College Board Review, 155,* 20-25.

Larke, P. (1990). *Cultural awareness inventory: Assessing the sensitivity of preservice teachers.* Paper presented at the annual meeting of the American Educational Research Association, Boston.

Liston, D., & Zeichner, K. (1991). *Teacher education and the social conditions of schooling.* New York: Routledge.

Melnick, S., & Zeichner, K. (1994). *Teacher education for cultural diversity: Enhancing the capacity of teacher education institutions to address diversity issues.* Paper presented at the annual meeting of the American Association of Colleges for Teacher Education, Chicago.

National Center for Research on Teacher Education. (1991). *Findings from the teachers education and learning to teach study.* East Lansing: College of Education, Michigan State University.

Nieto, S. (1992). *Affirming diversity: The sociopolitical context of multicultural education.* New York: Longman.

Paine, L. (1989). *Orientation towards diversity: What do prospective teachers bring?* (Research report 89-9). East Lansing: National Center for Research on Teacher Education, Michigan State University.

Quality Education for Minorities Project. (1990). *Education that works: An action plan for the education of minorities.* Cambridge, MA: Author.

Schneider, B. (1987). Tracing the provenance of teacher education. In T. Popkewitz (Ed.), *Critical studies in teacher education* (pp. 211-241). New York: Falmer.

Stoddart, T. (1990). The Los Angeles Unified School District Intern Program: Recruiting and preparing teachers for an urban context. *Peabody Journal of Education, 67*(3), 84-122.

Villegas, A. M. (1991). *Culturally responsive pedagogy for the 1990's and beyond.* Princeton, NJ: Educational Testing Service.

Villegas, A. M. (1993). *Restructuring teacher education for diversity: The innovative curriculum.* Paper presented at the annual meeting of the American Educational Research Association, Atlanta.

Zeichner, K. (1994). *Defining the achievement gap: Issues of pedagogy, definition of knowledge and the teaching-learning process.* Philadelphia, PA: Research for Better Schools.

Zeichner, K. (in press). Preparing teachers for cross-cultural teaching. In W. Hawley & A. Jackson (Eds.), *Toward a common destiny: Race and ethnic relations in American schools.* San Francisco: Jossey-Bass.

Zeichner, K., & Gore, J. (1990). Teacher socialization. In W. R. Houston (Ed.), *Handbook of research on teacher education* (pp. 329-348). New York: Macmillan.

Zimpher, N., & Ashburn, E. (1992). Countering parochialism among teacher candidates. In M. Dillworth (Ed.), *Diversity in teacher education* (pp. 40-62). San Francisco: Jossey-Bass.

4 Preparing the Urban Teacher: Reconceptualizing the Experience

Norvella P. Carter

Patricia J. Larke

Norvella P. Carter is Assistant Professor in the College of Education at Illinois State University and Director of the Chicago Metropolitan Teacher Education Center. Her research interests are urban education, multicultural education, and educating teachers for urban settings.

Patricia J. Larke is Associate Professor in the College of Education at Texas A&M University and Director of the Multicultural Mentoring Project (formerly Minority Mentorship Project). Her research interests are multicultural education and educating teachers for diverse classrooms.

ABSTRACT

Educating teachers for the urban experience is a major challenge for teacher education institutions. The teacher shortage has been critical for our schools as a whole, but the shortage in urban areas can be described as catastrophic. However, getting candidates with credentials to seek employment in urban settings is an even more intractable problem. Many education institutions are beginning to reconceptualize how they prepare the urban teacher. In this chapter, we discuss (a) a model of a redesigned urban teacher education center, (b) a description of a revised course that provided a knowledge and experience base about urban schools and communities, and (c) a case study of preservice teachers who did and did not seek employment in urban schools.

Educating teachers for the urban experience is clearly a challenge for all those preparing teachers. The teacher shortage has been an issue for many schools, but the shortage in urban areas has been catastrophic in recent years. However, getting candidates with credentials to seek employment in urban settings is an even more intractable problem, which is heightened by concerns about working in unsafe environments, with inadequate facilities and inadequate instructional supplies and equipment. These concerns have been dramatized by the media, and researchers have sometimes sought to "explain" urban conditions through deficit theories and by unchallenged stereotypes that promote racism and discrimination (Grant, 1989; Harris, Heid, Carter, & Brown, 1991; Kietovics & Nussel, 1994; Natriello & Zumwalt, 1993).

Urban school districts account for more than 50% of the total school districts and teaching population in the nation, and teacher education institutions are responsible for educating teachers for urban schools (Quality Education for Minorities Project, 1990). However, in many states over 80% of education graduates do not teach in urban settings (Haberman, 1991c; Kotsakis, 1991). In fact, it has been reported that graduates from most college and university teacher education programs have very little interest in urban school environments (Tillman, 1989). Many education institutions are beginning to reconceptualize how they prepare urban teachers. In this chapter, we offer an overview of urban education and teachers, a model of an urban teacher education center that was redesigned, a description of a revised course that provided a knowledge and experience base about urban schools and communities, and a case study of preservice teachers who did and did not pursue employment in urban schools.

Urban Education and Teachers:
An Overview

Although urban schools have existed since the development of teacher preparation programs, specific issues about urban education historically emerged only as a result of legal mandates, such as *Brown v. Board of Education* and Title VI and Title VII of the Civil Rights Act of 1964, and as a result of federal funding, such as the Elementary and Secondary Education Act of 1965. Such actions were instrumental in increasing the concern about urban education. Still, few studies have been conducted to examine the limited number of programs focusing on the education of preservice teachers for urban environments (Haberman, 1991a). Most traditional teacher education programs have focused on the preparation of teachers for monocultural classrooms with students from middle and upper socioeconomic backgrounds (Avery & Walker, 1993; Grant & Secada, 1990).

Studies have reported that three variables—(a) location of school within city, (b) demographic composition of the school-age population, and (c) the socioeconomic status of the community—challenged teacher education programs to prepare teachers for diverse environments (Carter & Carter, 1991; Grant, 1989). As studies and reports became more focused on critical issues of schools, research began to identify characteristics that were unique to urban schools (Brookover, 1982; Edmonds, 1979; Grant, 1989; Haberman, 1987). These studies reveal that the teaching environment was different in urban schools than in suburban or rural schools (Harris et al., 1991; Kietovics & Nussel, 1994). Unfortunately, many of the differences highlighted negative issues about teaching and learning in urban schools with the use of labels such as "ghetto," "deprived schools," and "impoverished" and references to students as "disadvantaged," "culturally deprived," and "disenfranchised."

During the late 1970s and early 1980s, researchers began to describe urban education and urban students in a more positive and equitable way. For example, Edmonds (1979) reported that urban schools can be effective schools when they have a strong administrative leadership, when they have a climate of expectation in which no children are permitted to fall below the minimum level of achievement, when there is an atmosphere that is orderly without being rigid and quiet without being oppressive, when pupil acquisition of basic skills takes precedence over all other school activities, and when pupil progress is monitored frequently.

With the rising concern about how to enhance the quality of education in urban schools, studies began to support the significance of teachers' behaviors and attitudes in the educational process (Gollnick & Chinn, 1986; Sleeter & Grant, 1994). Urban teachers were found to need high levels of cultural sensitivity, which would be demonstrated through their attitudes, behaviors, and instructional practices in the classroom (Larke, 1992; Zeichner, 1992).

Researchers have argued extensively that urban teachers need specific skills and preservice teachers need experiences to develop those specific skills (Grant, 1986; Haberman, 1991b; Shulman, 1986; Stallings & Quinn, 1991). Haberman (1991a, 1991b), for example, identifies seven characteristics of urban teachers that outweigh ability and instructional skills in teaching. He reports that urban teachers need to be persistent when seeking solutions to never-ending problems, exhibit a response to authority that supports student learning regardless of school policy, have the ability to apply generalizations about learning and development to a specific classroom situation, have an appealing approach to students in at-risk situations that indicates the teacher has a willingness to be accountable for teaching all children, have a professional orientation that necessitates teaching even the children they do not like or love, have a resistance to burnout and learn to remediate problems, and have a recognition of their own humanness.

It is becoming more widely understood that preservice teachers who aspire to become urban teachers should be provided with the necessary experiences to enable them to be effective in urban classrooms. We now turn to a new model that provides urban experiences to assist preservice teachers in learning to teach in urban settings.

Program Changes: The New Model

The teacher education program at a midwestern university was reflective of a growing number of large teacher education centers needing to redesign programs to prepare students to teach in urban settings with a diverse population. The program redesign focused on three areas: (a) the core experience, (b) the field experience, and (c) student teaching seminars (see Figure 4.1).

The core experience refers to coursework and preclinical field experience that takes place after the students have been accepted into the College of Education and occurs in the students' sophomore, junior, and senior years at the university. The traditional core experience required the students to spend 100 hours in the classroom before the student teaching experience. These 100 hours were spent in predominantly white middle-class settings where the socioeconomic status was similar to the university student's own experience. The students were not prepared for diverse classrooms and would not consider a student teaching placement in a multicultural setting.

In the new model, major changes took place to provide training for students who might consider teaching in diverse school settings. First,

THE CORE EXPERIENCE

Pre-Clinical Experiences

Urban School Setting
Diverse Suburban Setting

Multicultural Education Class

Urban Studies (history, child, environment)
Urban Methods Application
Urban Teaching Strategies

THE FIELD EXPERIENCE

Placement	Cooperating Teachers
Urban Expertise	Urban Setting
Diverse Suburban Setting	Positive Attitude
	Willing to Mentor
School Selection	**Supervisors**
University Professors	Urban Specialists
University Supervisors	Urban Practitioners on Loan
(Visitation, Observation, Interview)	
Cooperating Teacher Selection	**Professional Development**
Principal	Workshops for Teachers
University Faculty	Graduate Courses in Education
	Seminars/Resource Materials

STUDENT TEACHING SEMINARS

Informal Sessions

Sharing
Journals

Practical Application

Classroom Management
Resume/Mock Interviews/ Job Search

Figure 4.1. Program Redesign: Components of New Model

culturally diverse classrooms were incorporated as mandatory requirements for 18 of the 100 hours of preclinical experience. Second, buses were
made available to transport students to schools with diverse populations.
Many students traveled to major urban settings, located sometimes over
100 miles from campus, to spend the day observing and tutoring students
for preclinical credit toward their 100 hours. Some of the students formed

relationships with children in the schools during this period and developed a "pen pal" correspondence program with support from the university. The college students and children in the classrooms wrote letters to one another with postage provided by the university. In the first letter, the college students sent a variety of small gifts (i.e., gum, candy, pencils) that amounted to less than $5 in value.

In addition, multicultural education courses were required before students reached the student teaching experience. These courses enabled students to develop knowledge about urban children and how they learn. A wide variety of instructional strategies such as cooperative learning, whole language, and teaching and using instructional games adapted to the urban child were incorporated into the program as well.

The second major change was in student teacher placements. New school districts with diverse populations of students were selected as teacher training sites for student teachers. The selection of schools was based on a pool of recommendations provided by a team of university professors who had experience working with urban schools. The selection process included visitations to schools, observations in classrooms, and interviews of administrators and teachers. Positive climates and use of effective teaching practices in classrooms were criteria used to select school sites. Student teaching placements in urban and multicultural suburban school districts provided experiences for effective training of urban teachers and sometimes resulted in employment opportunities for student teachers following graduation.

Research reveals that positive, efficacious teachers play a major role in influencing the perceptions, attitudes, and behaviors of preservice teachers (Martin, 1989). Accordingly, teachers in urban school sites were selected as cooperating teachers on the basis of effective classroom practices as well as a willingness to share information in a positive and professional manner when the information dealt with sensitive or serious issues. The goal was to select cooperating teachers who would share their resources, interests, expertise, and knowledge in teaching diverse children. The university supported the professional development of the cooperating teachers by providing periodic workshops, graduate courses, seminars, and resource materials. In addition, assistance from a new team of university supervisors who had prior experience in urban and diverse classrooms provided guidance for student teachers. The goal was to surround student teachers with support from supervisors who had been competent, positive teachers in urban settings and who could contribute meaningful insights and experiences on a consistent basis. Some of the supervisors were actual practitioners who were on loan from school districts for one or two semesters to work for the university in preparing preservice teachers. For the practitioner on loan, a contract was negotiated with the school district to allow the teacher to work for the university for one year or one semester. After termination of the contract, the teacher returned to the district with new experiences that were shared with other teachers in the school district.

The third change was made in the student teaching seminars. In the traditional program, university supervisors taught seminars as formal classes, complete with reading assignments, written papers, and grades. Seminars were redesigned to be supportive of the students' ongoing field experience rather than resembling a formal class. Attendance was the only requirement, and class assignments were eliminated. This practice removed pressure and anxiety from the student teachers and created a supportive climate for their efforts during the student teaching experience. The students attended the seminars to gain information and share experiences. In addition, the university scheduled monthly seminars throughout the semester to allow students to express concerns and interact with practicing teachers who were invited to share their expertise. Topics such as classroom management, teaching and learning styles, and the job search were added to the seminar.

Opportunities to prepare for employment were provided through professional resume-writing sessions and mock interviews. Urban recruiters were invited as a special feature at the end of each semester. In fact, many students were offered employment before they completed their student teaching experience. At the close of the semester a formal review of the progress and effectiveness of each semester is conducted to determine if changes in school sites, seminar topics, or student teacher placement are needed.

The Course

A course entitled School Community Involvement was developed and offered as an elective and served to support preservice teachers in urban and suburban diverse student teaching placements. During the course, students' attitudes and perceptions about urban settings were examined through personal journals and class discussions. At the end of the semester, individual exit interviews were conducted. This course, which was taught by a professor who was a former urban principal and teacher, required school and community involvement through urban field experience and included a multicultural education component.

The course met once a week for 16 weeks. During the first three semesters it was offered, 24, 14, and 7 students, respectively, took the class, for a total of 45 students over the three-semester period. The decreasing number of student teachers in the program was due to the lower number of students admitted to the teacher education program. The course, which met 2 hours weekly, included minimal lectures, carefully selected guest speakers, three all-day field trips in urban schools and communities, and class discussion. Class discussion was designed as an integral component to help students debrief, critically analyze conditions of schools and communities, and challenge stereotypes about urban schools and communities.

Weekly journals were submitted by the students, and the professor responded to them. The students were encouraged to share truthfully and "from the heart" their feelings and opinions about student teaching and the course as long as they were respectful of others' feelings. The students were asked also not to "judge" one another and to respect the confidentiality of the classroom group.

Each semester, there were three field trips, one to a community agency and two to schools, one predominantly African American and the other predominantly Hispanic American. The trips to the urban schools were arranged so that the students, as a group, spent some time with the principal learning about the school and touring the building. The principal, having advance information concerning grade choice, assigned each student to a classroom where ½ day was spent with the teacher and students. The principal provided the names of all teachers and a class list of their pupils in advance to enable the university students to become familiar with the names of the children. The visiting university students were also informed in advance of the children's grade level so that appropriate instructional sessions and games could be planned. After lunch, the university student would spend the remainder of the day teaching and sharing games with the children under the supervision of the classroom teacher. The university students were required to have lesson plans for the instructional sessions and games evaluated before each field trip.

The second school trip was spent tutoring students and interviewing parents at a school. This provided the university students an opportunity to talk with some children individually and to gain greater insights into different cultures by spending time with the parents who volunteered in the building.

An additional trip was spent gathering information at a community center that serves one of the schools. Agencies such as the fire department, police department, public library, and local hospital all have information and materials available for teacher use. In some cases, representatives from the agency will do a workshop for the children or the school faculty identifying services for the school. The student was asked to visit the actual facility and prepare a written and oral report on the facility from a perspective of usefulness to teachers.

The purpose of the field trips was to provide greater exposure to a variety of urban settings. The visits with the parents and community agencies enhanced the students' knowledge of other aspects of urban teaching outside of the classroom.

Analysis of Experiences: A Case Study

The 45 preservice students in this study were Anglo, middle-class students who expressed a goal of teaching in suburbia. These students consented to student teaching in an urban school ($n = 19$) or a culturally/economically diverse suburban school ($n = 26$). Thirty-eight of the 45 students stated that they elected to become a part of this experience because of job availability in the school districts; therefore, immediate employment was their incentive. Although students self-identified themselves as middle or upper class, nine received financial aid. Forty-three of the 45 students were between the ages of 21 and 24, single with no children; two students (ages 34 and 35) were married with one child.

In the new course described as part of the teacher education program, students were asked to write in their journals weekly and were provided feedback from the instructor. Additional data were obtained from written assignments, class observations, and exit interviews. In addition, follow-up data were obtained from students who sought employment in urban schools.

The data were analyzed for key domains and further sorted into categorical units (Lincoln & Guba, 1985). Four topics emerged as points of notable difference between the students who pursued urban teaching positions (the pursuers) and those who did not seek urban jobs (the nonpursuers). These four topics were (a) the urban school experience, (b) view of the city, (c) cultural conflicts, and (d) school choice.

The Urban Experience. The first topic of contrast dealt with the urban school experience. Analysis revealed that 34 of the 36 nonpursuers lacked experience as well as exposure to urban schools. In addition, the nonpursuers wrote very little about their overall desire to learn more and gain greater experience in the urban setting. This is reflected in journal entries. For example:

> I have not been in an urban school before. I don't know what to expect.

> I have never stepped foot in an urban school. . . . It wasn't required and it didn't occur to me to seek information in that area.

> Prior experiences in my teaching endeavors have never brought me to the urban school setting. There really wasn't much said about it before now.

Six of the nine pursuers had previous experiences in urban schools. Although none of them had clinical experiences, all six had attended an urban school at some time during their kindergarten through high school experience. The other three pursuers responded differently from the nonpursuers in the sense that they took time to reflect upon their lack of exposure and experience in urban schools. Two did not feel that it was a coincidence that their paths happened to miss the cities near their living environment. Their journal entries are illustrative:

> I must admit that I have not been in a city, but I always wondered why the clinical experiences at the University did not include city schools. When I inquired, some of the professors said they did not know why, others said the city was too far away. I feel somewhat disadvantaged by my lack of experience. Even though I don't teach there, I want to know more about it as a future teacher.

> My experience in city schools is zero, but I am looking forward to the field trips. I feel that it is exciting to explore new territory. I do not understand why an institution as large as ours would wait until graduation to give us this exposure and training. I do not believe there is sincere interest in urban areas.

> This experience will be a new one for me. That is why the school visits are so important. I want to spend time with the children. I want to formulate my own views . . . apart from the media and what I've heard.

These responses showed a definite contrast between the two sets of students. Their responses are important because studies indicate that perceptions and attitudes about schools are influenced and shaped by personal knowledge (Swetnam, 1992). According to the annual Gallup Poll of the Public's Attitudes Toward the Public Schools, the percentage of schools graded A or B by citizens decreased as citizens' personal knowledge of the schools became more remote. The citizens in this poll rated the school that their oldest child attended at 72% above the average, the local public schools at 41% above average, and the public schools in the nation at 21% above average (Elam & Gallup, 1990). These authors concluded that the greater one's personal knowledge was about the public schools (for example, knowledge that does not come from the media), the better one likes and respects the schools. According to Swetnam (1992), people who do not have personal knowledge or experience have a tendency to form their attitudes and perceptions based on media representation that could be fictional. There is a definite dearth of positive information about city schools and urban areas in general. It is conceivable that the students' lack of exposure to urban schools could leave many preservice teachers vulnerable to stereotyping and resistant to opportunities for employment.

View of the City. The second area of contrast was revealed when the students were asked to include in their journals a discussion of their personal view of the city. It must be noted that 27 of the 36 nonpursuers took this opportunity to write about their fear of the city. Examples were:

> I have heard so much about the city, most of it negative. If you had not indicated that we all were going on the bus together for the field trips, I would have dropped this class. I can imagine driving around a neighborhood in the city looking for a school. I could end up in the wrong neighborhood, I could get mugged. . . . My personal view of the city is that it is filled with drugs and illegal weapons.

I must admit that I am very concerned about safety in the city.

I did not say anything in class, but I feel the city is unsafe. I want to think positively, but the newspaper and news broadcasts tell horror stories daily. . . . The city is dangerous.

All nine pursuers, however, responded to this topic in positive terms. They detailed personal experiences such as visits to the museums, cultural events, shopping sprees, unforgettable sports events, visits with city friends and relatives, and trips to special restaurants. One student wrote:

Whenever I go to the loop [the downtown section of the city] I become exhilarated. The lake is beautiful, the buildings are architectural wonders. . . . I love the hustle and bustle.

These university students seemed genuinely to enjoy several aspects of their students. They had experiences to share. Their personal view was related to the first contrast discussed in the sense that they had exposure and experiences in the city. The pursuers did not mention fear or safety issues in their journals.

Cultural Conflicts. The third area of contrast dealt with cultural conflicts. The nonpursuers were excited about the new experience initially but grew frustrated after the novelty disappeared. Responses indicated that conflicts did emerge:

This was fun at first, but it has become tedious. Some of the students do not speak English at all. The daily tutoring of simple English is not what I planned in my student teaching experience. The pace is too slow.

Everything that I do has to deal with Black people. I thought this was great for Black History Month, but other than that I think the issues are what's important rather than a focus on Blacks. I realize this is an Afro-American School, but there are many important issues for current events that do not necessarily deal with only Black people.

Some of my classroom children have had experience with shooting, gangs and the law. . . . They talk about it too much. . . . They have so many problems. . . . They should concentrate on more positive topics. . . . They make me feel sad and depressed. . . . I feel so sorry for some of these children. . . . I understand why they have problems learning. . . . This is an unusual suburban school.

These children can stand this type of life. . . . I can't.

Many of the preservice teachers who were placed in suburban schools with diverse populations suffered from culture shock and manifested the same symptoms as their urban counterparts. Eighteen students seemed to have consuming cultural conflicts, as indicated by the numerous journal entries in which they discussed their own feelings and sufferings. They said little about adaptation, ways of coping, or desire to contribute to the child's well being. The students were very self-centered and self-focused.

All nine pursuers met with cultural conflicts also. However, the attitudes with which they faced conflicts were strikingly different as indicated by these entries:

I plan to accompany my cooperating teacher when she visits the home of a student. . . . I am a little nervous about the visit. . . . I asked her [the cooperating teacher] a dozen questions because I don't want to say the wrong thing. . . . We talked about body language. . . . My hope is that I do not offend anyone.

I plan to take a course in African American history this summer. . . . I will need it in order to be effective.

I have learned more Spanish in one semester than four years in high school. . . . I need to improve . . . I do not want barriers of any kind between the children and myself.

According to Haberman (1991c), teaching requires a level of maturity that enables one to be concerned about the development and nurturing of others. He promotes the recruitment of older students for urban teachers. He identifies late adolescent youth and young adults as appropriately concerned with the separation of themselves from parents and the development of their own identities. He suggests that teachers over the age of 25 are more appropriately prepared to teach because they have the ability to focus on someone other than themselves. Although there were only two older preservice teachers in this study, it should be noted that they were both among the pursuer group.

School Choice. The final area that emerged as a contrast between the pursuers and the nonpursuers was school choice. The students were asked if they would accept a position in their preservice school. In addition, they were asked to explain in detail why they would or would not accept a teaching position. The following responses were written by the nonpursuers:

I found that I don't want urban or suburban children, just affluent.

If I had the opportunity to teach in this school, I would not. I grew up in an affluent district. I am used to having the most advanced equipment and tests, as well as unlimited supplies. I am also privileged to be a part of a very active and concerned community. The students are highly motivated and have very few discipline problems. I would not be content in a school that isn't top notch. I realize I am being selfish and idealistic, but I don't want to settle for less.

I would not work here. . . . I couldn't handle being in a school indefinitely where all the doors are kept locked and teachers spend most of the day dealing with depressing problems. I don't want to be part of a school where the materials are over ten years old and supplies are extremely limited. I simply want a school where I can fit in with my peers and students.

If I had an opportunity to teach in this setting, I would deny it. I don't think that I would want to work in a school where supplies are limited. Also, the fact that they put chains on the doors during school hours really bothers me. I was never exposed to that sort of situation when I was young. I would never want to fear coming to work everyday. Even though, I would never work in this situation, I feel it was a good experience for me and any future student teachers.

It was a great college experience but I would be embarrassed to tell my friends and family that I work here.

For some of the nonpursuers, the experience in the school was good, but where employment was concerned, the wealth and social status of the school district determined their personal value and worth as a teacher. Nonpursuers who had this problem were confused in their philosophical orientation toward how to establish their worth.

It should be noted that all of the 45 university students functioned well in the classroom according to the supervisors' and cooperating teachers' reports. All received average or above average grades. When asked their opinion about the overall experience during their exit interview, 34 students indicated that all student teachers should have similar experiences. The students' writing revealed that the nonpursuers thought it was a great experience because "it would look good on their resume" or would "show that they were well-rounded to an employer."

The pursuers revealed a different mind-set. They discussed their school choice from another perspective:

> This has been the best semester of my college experience. I have learned a great deal about myself, children, and my teaching ability. If given the opportunity, I would take a job in this school. . . . I never gave up. There were a couple of times I was ready to throw in the towel, but I stuck with it. I figured that I owed it to the students and myself to finish what I started.

> If I had the opportunity to teach in a school such as this, I would take it. This experience opened my eyes to the fact that I enjoy this type of setting. I developed an excellent rapport with the children and some parents too. . . . Last semester, I expected to teach in suburbia . . . that has changed. . . . I will definitely apply for a position in the city.

> I really feel like my students learned something from me this semester. . . . The children in my fourth grade class were so active, I didn't think I could handle it, at first. . . . My cooperating teacher was excellent. She allowed me to gain confidence and helped me utilize instructional methods that were never taught at the University. . . . I believe I could teach anywhere. . . . I would seriously consider this school if given the opportunity to work here.

These preservice teachers began the semester with a goal of teaching in suburbia. The new teacher education model enabled them to change their minds before the semester ended or confirm their fears. It appears that if they had not been granted an opportunity to work in urban and suburban diverse settings, the cities, in all probability, would have lost the services of the nine who decided to pursue teaching in an urban setting. Granted, this does not begin to address the issue of teacher effectiveness, but there must be a willing perspective and disposition before greater issues can be examined.

Implications for Teacher Education

The results of this study indicate that some preservice teachers would be eager urban candidates if given the support, training, and encouragement through teacher education programs. Support, training, and encouragement can occur by providing early exposure and experience in urban settings, positive urban environments for preservice teaching, support and supervision from university faculty and school personnel who are experts in urban education, and multicultural education courses throughout their college experiences to provide students a philosophy and process to accept and respect student diversity in schools while simultaneously critically examining an educational system that perpetuates inequality for many children.

An analysis of the student journals indicates that there were differences in attitudes or perceptions between students who pursued urban employment and those who did not. In essence, it was the manner in which these students responded to the same topic that made the distinction among them. The follow-up data received from the university students after graduation revealed that nine actually applied to urban school districts for employment considerations. Thus, 20% of the students in the program obtained employment in urban schools, seven in their home state and two out of state.

Although all of the participants were educated for urban settings, only nine selected to participate in the quest for urban teaching positions. It is important to note that when addressing the issue of preparation of teachers for employment, if selection is not considered, then training may be in vain. Overall, a profile of the pursuers revealed five common characteristics about these students. The students usually had exposure or experience in urban settings, they did not fear the city, they accepted and respected cultural differences, they did not base school value on material goods, and they had a sense of self-efficacy. However, further study is needed to establish both the effectiveness and longevity of these nine urban teachers.

In summary, if colleges and universities are going to assume the responsibility for supplying adequate numbers of teachers with credentials for our nations' classrooms, selection and preparation of future graduates must be considered. Major institutions that graduate large numbers of preservice teachers must face the challenge of identifying students who are willing to enter the urban setting. In addition, students may be capable of mastering the training, but if their attitudes are not open to urban children and schools, the training is useless. Teachers seeking other professions while urban classrooms have vacancies is a trend that must be reversed. It is time for teacher education institutions to reconceptualize the way teachers are prepared if, for no other reason, than for the children and adults who look to educators to educate them to live in a culturally pluralistic society. Therefore, preparing teachers for urban schools must be viewed as a distinctive component of teacher education programs, and rather than adhering to the traditional standards involving general guidelines, a new model with specialized criteria must be embraced. Utilizing various components of this evolving model may be useful in modifying existing programs to allow preservice teachers who desire a career in urban areas to be supported, trained, and encouraged.

References

Avery, P., & Walker, C. (1993). Prospective teachers' perception of ethnic and gender differences in academic achievement. *Journal of Teacher Education, 44*(1), 27-37.

Brookover, W. (1982). *Creating effective schools.* Holmes Beach, FL: Learning Publications.

Carter, D., & Carter, L. (1991). Bilingually prepared teachers and students: In search of diversity. In J. Harris, C. Heid, D. Carter, & F. Brown (Eds.), *Readings on the state of education in urban America* (pp. 67-74). Bloomington: Indiana University, Center for Urban and Multicultural Education.

Edmonds, R. (1979). Effective schools for the urban poor. *Educational Leadership, 9*(1), 1-14.

Elam, S., & Gallup, A. (1990). The 22nd gallup poll of the public's attitudes toward the public schools. *Phi Delta Kappan, 72*(1), 51.

Gollnick, D., & Chinn, P. (1986). *Multicultural education in a pluralistic society.* Columbus, OH: Charles E. Merrill.

Grant, C. (1986). Education that is multicultural: Isn't that what we mean? *Journal of Teacher Education, 29,* 45-48.

Grant, C. (1989). Equity, equality and classroom life. In W. G. Secada (Ed.), *Equity in education* (pp. 89-102). London: Falmer.

Grant, C., & Secada, W. (1990). Preparing teachers for diversity. In W. R. Houston (Ed.), *Handbook of research on teacher education* (pp. 403-422). New York: Macmillan.

Haberman, M. (1987). *Recruiting and selecting teachers for urban schools.* New York: ERIC Clearinghouse on Urban Education, Institute for Urban and Minority Education.

Haberman, M. (1991a). *A brief review of the history and development of the urban teacher selection interview.* Unpublished manuscript.

Haberman, M. (1991b). *The dimensions of excellence in programs of teacher education.* Paper presented at the First Annual Conference on Alternative Certification, South Padre Island, Texas.

Haberman, M. (1991c). The pedagogy of poverty and good teaching. *Phi Delta Kappan, 73*(4), 290-294.

Harris, J., Heid, C., Carter, D., & Brown, F. (Eds). (1991). *Readings on the state of education in urban America.* Bloomington: Indiana University, Center for Urban and Multicultural Education.

Kietovics, J., & Nussel, E. (1994). *Transforming urban education.* Needham Heights, MD: Allyn & Bacon.

Kotsakis, J. (1991, November 5). Interns bring talent and enthusiasm to urban schools. *Chicago Union Teacher,* p. 7.

Larke, P. (1992). Effective multicultural teachers: Meeting the challenges of diverse classrooms. *Equity and Excellence, 25*(2), 133-138.

Lincoln, Y., & Guba, E. (1985). *Naturalistic inquiry.* Newbury Park, CA: Sage.

Martin, O. (1989). *Does teacher efficacy begin with teacher education? Implications from student teacher candidates.* Paper presented at the annual meeting of the Mid-South Educational Research Association, Little Rock, AR.

Natriello, G., & Zumwalt, K. (1993). New teachers for urban schools? The contribution of the provisional teacher program in New Jersey. *Education and Urban Society, 26*(1), 49-62.

Quality Education for Minorities Project. (1990). *Education that works: An action plan for the education of minorities.* Cambridge: Massachusetts Institute of Technology.

Shulman, L. (1986). Paradigms and research programs: A contemporary perspective. In M. Wittrock (Ed.), *Handbook of research on teaching* (pp. 3-36). New York: Macmillan.

Sleeter, C., & Grant, C. (1994). *Making choices for multicultural education: Five approaches to race, class, and gender.* New York: Macmillan.

Stallings, J., & Quinn, L. (1991). Learning how to teach in the inner city. *Educational Leadership, 47*(4), 25-27.

Swetnam, L. (1992). Media distortion of the teacher image. *Clearing House, 66*(1), 30-32.

Tillman, J. (1989). Preparing effective teachers for urban schools: A quintessential role for NCATE. *Action in Teacher Education, 11*(2), 39-40.

Zeichner, K. (1992). *Educating teachers for cultural diversity.* East Lansing: National Center for Research on Teacher Learning, Michigan State University, and the Wisconsin Center for Educational Research.

5 Project MASTER:
Peer Coaching and Collaboration as Catalysts for Professional Growth in Urban High Schools

Judith A. Ponticell

George E. Olson

Patricia S. Charlier

Judith A. Ponticell is Assistant Professor in the College of Education at Texas Tech University. She studies belief systems and their relation to classroom and school practices, adult cognition and its relation to learning, and individual and organizational change processes.

George E. Olson is Dean of the College of Education at Roosevelt University in Chicago. His interests include professional development and school-university partnerships.

Patricia S. Charlier is Professor Emeritus in the College of Education at the University of Illinois at Chicago. Her research interests are in supervision and teacher leadership.

ABSTRACT

Project MASTER (Mathematics and Science Teachers Education Renewal) was designed to provide a climate in urban high schools where collaboration, risk taking, and experimentation were valued, supported, and practiced. The project design included workshops and seminars in effective teaching strategies with at-risk students, individual consultations with supervision and teacher education specialists, peer coaching, and a collegial support system within and among each of the 10 participating high schools. Data were collected through questionnaires, inventories, classroom observation notes, conferencing notes, participant observation notes, and semistructured and open-ended interviews. Data were analyzed using frequency of response and constant comparative analysis and reveal teachers' perceptions of professional growth, teachers' expectations for and experiences with peer coaching, teachers' experimentation with changes in classroom practice, and teachers' perceptions of peer coaching and collaboration as a catalyst for professional growth. The project increased teachers' professional orientation toward teaching, particularly in their value for critical examination of the effects of their classroom practices on students and student learning.

Recent literature on teacher renewal and professional growth suggests that many urban teachers need meaningful support to recapture their belief in students' ability to learn, renew their sense of purpose, rebuild lost confidence, and risk examining their classroom practices (Bolin & Falk, 1987; Levine, 1989; Maeroff, 1988; Ponticell, 1994). But what is meaningful support?

Staff development programs in schools have largely been "one-shot, quick-fix" episodes of teacher inservice training or rare classroom observations for summative evaluation. Both modes of professional development play a small and ineffectual role in the professional growth of teachers (Busching & Rowls, 1987; Howey & Vaughn, 1983; Karant, 1989; Zimpher, 1988). Opportunities for teachers to engage in ongoing renewal in practice appear to be few.

In addition, various studies have found that teachers' beliefs and dispositions are important factors influencing how individual teachers define and respond to their teaching contexts (e.g., see review in Clark & Peterson, 1986). Change-oriented processes are concerned with such influences, particularly with regard to the relation of these beliefs and dispositions to the individual's self-image (Schein, 1964). Change efforts, to be successful, must take into account the individual's perceptions, beliefs, and dispositions. Successful change efforts are based upon ideas, perceptions, and local problems important to those expected to enact change (Bennis, Benne, & Chin, 1961; Deal, 1986; Duffy & Roehler, 1986).

The above considerations led to the design of a professional development project in 10 Chicago high schools, Project MASTER (Mathematics and Science Teachers Education Renewal) supported by a grant from the Chicago public schools. Project MASTER began with cautious expectations for positive impact on teachers' beliefs about professional growth and improvement of classroom practice. Over 3 years, the project produced dramatic and unanticipated changes, particularly in opening urban classroom doors and breaking the professional isolation strongly felt by inner-city high school teachers. What factors motivated these urban teachers to change their beliefs about professional development and examine the effectiveness of their classroom practices?

Project Objectives

Project MASTER was designed to provide a climate in urban high schools where collaboration, risk taking, and experimentation were valued, supported, and practiced. The project design included workshops and seminars in effective teaching strategies with at-risk students, individual consultations with supervision and teacher education specialists, peer coaching, and a collegial support system within and among each of the 10 schools participating in the project.

Eight teachers (four in mathematics and four in science) from each of 10 schools volunteered to participate in the project because they were "curious about it" or "interested in trying something new." The majority of the participants ($n = 80$) had more than 12 years of teaching experience in the Chicago public schools. In each school, the teachers formed collegial support groups or professional cadres. A mathematics cadre was led by a mathematics department chair or lead teacher, and a science cadre was led by a science department chair or lead teacher.

Project activities were designed to develop both a common knowledge base and a structure for professional interaction. Participants engaged in reading and discussion of effective teaching research and attended workshops conducted by modeling these teaching strategies. The core professional development strategy was peer coaching, using a modified clinical supervision model designed to focus on peer-to-peer situational problem solving. Cadre participants were trained in conferencing skills, classroom observation and data collection, and instructional analysis. University faculty associated with the project acted as in-house mentors or "master coaches," modeling the coaching strategies that teachers were learning and supporting cadre activities. In addition to practicing coaching skills and experimenting with new teaching strategies in their own schools, participants engaged in cross-school visiting days during which they practiced their coaching and instructional analysis skills with project participants in other schools. Teachers were provided with multiple opportunities to articulate and examine their beliefs about teaching, learning, and teacher growth. Also, techniques and strategies for reflective analysis of classroom practice and strategies for collaboration were discussed and modeled. Schools were provided with in-house assistance to develop their own professional growth plans.

Theoretical Framework

Emerging views of supervision and the professional growth of teachers suggest that teachers grow through an interactive process of learning from one another in "critical learning communities" initiated, developed, and sustained by the teachers within individual schools (Garman, 1986; Holland, 1988; Smyth, 1988). Further, current reforms focusing on the professional model of teaching suggest that staff development cannot be a one-shot inspection of practice. Rather, professional development must be an ongoing *discovery in practice* where teachers engage in a process of interaction and inquiry in work that is perceived as dynamic (Busching & Rowls, 1987; Karant, 1989; Lieberman, 1986; Zimpher, 1988). Such inquiry focuses on the teacher looking inward and examining both professional practices and the meanings one attaches to those practices in the contexts in which they are engaged.

Much of teachers' confidence and willingness to maintain commitment or to confront change and challenge depends upon the meaning they give to their own teaching success or failure. As bureaucratic management of urban schools increases, opportunities decrease for "teachers to exercise influence and thus to develop a sense of ownership of their work" (Frymier, 1987, p. 12). Moreover, persons who realize someone else is making their decisions are apt to react with resistance and entrenchment (Jung, 1978).

In urban schools that have "lost the centrality of teachers," one solution is to "empower teachers, to help them develop an internalized locus of control" (Frymier, 1987, p. 14). From personal empowerment develops a professional orientation toward teaching (Maeroff, 1988). The concept of locus of control (Rotter, 1954) emphasizes individuals' beliefs about whether outcomes are independent of one's actions (external) or dependent upon one's actions (internal). Further, as Bandura (1977) noted, "self-produced" influences are significant contributors to goal selection and attainment. If individuals experience what are perceived as uncontrollable outcomes, they have difficulty in recognizing later outcomes as due to their own actions (Hiroto & Seligman, 1975). For those who perceive a general absence of relationship between action and outcome, a "what's the use of trying" attitude is frequently generated to cope with feelings of hopelessness (Jung, 1978).

The learning process in which teaching professionals engage should be a process of interaction and mediation, whereby individuals are "empowered" by their collegial learning (Garman, 1986; Garman, Glickman, Hunter, & Haggerson, 1987). This learning is not only recollection and reflection, but also the generation of new knowledge. If we think of change, as Shroyer (1990) suggests, as a process of clarification of the personal meaning one attaches to one's actions, then the foundation for changing individual behavior lies in the understandings one develops about one's values, power, and control in relation to alternatives among actions that might produce desired outcomes.

Enhancing—or changing—teachers' beliefs and perceptions about their work and teaching contexts and the decisions they make are key factors prerequisite to changing instructional behaviors (Costa & Garmston, 1984). The typical one-shot workshop approach to staff development familiar to most teachers lacks the continuity of experience necessary for such inquiry-based learning and for seeing growth over time. Hunt (1978) suggested that effective approaches to staff development must "begin with an understanding of the practitioner and his [or her] implicit theories about the world of practice" (p. 88). This makes sense with regard to what we know about teachers, particularly experienced teachers, as learners.

Focusing on one's own teaching and interactions with peers becomes more important as teachers gain years of teaching experience (Smylie, 1989), as do developing clearer images of "who I am" and defining a "consistent sense of self" (Bullough, Knowles, & Crow, 1989). Further, interactions with peers create an "occupational ethos" that shapes what teachers choose to do in their classrooms (Cuban, 1984) and what teachers choose to learn (Joyce & McKibbin, 1982).

Peer coaching is based upon research findings that indicate teachers generally identify other teachers as their primary sources of assistance and information when learning about teaching (Smylie, 1989; Showers, 1985). Teachers seek informal sharing and support relationships naturally. Coaching provides a structure for collaborative professional development and for improving a school's professional culture through collaboration. The "practice of public teaching" provides teachers with opportunities to develop common language and understandings about their professional practice and "contributes to school norms of collegiality and experimentation" (Showers, 1985, p. 46).

The design of Project MASTER developed both a common knowledge base and structure for professional interaction among teachers within and across the 10 participating high schools. The research-based workshops and seminars provided both information and demonstration of effective teaching strategies with at-risk students. Training and practice in classroom observation, data collection, and conferencing focused on peer-to- peer problem solving and instructional analysis. Techniques and structures for reflective analysis of individual classroom practices and strategies for cooperative professional development strengthened the view of teacher as reflective professional—a view rarely demonstrated for the urban teachers participating in the project.

Data Collection and Analysis

Participants completed open-ended pre- and postproject questionnaires. At the start of the project, respondents were asked to describe in detail their educational backgrounds, teaching aspirations, beliefs about teaching and learning, teaching experiences, staff development experiences, and project expectations. To assess to what extent participants' knowledge, skills, and beliefs had changed as a result of project participation, participants were also asked to describe their teaching aspirations, beliefs about teaching and learning, and project experiences at the end of the project.

Participants also completed open-ended postactivity reaction surveys to assess interest and attitude changes as they moved through the various professional development activities. Attitude inventories captured participants' perceptions of changes in their own teaching beliefs and practices. These data, together with university faculty participant observation notes, classroom observation data, and conferencing notes, provided an indication of changes in belief and practice over time. Semistructured interviews were conducted with project participants to obtain clarification and expansion of their written responses on questionnaires and inventories. Open-ended interviews were conducted with a random selection of 35 participants early in the project to capture teachers' perceptions of professional growth.

Data were analyzed using frequency of responses to interpret results of inventories and questionnaires. Constant comparative analysis, allowing unitizing and categorizing of patterns and themes in the data, was used to interpret interview responses and participant observation notes, as well as to identify changes in teachers' beliefs and teaching practices as captured in classroom observation and conference notes. Only patterns and themes reflected by all 80 teachers are reported in the findings section.

Data tell a variety of stories about teachers' perceptions of professional growth, teachers' expectations for and experiences with peer coaching, teachers' experimentation with changes in classroom practices, and teachers' perceptions of peer coaching and collaboration as catalysts for professional growth.

Findings

Teachers' Perceptions of Professional Growth. Open-ended interviews with a random selection of 35 teachers revealed teachers' perceptions of what professional growth means and might mean. Early in the project teachers perceived professional growth as something that was done to them. It was clearly equated with summative teacher evaluation and seen as frustrating, threatening, and generally meaningless. The view of professional growth as a "polite word" for inspection was most commonly shared. Teachers shared an image of "somebody sitting in my class and making judgments on me." These judgments were perceived as useless, lacking in any "really helpful information." Administrators simply "come in to see that you're doing things right . . . make sure you're toeing the mark . . . and find places to make corrections."

These experienced teachers expressed a desire for more self-directed and collaborative opportunities to "review, examine, and renew" their teaching. For these experienced teachers, it was important to be trusted with leadership. Self-directed and collegial roles for teachers in their own improvement were perceived as more useful and meaningful. Observing other teachers "in the same situation" was more meaningful than rating by a supervisor or administrator. Teachers also expressed value for being able to watch "a fabulous teacher" who is "very enthused about what he/she teaches and successful with lots of kids." .

Watching other teachers generates "ideas, lots of things to think about" that "you just don't think about while you're up there teaching." Feedback from "descriptive comments" and discussion or "learning by example" were viewed positively by the teachers interviewed. Clearly, teachers preferred a collegial approach to professional growth: "Let's learn from one another." More than half the teachers spoke of a need to be "inspired" and supported to take a chance and "really dig into" their teaching practices.

Teachers' Expectations for and Experiences With Peer Coaching. Teachers expected to find out about new and improved teaching strategies and to receive a motivational "shot in the arm." Teachers also expected to learn more about their peers and to "learn something" from them. Participants hoped to find "commonality" among peers. Teachers' expectations, however, were couched within a context of powerful obstacles. Classroom observation was viewed with considerable suspicion, with fear of "going into a friend's room and finding something wrong."

Teachers' perspectives on their experiences with peer coaching generally began with talking about changes in their relationships with colleagues. The dominant theme was that "professional isolation was broken." Teachers commented:

> Observing, exchanging information and views with others, discussion with other teachers—we learned we are not alone.
>
> We ask questions more freely, we communicate more willingly, less formal. . . . We have a chance to share, to get together with each other as a staff; this helped us become a team and help each other.
>
> The program gave us a reason and way to deal with problems together. It is difficult to approach other teachers or provide help. Our attitudes toward such help have changed.

Only after classroom doors were "open" to colleagues did trust develop, and with it, motivation and willingness to risk looking more closely at classroom teaching. Teachers noted:

I isolated myself. . . . Because of this program, there is more a community of needs, of people out there to help. . . . A trust among us has developed.

I think this project had an impact on my professional role as (1) at least two colleagues allowed me to express my professional interests beyond ordering texts and scheduling teacher programs, (2) two colleagues learned to trust me enough to express their ideas, and (3) the taboo of sharing by observing and two-way evaluation was shaken.

The project strengthened my understanding of instructional leadership and my own instructional leadership skills. The focus was on improving instruction, and I became more aware of certain aspects of teaching through observation.

Teachers' Experimentation With Changes in Classroom Practice. At the outset of the project, teachers reported consistently low perceptions of the at-risk students they taught. Students were perceived as "not putting forth enough effort" and "lacking discipline." Students came from "poor" elementary schools "poorly prepared" and "not knowing the basics." Students were also perceived as acquiring negative attitudes from "parents who don't care about school." Urban at-risk students were described simply as refusing to learn and study, "spoiled and too outspoken, rebellious against authority."

Classrooms were routine at the outset of the project. Five to 15 minutes of instructional time was taken up with "administrivia." The remainder of the class was spent in lecture, demonstration at the board, and assigned seatwork. Classroom discourse was largely teacher initiated with four or five "key students" who could "move the lesson along."

Teachers "covered" textbook pages and interacted with those students who signaled that they wanted to be part of the lesson. Classes were described by teachers as "going well" when students are "quiet and most are working on assignments." In general, teachers taught "the ones who want to learn." Lack of student involvement, homework, and poor performance on tests was attributed to "lazy, unmotivated kids."

Students were generally pleasant and nondisruptive. They came to school although many times teachers wondered why. Students seemed to equate presence in the classroom with all that was required for safe passage through the school system. While the teacher was lecturing and leading those who elected to participate in the class through boardwork or seatwork, many other students simply did other things. They did not throw the room up for grabs as long as they were left alone to write letters to friends, daydream, sleep, chat quietly with peers, or look through magazines or newspapers. They cooperated, did some work here and there, and took required tests.

Teachers' experiences with peer coaching focused their attention on the outcomes of their day-to-day interactions with students. As teachers experimented with more student-centered approaches to teaching, they observed changes in their own classrooms. For example:

1. *Increasing student involvement.* Teachers devised ways of calling on more students and sticking with students who were attempting an answer. They varied their patterns and methods for calling on students. Some used systems by which students all had an equal chance of being called through "luck of the draw" index cards on which teachers recorded students' participation points. Many teachers developed games and rewarded team competition. Noise increased, and teachers became more comfortable with it.

2. *Student-teacher interactions.* Teachers changed the tone of student-teacher interactions. It was not uncommon at the outset of the project to spend 40 minutes in a classroom and never hear students praised for doing something well. Teachers experimented with specifically telling students when they had done something well and what was good about what they had done. They also discouraged negative student-to-student comments, modeling simple courtesy.

3. *Classroom discourse.* Teachers more frequently asked for students' ideas and opinions and were more willing to let students grapple with a problem, rather than giving them step-by-step skills for finding the answer. Classroom discourse changed most noticeably in students initiating questions and in teachers asking students to explain how they had come up with the answers they gave. Teachers also employed peer and cooperative learning strategies, encouraging students to verbalize what they knew and to solve problems and learn concepts together.

4. *Monitoring student performance.* Rather than sitting at their desks, teachers practiced moving about the room, monitoring student work. They paid particular attention to how students were working and practiced giving specific encouragement or help to students.

5. *Wasting less time.* Teachers focused attention on "wasting less time" in the classroom by devising ways to engage students in warm-up or retention activities during the first 5 minutes of the class. This enabled them to take attendance, check with late or absent students, and set a pattern for early participation in the class.

6. *Purpose-clear lessons.* Teachers worked at structuring their lessons with clear review, objectives, demonstration, and practice time. This allowed them to recover minutes at the end of the class for giving specific homework directions and examples before sending students out of the room. Early in the project the typical end of the period was a flurry of teachers rattling off homework assignments to students as they ran out the door. Teachers, in general, agreed that "better and consistent routines" and "better structure to lessons" helped them to get students on task.

7. *Attention to student thinking.* Greater attention was given to how students think about what they are being asked to learn or do, rather than to students "getting the right answer." Teachers asked fewer "fill in the blank" questions and more open-ended questions. Teachers worked consciously at providing students with thinking time before asking for responses. Teachers also discovered that listening to students' explanations of how they were solving problems or finding answers told them much about what students did and did not understand. Also, students listening to other students proved to be an untapped resource for reteaching or repeating concepts. Initially uncomfortable with students "who learned better by listening to another student than by listening to me," teachers soon observed that they could use student explanations as quick assessments of levels of understanding and as springboards for clarifying or reteaching.

Generally, teachers became more aware of focusing on students rather than on "covering material." This created considerable conflict for many teachers. They strongly perceived intense pressure to "cover" the pages in the textbook and teach students "simple right answers." They knew from observing each others' classrooms that not many students participated when the purpose of instruction was finding those simple right answers. More students were engaged in learning when they were active. But giving students sufficient time and space to be active in their own learning meant "covering" fewer pages. Differences among teachers were greatest in their willingness to change this aspect of classroom instruction.

Teachers' Perceptions of Peer Coaching and Collaboration as a Catalyst for Professional Growth. At the outset of the project, many teachers perceived themselves and their colleagues as "too burned out," with "low expectations" that meant they "tended to settle for too little." Others saw themselves and their colleagues as lacking sufficient preparation for the urban classroom and lacking greatly in motivation to do anything differently. Poor communication, little administrative or system support, low levels of resources, low motivation of inner-city students, and no means of "useful evaluation" were cited as the most frequent deterrents to innovation and change. Project MASTER, in essence, "sounded good," but would most likely "produce very little change."

Generally, teachers' suspicion and skepticism regarding the coaching process were replaced by genuine appreciation for the practice of "looking in classrooms." Teachers commented:

> The importance of the observing process with conferencing was its purpose of improving one's own classroom practice.
>
> Each time we went to observe other teachers' classrooms, we learned other strategies and other situations.

The nonthreatening climate in which the teachers observed one another and talked about their teaching, the degree of teacher control over the focus of the observations, and the collaboration built into the coaching process were considered extremely important to teacher change. Some teachers noted:

> Administrators don't customize for teachers. There are a lot of minuses. It is a big problem for a system to address the individual. This program has helped us to help each other.
>
> Observation is not a one-way street. We teachers need to discuss problems more. We thought critiquing each other's practice would be very stressful. We found we could do this together.

In addition to perceiving the peer coaching process as a positive experience, teachers perceived a "possible link" between their own growth as teachers and their students' behaviors. During and at the end of the project, teachers reported "unexpected influences" on their students. Most commonly teachers talked about discovering a relationship between teacher change and student change. Teachers commented:

> Through observations I was able to get an idea of how I was coming across to the kids and also get suggestions that made sense to me to use later on.
>
> I am convinced students are aware of good teachers, teachers who are changing positively, and students respond to their efforts.
>
> I do more review with students, go over homework more. Students in response are more motivated.
>
> There is conscious questioning concerning making students think. I ask more questions, better questions, and wait for students' answers.
>
> Techniques emphasizing lesson structure have enabled us to get the students to do what we want them to do. We use more hands-on activities, and students are more motivated. . . . I am determined to try more experiments.
>
> Students are doing a better job with their homework. . . . I have been successful in getting students here on time.
>
> I am aware of so many small things that will get kids to work. I think they are responding better. . . . I have to motivate my kids; this is what I've learned. The project has opened my eyes to positive change for our kids.
>
> It helped me not to give up on the kids and my goals for them. I finally got these kids involved, because I am.
>
> The project has made me more aware of how I present subject matter in my own class and more alert as to what each student is doing during my class.
>
> Visiting other teachers makes us more aware of our own teaching, more conscious.

Association with colleagues was initially seen as a way to "enlighten one's daily spirit, lighten the burden." But as the project progressed, collaboration with colleagues was seen as a way to "widen the vision" one has of the classroom and one's own teaching. In addition, teachers reported that collaboration served as renewal for professional growth. In particular, these teachers both expressed and assumed strong advocacy roles for collegial interaction and instructional improvement in their schools. For example,

My belief in the need for inservice and supervision and ongoing staff development has been strengthened, and I will continue to campaign on this subject.

Collegiality helps stem erosion of attitudes. I have wanted to quit, but I have new ideas to try, ones that have worked. This has shown me I can try new things and not stay in the same place, but grow.

I am scheduling our department to meet on a regular basis. Topics already discussed are curriculum planning, management of records, test evaluation. . . . We are on a "colleague in action program" to offer and request regular help from each other.

We have already planned discussion with all the department chairs at the school on coaching, its goals and processes.

We value seeing each other's and our own strengths and weaknesses. We can take these things we learned and *use* them as a result.

Discussion and Implications

For the 80 high school teachers who participated in this project, discovering the value of observing others teaching, being observed, learning how to collect and analyze classroom data, and discussing what was seen and felt together were surprising. The process of not only looking in classrooms but also analyzing and designing alternative instructional strategies with colleagues heightened teachers' awareness of their inattention to their own classrooms. The "practice of public teaching," as suggested by Showers (1985), did renew these experienced teachers' interest in their own teaching. Many had been flying for years on automatic pilot; the peer coaching process raised their consciousness of the quality of their own teaching efforts.

For experienced, veteran teachers the routineness and inattention to their day-to-day teaching is not surprising. Teachers with more than 15 years teaching experience frequently feel a sense of growing monotony (Huberman, 1989; Krupp, 1987). Teaching and working in schools becomes routine, and perceptions of mastery ("I've learned all there is to know") reduce the need for growth as competence is generally taken for granted. However, accompanying this more relaxed view of teaching is a sense of constraint and a greater resistance to change. Experienced teachers tend to focus on the quality of daily work life rather than on the outcomes of their work (Levine, 1989).

This inattention to the effects of teaching appears to be accompanied by both feelings of ineffectiveness and focus on external causes (e.g., "lazy and incapable students"). Five key features of the peer coaching process emerged as important in helping these experienced teachers to refocus their attention on the effects of their teaching: (a) the control of the individual teacher over the focus and purpose of the observation; (b) the noninspection context of the peer relationship; (c) the tailoring of the process to aspects of the individual teachers' own teaching; (d) the training provided in descriptive data collection and nonconfrontational conferencing techniques; and (e) the in-house support from university faculty and central office staff that demonstrated a value for change over time, rather than change on a deadline.

Teachers' morale was low. They perceived that their students were unmotivated and that others external to their classrooms did not respect or value teachers or schools. They were impatient and frustrated with others who expect changes overnight. Interestingly, their inattention to the day-to-day effects of their teaching created this same expectation for their students—all students should perform well enough to attend Harvard, and those that didn't perform that well simply needed to change overnight. Both peer coaching and collaboration with colleagues enabled teachers to see "so many small things" that signaled growth over time. This proved significantly motivating for teachers as these small successes with at-risk students rekindled their belief in their own instrumentality in promoting student learning, a finding confirmed by previous studies of teacher efficacy (e.g., Bandura, 1977; Smylie, 1988).

The role of university faculty and central office staff in this project contributed to teacher motivation. Teachers' perceptions that they were not valued diminished their own self-esteem. The commitment of university faculty and central office staff to work in schools and with teachers was perceived as value placed on urban classroom teaching, and this was instrumental in renewing teachers' dormant respect for their own teaching. This reflects earlier Rand Corporation research that suggested universities might be more effective in their relationships with schools if they were part of ongoing staff development processes at the school, particularly by providing concrete help and classroom follow-up (McLaughlin & Marsh, 1978).

In addition, Hall's (1986) study of midcareer needs in the workplace found four characteristics of the work environment that promote career growth: (a) choice and exploration, (b) recognition, (c) experience-enhancing roles, and (d) collegiality. The visibility of central office staff in these high school classrooms provided both recognition and collegiality with education resources otherwise perceived as useless in a large urban system. Assistance plays a key role in change-oriented programs. Huberman and Miles (1984) noted several key types of assistance related to individual change: external conferences, inservice training, visits, committee structures, team meetings, peer consultation, access to external consultants, and access to central office personnel. The in-house nature of the involvement of both university faculty and central office staff, and the assistance they provided as teachers experimented with new strategies in their classrooms, communicated value for urban teachers and their experiences.

Teachers' experiences with professional development in their schools had clearly been one-shot workshops and scarce evaluation. The majority of these teachers had been observed and evaluated only once or twice in more than 10 years. It was important to these teachers to be able to "see growth over time." The long-term nature of this project, together with the high degree of teacher control over the focus and purpose of classroom observations, created a nonthreatening climate in which teachers perceived themselves as being supported in "improving one's own classroom instruction." The coaching and collaborative processes attended to the differences among teachers and schools and addressed the individual. That individual growth and change would take time was a given structured into the design of the project.

The importance of building collegial trust was also clear. The strongly expressed desire to "learn from one another" assumed a context of discussion and problem solving for the purpose of helping the individual teacher and building "commonality" in the group. Teachers' increased trust in turning to colleagues to "offer and request help" promoted risk taking and "shook" the tendency to equate classroom observation with inspection. Rather, observation and professional, collegial dialogue became a tool for ongoing professional growth.

Teachers perceived that there was a "rightness" and "wrongness" to teaching, mostly because their experiences with classroom observation were linked to evaluation for inspection. The peer coaching process and collegial dialogue provided teachers with a broader vision of teaching. Teachers "learned other strategies and other situations" each time they went into one another's classrooms. In doing so, teachers gained things to think about that resulted both in new ideas and a climate in which to try them. The increased comfort of these teachers with risk taking and experimentation was important. These teachers engaged both in individual reflection and in interactive, critical examination of their teaching practices with support from their peers and significant external others from universities and the central office.

Current educational reform (e.g., Donaldson, 1991; Fullan & Hargreaves, 1991; Rost, 1991; Sizer, 1992) focuses heavily on the empowerment and leadership of teachers, and on their ability and disposition to change current classroom structures and practices. Peer support and specific training and practice in classroom observation and instructional analysis led teachers to develop alternate instructional strategies and to engage in systematic review of the success of those strategies. From a teacher-as-learner perspective, the attention to the individual teacher's context reflects the "boundedly rational" nature of teacher learning (Shulman & Carey, 1984). The individuals' construction and reconstruction of images of their own teaching, personal values, and personal meanings are significant to teacher growth and change. Teachers' practical theories (Sanders & McCutcheon, 1986) and practical knowledge (Clandinin, 1986) provide the conceptual structure and vision that give teachers reasons to learn, to act, and to change. Both peer coaching and the collaborative networks supported by the project provided a climate for learning-of-self-in-context.

The results of this study of peer coaching and collaboration in urban high schools suggest that such strategies can be powerful tools for empowering teachers to resist hopelessness, changing teacher attitudes about how to promote successful student learning, and changing instructional behavior. In addition, teachers observing other teachers and engaging in critical dialogue around common classroom concerns is a successful strategy for renewing beliefs and for rekindling teachers' willingness to risk rethinking their own instructional routines.

Probably the most significant drawbacks to ongoing, formative professional development in schools, particularly in large urban school systems, are time and resources. But these drawbacks are largely focused on the assumption that administrators and supervisors alone can be responsible and competent in this role. Peer coaching, collaborative teacher study groups, and problem-solving networks present strategies for better utilizing teachers themselves as resources. Such strategies provide a context in which teachers can exercise choice; explore their potential for growth and influence; gain recognition of their successes; enrich skills and develop new competencies; and enhance the trust, support, and collaboration that reduce professional isolation.

Empowerment begins with a professional orientation toward teaching. Or as Garman (1986) explains: "The teacher who maintains a reflective approach toward his or her practice continues to develop a mature professional identity. By understanding and articulating the rationale one holds for action, and then acting in reasonably consistent ways, the professional gains a power and control over his or her own destiny" (p. 18).

The findings of this 3-year project in urban high schools suggest that breaking the barriers of professional isolation in large high schools may be a key step to revitalizing urban teachers and refocusing their attention on taking control of their own growth. This project demonstrates that when teachers take control of their own professional growth, their sense of instrumentality in promoting successful student learning increases. Although the link between teacher growth and student growth is nebulous at best, that people change slowly as a result of their evolving beliefs, feelings, attitudes, values, visions, and experiences is a well-supported construct of individual and organizational change (e.g., Duffy & Roehler, 1986; Fullan, 1982; March & Simon, 1958; Schein, 1964). Our study suggests that it is time to get a clearer picture of the relation between teacher as learner and student as learner, and changes in classroom practice and student achievement.

References

Bandura, A. (1977). Self-efficacy: Toward a unifying theory of behavioral change. *Psychological Review, 84*(2), 191-215.

Bennis, W. G., Benne, K. D., & Chin, R. (Eds.). (1961). *The planning of change: Readings in the applied behavioral sciences.* New York: Holt, Rinehart & Winston.

Bolin, F., & Falk, J. (1987). *Teacher renewal.* New York: Teachers College Press.

Bullough, R. V., Knowles, J. G., & Crow, N. A. (1989). Teacher self-concept and student culture in the first year of teaching. *Teachers College Record, 91*(2), 209-233.

Busching, B., & Rowls, M. (1987). Teachers: Professional partners in school reform. *Action in Teacher Education, 9*(3), 13-24.

Clandinin, J. (1986). *Classroom practice: Teacher images in action.* London: Falmer.

Clark, C. M., & Peterson, P. L. (1986). Teachers' thought processes. In M. Wittrock (Ed.), *Handbook of research on teaching* (pp. 255-296). New York: Macmillan.

Costa, A., & Garmston, R. (1984). *The art of cognitive coaching: Supervision for intelligent teaching.* Sacramento: California State University.

Cuban, L. (1984). *How teachers taught: Constancy and change in American classrooms 1890-1980.* New York: Longman.

Deal, T. (1986). Educational change: Revival tent, tinkertoys, jungle, or carnival? In A. Lieberman (Ed.), *Rethinking school improvement: Research, craft, and concept* (pp. 115-128). New York: Teachers College Press.

Donaldson, G. (1991). *Learning to lead: The dynamics of the high school principalship.* Westport, CT: Greenwood.

Duffy, G., & Roehler, L. (1986). Constraints on teacher change. *Journal of Teacher Education, 37*(1), 55-58.

Frymier, J. (1987). Bureaucracy and the neutering of teachers. *Phi Delta Kappan, 69*(1), 9-14.

Fullan, M. (1982). *The meaning of educational change.* New York: Teachers College Press.

Fullan, M., & Hargreaves, A. (1991). *What's worth fighting for? Working together for your school.* Andover, MD: Regional Laboratory of the Northeast and Islands.

Garman, N. B. (1986). Reflection, the heart of clinical supervision: A modern rationale for professional practice. *Journal of Curriculum and Supervision, 2*(1), 1-24.

Garman, N. B., Glickman, C.D., Hunter, M., & Haggerson, N. L. (1987). Conflicting conceptions of clinical supervision and the enhancement of professional growth and renewal: Point and counterpoint. *Journal of Curriculum and Supervision, 2*(2), 152-177.

Hall, D. (Ed.). (1986). *Career development in organizations.* San Francisco: Jossey-Bass.

Hiroto, D. S., & Seligman, M.E.P. (1975). Generality of learned helplessness in man. *Journal of Personality and Social Psychology, 31,* 311-327.

Holland, P. E. (1988). Keeping faith with Cogan: Current theorizing in a maturing practice of clinical supervision. *Journal of Curriculum and Supervision, 3*(2), 97-108.

Howey, K., & Vaughn, J. (1983). Current patterns of staff development. In G. Griffin (Ed.), *Staff development: Eighty-second yearbook of the National Society for the Study of Education, Part II* (pp. 92-117). Chicago: University of Chicago Press.

Huberman, M. (1989). The professional life cycle of teachers. *Teachers College Record, 91*(1), 31-57.

Huberman, M., & Miles, M. (1984). *Innovation up close.* New York: Plenum.

Hunt, D. E. (1978). Conceptual level theory and research as guides to educational practice. *Interchange, 8*(4), 78-90.

Joyce, B., & McKibbin, M. (1982). Teacher growth states and school environments. *Educational Leadership, 40*(3), 36-41.

Jung, J. (1978). *Understanding human motivation.* New York: Macmillan.

Karant, V. I. (1989). Supervision in an age of teacher empowerment. *Educational Leadership, 46*(8), 27-29.

Krupp, J. A. (1987). Understanding and motivating personnel in the second half of life. *Journal of Education, 169*(1), 20-46.

Levine, S. L. (1989). *Promoting adult growth in schools: The promise of professional development.* Needham Heights, MA: Allyn & Bacon.

Lieberman, A. (Ed.). (1986). *Rethinking school improvement: Research, craft, and concept.* New York: Teachers College Press.

Maeroff, G. I. (1988). *The empowerment of teachers: Overcoming the crisis of confidence.* New York: Teachers College Press.

March, J. G., & Simon, H. A. (1958). *Organizations.* New York: John Wiley.

McLaughlin, M. W., & Marsh, D. D. (1978). Staff development and school change. *Teachers College Record, 80*(1), 69-94.

Ponticell, J. A. (1994). Seeing and believing: Using collegial coaching and videotaping to improve instruction in an urban high school. In M. J. O'Hair & S. Odell (Eds.), *Partnerships in education: Teacher education yearbook II.* Fort Worth, TX: Harcourt Brace.

Rost, J. (1991). *Leadership for the 21st century.* New York: Praeger.

Rotter, J. B. (1954). *Social learning and clinical psychology.* Englewood Cliffs, NJ: Prentice-Hall.

Sanders, D. P., & McCutcheon, G. (1986). The development of practical theories of teaching. *Journal of Curriculum and Supervision, 2*(1), 50-67.

Schein, E. H. (1964). The mechanisms of change. In W. G. Bennis, E. H. Schein, R. Steele, & E. Berlew (Eds.), *Interpersonal dynamics* (pp. 98-107). Homewood, IL: Dorsey.

Showers, B. (1985). Teachers coaching teachers. *Educational Leadership, 42*(7), 43-48.

Shroyer, M. G. (1990). Effective staff development for effective organizational development. *Journal of Staff Development, 11*(1), 2-6.

Shulman, L., & Carey, N. (1984). Psychology and the limitations of individual rationality: Implications for the study of reasoning and civility. *Review of Educational Research, 54*(4), 501-525.

Sizer, T. (1992). *Horace's school: Redesigning the American high school.* Boston: Houghton Mifflin.

Smylie, M. A. (1988). The enhancement function of staff development: Organizational and psychological antecedents to individual teacher change. *American Educational Research Journal, 25*(1), 1-30.

Smylie, M. A. (1989). Teachers' views of the effectiveness of sources of learning to teach. *Elementary School Journal, 89*(5), 543-558.

Smyth, W. J. (1988). A "critical" perspective for clinical supervision. *Journal of Curriculum and Supervision, 3*(2), 136-156.

Zimpher, N. L. (1988). A design for the professional development of teacher leaders. *Journal of Teacher Education, 39*(1), 53-60.

6 Preservice Teachers and Coursework: When Is Getting It Right Wrong?

Diane Holt-Reynolds

Diane Holt-Reynolds is Assistant Professor of Teacher Education with the College of Education at Michigan State University. She works primarily with the teacher certification program, focusing attention on coursework as an opportunity to engage preservice teachers in identifying, questioning, and professionalizing their beliefs about their roles as teachers and students' roles as learners. She is also a senior researcher with the National Center for Research on Teacher Learning. Her projects there include a longitudinal study of how undergraduate English majors develop disciplinary understanding and teaching expertise and a second research study focusing on preservice teachers' learning in a content area reading course she teaches. She worked in a public high school in southern Indiana teaching English and theater arts for 13 years.

ABSTRACT

What do teacher educators hope to accomplish with those who come to us for help as they learn to be teachers? How are we judging whether the preservice teachers who involve themselves in the coursework for which we are responsible are "getting" it? These questions formed the structure for inquiring into and thinking about the practice of teacher education. The data reported here reveal discrepancies between what one teacher educator seemed to offer as rationales and theories for implementing reading-to-learn, writing-to-learn, and discussing-to-learn strategies in classrooms and the rationales nine preservice teachers offered for valuing those same strategies.

The data suggest that our estimations of what preservice teachers actually learn from coursework change if we take as evidence their abilities to adopt the professional rationales supporting instructional strategies rather than their abilities to demonstrate functional expertise at matching a strategy to appropriate subject matter uses. The tension between teaching preservice teachers technical skills and helping them develop professional arguments for explaining the value or importance of the instructional strategies those skills support raises questions we as teacher educators might consider as we examine our programs and roles.

Pedagogical shifts that are startlingly dramatic in retrospect can be ever so subtle as we live through them. Many of us can remember a time when "learning" meant reproducing a set of "right" answers to teachers' questions; "teaching," therefore, meant inviting students to rehearse those answers—in interesting and memorable ways, of course. Those were the days when as new teachers we were encouraged to, harangued about, rewarded for, and evaluated by how well we could plan teaching episodes around straightforward behavioral objectives that detailed how students would respond given particular tasks in specified contexts. We learned to think objectives, to write them, and to feel guilty if we engaged students in any activities not clothed in them.

I began my career in this milieu as a teacher of high school English. It was not long before I became far too busy doing the work of teaching to notice that I was spending less time drafting objectives and more time listening to students as they struggled to "see" literature as I saw it. Eventually all of my energies worked toward trying to "see" literature as students saw it. I forgot to remember objectives.

Now, in spite of the fact that I am a teacher educator acting out of theories of constructed knowledge and convinced of the power of lived experiences as bases for that construction, I find myself looking at my work and asking questions that bear at least a family resemblance to the objectives-based questions that were such a formative part of my past: What do I hope to accomplish with those who come to study teaching? What do I want them to learn to do? How do I expect them to demonstrate that learning—and under what conditions? How will I know whether the preservice teachers I teach are "getting it"?

These questions have taken shape, grown, and become increasingly urgent. If preservice teachers are constructing ideas about their future practice while engaged with teacher educators in formal coursework, and if prior beliefs based on personal history are active in that constructing process, then what happens in a university course where beliefs and new ideas interact? Do lay beliefs wane and vanish in the brilliance of ideas that represent the professional knowledge base? Do new ideas seem like extensions of prior beliefs so that there remain no distinctions to bother about? Do preservice teachers add new ideas to their repertoire without either revising old ones or thinking critically about new ones? What happens inside preservice teachers' heads as they engage with coursework and try to "get it"?

As I explore and come to understand more clearly the implications of data I collected through interviews with nine preservice teachers as they worked their way through one teacher education course, I am struck by the processes these preservice teachers used for constructing meaning in a coursework setting. Although the actual beliefs they held prior to university study are compelling and the ideas they encountered in the course provide a context for looking at their subsequent sense making, it is the processes themselves I explore in this chapter.

Given what their professor hoped to teach, given the principles he valued and made accessible through the course he taught, what did the preservice teachers do to make those ideas seem sensible to themselves? They "got it right" by all external indicators. Their assignments and in-class comments were exemplary. But did they "get it right" internally? If we use their professor's intended outcomes as a standard, then the answer is no. In this chapter, I examine *how* preservice teachers used their ideas based on personal history and show how the use of these ideas led preservice teachers to value course ideas based on rationales that differed greatly from those of their professor and yet failed to help them identify those differences.

A Case Study

The course was Content Area Reading. Informal data collected during previous iterations of this course suggested that the preservice teachers who typically enrolled held powerful beliefs about what teaching, classrooms, and students should be like. As the course had no field component and was not part of a sequence of courses designed to build beliefs about "good" teaching, it seemed likely that the source for these beliefs might be preservice teachers' previous experiences in classrooms as students.

The nine preservice teachers who participated in this study were all secondary, subject matter majors. None had any field experiences to inform their thinking. Therefore, these nine were appropriate resources for my inquiry into the interaction of biography or personal histories (see Bullough, 1989, 1990; Knowles, 1990; Knowles & Hoefler, 1989) with teacher education coursework.

Each of the nine talked with me on six occasions across the semester. We spent two interview sessions talking about their experiences as learners in home, community, and school settings. We focused the next three interview sessions on specific aspects of the course. We discussed in-class events and speakers, reviewed the stories of how each had developed class assignments, and reopened discussions that had originated in the class. Our final session was devoted to their evaluation of 35 statements their professor had made throughout the course. These statements embodied his research-based theories about teaching and learning and included suggestions he had made for using reading, writing, and discussing as tools for learning subject matter.

Thus, I became privy to many of the private, personal reactions and responses these nine had to the concepts they encountered in the course. I was privileged to hear *what* they believed Professor Barnett (a pseudonym) had advocated—their reconstruction of his arguments—and *how* they arrived at decisions about the potential value of the reading-to-learn and writing-to-learn strategies and techniques he had advocated teaching high school students to use—their processes for evaluating those arguments.

Because both the course itself as well as the interviews were audiotaped and completely transcribed, I have had ample opportunity to revisit those conversations, to look closely at the relationship between what Barnett said, what these preservice teachers reported that they heard, and their rationales for supporting the decisions they made about course ideas. If Barnett's objective was to "sell" specific instructional strategies as decontextualized, discrete practices, useful as additions to a wide range of preexisting pedagogical goals, then these nine "got it"—his objective— "right." If, however, his objectives included passing along an intact set of principles for guiding decisions about which instructional practices might be most productive when helping high school students negotiate text in order to learn, then these nine got it "wrong."

The discrepancies were large between what Barnett offered as rationales and theories for implementing reading-to-learn, writing-to-learn, and discussing-to-learn strategies in classrooms and the rationales these nine preservice teachers offered for valuing those same strategies. What lessons we as teacher educators take from these discrepancies depends on how we view our roles as teachers of those who hope to teach, on what goals or objectives we imagine lie beneath the programs of teacher education within which we work, and on how we frame the task of learning teaching.

In this chapter, I first share the thinking of these nine preservice teachers as they explained that thinking to me. Thus, the first section of the chapter details their responses to course ideas and contrasts their rationales for making positive decisions about those ideas with Barnett's rationales for recommending them in the first place. It is these contrasts that seem most important to notice.

The data imply that *how* these preservice teachers arrived at their conclusions is far more significant than *what* those conclusions actually came to be. I have, therefore, devoted the second half of the chapter to exploration of the relationship between how these preservice teachers apparently made sense of coursework without noticing or confronting the differences between their constructions and those of their professor and our assumptions as teacher educators. It may well be time for us as teacher educators to reassess our assumptions, to define anew our objectives and to look closely at what "it" is that we find ourselves busy trying to achieve with the preservice teachers we intend to help, guide, or mentor as they learn to teach.

Looking at the Data

Before taking a detailed look at the relationship between the rationales these preservice teachers offered in defense of their positive decisions about many ideas they encountered in this content area reading course and the rationales offered by their professor, it is important to understand what these data cannot be expected to illuminate. No attempt was made in the data-gathering process to collect evidence that would allow a later evaluation of the quality of Professor Barnett's instruction or of the appropriateness of his arguments. This was not a study of one teacher educator's effectiveness. It was instead an attempt to document the processes and resulting rationales these preservice teachers employed for determining the potential value of instructional principles they encountered through the coursework.

Questions have long plagued us about how to explain the discontinuity we see when preservice teachers leave the university and begin field practice. Preservice teachers appear to have learned new, research-based ways of engaging students with subject matter while at the university but fail to produce those new teacher actions in live classrooms (see Bullough, in press; Hollingsworth, 1989; Hoy, 1968; Knowles, 1988; Shipman, 1967; Zeichner & Tabachnick, 1981). Looking closely at preservice teachers' self-reports of their thinking about one course while it was in progress seemed an appropriate way to document the quality and character of that learning/thinking prior to any effects that might be introduced by socialization variables (see Zeichner, 1983) or site constraints inherent to field practice.

Emphasis here on the discrepancies between what Barnett offered and what these preservice teachers reported valuing is intended to challenge our assumptions about how preservice teachers manage coursework rather than to defend the position of either Barnett or the preservice teacher whose decision is discussed. The implications to us as teacher educators of the differences between the rationales Barnett offered to support his suggestions and those these preservice teachers offered as reasons for valuing Barnett's suggestions are enough to consider here without also tackling questions of whether one set of rationales is more desirable than the other.

In an effort to make these data accessible to readers, I briefly outline the context in which Barnett taught and report these preservice teachers' responses by organizing them around the dominant, most frequently expressed themes (see Barritt, Beekman, Bleeker, & Mulderij, 1985) expressed in those responses.

Content Area Reading—A Context

Barnett used this course in content area reading as an opportunity to invite preservice teachers who will eventually teach in a variety of subject matter contexts to consider strategies that will help inexperienced readers gain metacognitive control over their own reading processes. He advocated teaching high school readers how to read to learn as an alternative to circumventing difficult texts via teacher telling or lecturing. He proposed that writing and small group peer discussion might be useful tools for instruction.

Barnett worked from a constructivist stance even though he did not make this stance explicit. He used phrases like "making meaning" or "personalizing learning." Class sessions were 3 hours long, 3 days a week, as this was a summer semester course. In class, Barnett frequently asked those enrolled to work in small groups to try out a strategy. He invited subject matter specialists to speak as guest lecturers. He used an interactive journal as a forum for discussing assigned readings. Those enrolled submitted an I-Search (see Macrorie, 1988)—a narrative, process-focused reformation of traditional research papers—and a final project. This project consisted of a series of lessons, or a unit, on a topic of choice and was intended as a vehicle for those enrolled to use to demonstrate their abilities to transform course ideas into appropriate, subject matter-specific forms.

Enrollment included experienced teachers, several beginning teachers who had completed student teaching, and 11 preservice teachers. Two of these declined participation in this study due to heavy class loads and a short term. The remaining nine were the participants whose thinking I have used as data here.

Content Area Reading—Some Responses

During Interviews 3, 4, and 5, each individual was asked to explain his or her response to and current thinking about the ideas presented most recently in the lecture/seminar time or through the assigned readings. In the process of these rather lengthy conversations, the rationales for emerging points of view, the relevant explicit or implicit beliefs that functioned as the underriding premises for these rationales, and the conclusions individual preservice teachers were reaching emerged.

"These ideas seem natural." Their general reactions to the course, the readings, the activities, and the assignments were positive. Several of those with whom I spoke found the course "natural" and were even puzzled about why Barnett might want to focus on such "obvious" ideas. The examples below illustrate the lack of tension these preservice teachers felt between their lay beliefs about teaching and the research-based principles Barnett advocated. They talk as if there is little "it" to respond to or have an opinion about. Their comments here as well as those cited throughout this chapter include the pseudonym selected by the participant as well as an indication of his or her subject matter major.

> I expected this to be another junky education course, but what he's talking about makes sense to me. It doesn't seem like a theory that people *should* use but [that] has no backing. It will come natural to me because that's how I learn myself. (Corinne, English)

I have really enjoyed the class. I think it's quite useful so far. A prereading activity seems natural. What it accomplishes seems like it would be a natural thing to do. (Charlie, English)

In a lot of [the articles], the stuff seemed quite obvious to me—that textbooks are bad. I'm not sure why we're getting into this. It's somewhat obvious that we can't have people learning [by] just memorizing things. That's logical. (Will, math)

Not all of their commentary treated Barnett's ideas as mundane. Several preservice teachers noted that at least some of the ideas they were encountering were both new and potentially useful. The relatively unproblematic reaction to course ideas indicated here suggests that these preservice teachers recognized ideas as new without necessarily sensing any potential discrepancies between these new ideas and the previously constructed beliefs about teaching they brought with them into the course. Their reactions suggest that everything is fine; new ideas can be added to older ideas rather easily without negotiating or working through any differences between the sets of ideas.

[Prereading] is new to me. I hadn't thought about utilizing something before reading. Every method we've talked about in this course seems to me like, "Yes! This is going to work." I think what we are learning is really important. (Charlie, English)

The whole concept of combining reading, writing, and discussion is [new to me]. And journals—they are old, but this is a new way of thinking about [them]. With this new way of thinking, you can blend things together. (Jeneane, English)

What [Professor Barnett is] doing is important, relevant, interesting, and fun. I think it will help me. Thinking about how written things are organized, I have an intuitive knowledge, but it isn't anything I [had] really thought about trying to teach to somebody. (Lauren, English)

Such positive responses were the norm. Many of Barnett's ideas and recommendations for teaching strategies were indeed valued—almost immediately and without any debate—by those enrolled in the course. However, the rationales these preservice teachers gave for valuing the specific teaching actions or strategies that Barnett advocated seldom matched Barnett's rationales.

"*These ideas serve my goals.*" The recognition of "implicit theories" (Clark, 1988) about teaching is long standing. These are the logical consequences of the thousands of hours preservice teachers have already spent "studying" teaching via observation (Lortie, 1975) before they ever enroll in the first formal teacher education course or experience. What has been less clear is *how* preservice teachers use these lay theories or beliefs about good teaching to help them make sense of coursework. Because I asked them how they knew to value some ideas and discard others as less useful, these preservice teachers worked very hard to help me understand. In so doing, they revealed the predominance of lay beliefs over course-based rationales.

The most process-revealing theme common to these preservice teachers' rationales was, "These ideas are good because they help me do what I already thought a teacher should do." The process of making sense of coursework seemed to involve a conscious comparison between what the preservice teacher already believed or valued and the potential of any course-based idea for fostering that previously developed value. When these preservice teachers made a positive decision about a strategy they had encountered as part of this course, they explicitly linked their decision to a previously constructed goal for teaching based on their personal history. Preservice teachers who entered the course eager to become interesting teachers valued strategies that they reasoned could make material interesting to students. Others, who hoped to become caring teachers with rich personal connections to students, valued strategies that they reasoned could open dialogue or signal their attitude of caring and concern for students.

Some concrete examples may help clarify. Lauren, Charlie, and Jeneane, all English majors, came into the course with particularly strong, well-thought-out goals for their teaching. Each returned to this previously developed goal as the basis for making a decision about the potential value of course ideas. Each decided positively about particular ideas because each believed that the ideas and strategies they had encountered via Barnett would help them further personally constructed, preexisting goals.

Lauren's statement was typical: "Developing strategies that help students learn both content and a process to think about the content is the number one thing [Barnett] has taught. That's sort of another way of saying, 'Give them the tools.' " Giving students tools had been a dominant metaphor for Lauren from the start of the course. She entered the course believing in the importance of giving students "little tricks of the trade" and basic strategies for learning independently—she called these "tools." Lauren's translation of Barnett's rationale does not differ too much from it; however, her process for judging his idea involves measuring its validity by her own, personal beliefs. "Teaching as tool giving" was her metaphor, not Barnett's. Using it, in this case, did little to alter Barnett's intentions. The process of comparing course-based ideas to personal theories served Lauren well.

Charlie too had a tendency to recast Barnett's ideas into language that reflected goals to which he was committed even as he entered the course. From our first interview together, he expressed his interest in how an English curriculum might provide an opportunity for students to think critically about social issues. "For everything you want to do you could think of a reading and writing or discussing activity that could do it. I'm excited about doing those things because they accomplish the critical thinking and learning goals."

As in Lauren's case, when Charlie utilized his lay theories or goals, these helped him reach rationales that, although not reflective of Barnett's actual language, were close approximations of and mirrored Barnett's rationales. In these instances, it did no disservice to Barnett's ideas, theories, arguments, or list of suggested activities and strategies for either Lauren or Charlie to translate his language into her/his own system of metaphors and analogies.

However, some preservice teachers actually valued a course-based strategy because they perceived its ability to serve a goal they valued but that Barnett publicly and repeatedly acknowledged as something he hoped to eradicate! Lectures were a format all these preservice teachers valued if lecturing could be made "interesting." They ultimately valued some teaching strategies that Barnett intended as substitutions for lecturing. They valued small-group work and writing to learn because these could be used in conjunction with lecturing and so render lecturing less onerous to students.

The positive character of most of their decisions about course-based strategies is easy to see in these data. However, valuing course-based ideas may not mean much if preservice teachers' rationales in support of those practices vary greatly from the rationales implied by the professional knowledge base. These preservice teachers' arguments for supporting their positive decisions rested on their prior beliefs—on associations they had already built between student reactions they valued and teacher behaviors they believed could cause those reactions (see Holt-Reynolds,

1992; Knowles & Holt-Reynolds, 1991). Their rationales did not match or reflect those of their professor.

Jeneane used the same basic process—deciding about the value of course ideas by looking to see if they might serve preexisting goals—but with very different results. Her own goals for future teaching, based on her personal history, involved establishing conditions and states of mind such as tolerance for diversity, comfortableness, and shared authority. These were important to her, and Jeneane consistently appropriated Barnett's ideas to serve these goals. Her comments reveal her rationales for making positive decisions about the value of several writing-to-learn strategies. I have cited them extensively because they are examples of how all nine preservice teachers used beliefs about good teaching based on their personal history as bases for defending the value of course ideas rather than the rationales Barnett extended.

> In my class, I would use writing to learn for students to become comfortable with writing and to feel good about their own writing. . . . I am so concerned with students feeling comfortable and students wanting to do something. [The I-Search] is an assignment that students would enjoy and get a lot from. . . . It's letting them figure out what's comfortable for them in writing. . . . It's important to let students know that just because a person is an author, it does not mean they are an authority. I think an I-search can show students how much is available. . . . It's a lot easier to write like that, so that it can't be wrong because there is no form.

This last statement was especially far removed from Barnett's rationale for informal writing. He advocated the I-Search because writing informally would allow students to concentrate their efforts on content rather than form, not because informal writing is impossible to get "wrong." Jeneane made a positive decision about the value of the I-Search and writing to learn in general, but she based her decision on beliefs and attributions about its ability to serve her own, previously constructed goals.

All of the other preservice teachers in this study appropriated strategies to serve ends other than those Barnett had advocated. Based on their personal history they developed rationales for favoring these strategies with little or no modification to their preexisting beliefs about teaching or learning.

"These strategies will be interesting to students." One of the most frequently appearing personal history-based rationales involved *interestingness*. These preservice teachers argued that a variety of strategies would be good to use because they would promote students' interest in the class or enjoyment of the class. All nine entered the course reporting that they believed that when teachers or activities are interesting, students will learn. Therefore, they reasoned, if a strategy might be interesting to students, it would be good to use. Fostering students' interest functioned as a type of goal in itself. Jane offered an example of this argument.

> Journal writing and I-Searches [are] going to be a lot more fun to write. Students will get more excited about [the I-Search] than they would about a research paper. To know that their teacher really cares about how their classrooms are.

Throughout this chapter, preservice teachers' tendencies to advocate a strategy because they believed it would promote students' interest is evident. The belief that a strategy would be "fun" or "exciting" is laced throughout their comments and rationales. The priority of "interestingness" pervaded these preservice teachers' language; no other concept appeared as frequently in our conversations.

Barnett did preface his rationale for I-Searches by noting the value of encouraging students to find out about subjects they are interested in. But Barnett went on to tie interest to authenticity of reading and writing activities. The second half of his argument did not surface in the language of these preservice teachers.

"These ideas are different from traditional methods." Many of these preservice teachers reasoned that a strategy would be valuable because they believed it would be perceived by students as "different."

> Fun kinds of different projects that involve using math—kind of like the assignments we were thinking up yesterday—I can see how the creative ones would be good for a change of pace. (Beth, math)
>
> I think a good way to start a class would be to use the discussion methods that we were talking about this morning just to break down some barriers. It would kind of throw students for a loop. (Jeneane, English)

Jeneane was referring to a demonstration activity Barnett used to model how teachers could directly instruct students in how to use small groups as learning tools. He advocated the activity as a means for focusing students' attention on their own small-group processes and for eliciting explicit conversation detailing what productive small-group behaviors might look like. Jeneane reported none of his thinking or reasoning.

She did continue to invoke the belief that doing something different is good in and of itself. She used this belief as part of her rationale for minimizing her use of lecturing.

> [Lecturing] wouldn't aid my students in the way they need to be aided. It would be detrimental to them because they go through 13 years of schooling and a lot of it is lecturing or telling. When they get to college, it's the same thing. If there is one class where teachers do something out of the ordinary, something that is not the norm, I think that can really enhance and aid a student in learning.

Jeneane's rationale is presented in full here. She did not add that lecturing should be avoided because students are passive or uninvolved with making meaning while teachers lecture. That was Barnett's rationale. Jeneane's rationale tied learning to the state of being different. Others shared her point of view.

> I got the feeling that [students] would like [my final project]. They would think it was different. (Corinne, English)
>
> I think [the discussion model activity] was fun. I think kids would have enjoyed it. It's sort of a novel thing. If you're kind of getting into a rut, it would be something good to do for a day. . . . [My final project] has value. [Students] would enjoy it if they could get into it. It's better than just the same thing all the time. It's good to shake them up a little bit. (Jane, English)

Before leaving this rationale, it is worth noting that a commitment to *interestingness* is certainly not in itself a bad or undesirable aspiration. These data are not cited to suggest that there is anything wrong with the beliefs preservice teachers held. Rather, these data are cited to demonstrate the difference between the rationales preservice teachers adopted as defense of a potential practice and the rationales Barnett expressed as he taught their course. When these preservice teachers referenced their beliefs as standards for judging course ideas, the result was an acceptance of those ideas but the loss of the research-based rationales that initially supported them.

"These ideas provide bonuses for teachers." The final group of rationales that these particular preservice teachers offered for using the strategies from the content area reading course centered around bonus features they reported that they saw as inherent to the strategy. Beth and Dave talked about writing in math classrooms as a way to allow the teacher to "motivate" students to read the math textbook.

> I think if students knew that we'll write about [the reading assignment] tomorrow, they might be more motivated to stick with it. (Beth, math)
>
> Every once in a while, I think that they have to be aware that I know that they are just skipping the text [assignments]. (Dave, math)

All three math majors also talked about writing as a way for the teacher to know whether students understood material—as a sort of informal test.

> By writing in this journal and saying that you don't understand something, it would be good. As a teacher you can see exactly where the kids are having a problem. Having kids [write] an essay about a math problem [would be] a way of seeing if they really understand something. (Dave, math)
>
> [Put] students in the groups like we had yesterday; discuss what they got out of [the reading]. See if they got what you wanted them to get. I think that's one way to use it. (Beth, math)
>
> From [writing], you really can tell if a student really does understand what they are talking about. (Will, math)

Barnett's rationale for writing to learn argued that students' writing allows them to learn for themselves. He attempted to distinguish writing to learn from traditional, testlike writing to show learning. Using writing diagnostically as these math majors advocated may or may not actually violate his argument depending on whether they intend to grade that writing. What is significant here is that none of these three math majors' rationales for positive decisions about the potential of writing in math classrooms included or reframed Barnett's argument. In fact, each noted that she/he was not sure whether writing actually would help students learn math concepts directly. Will did add that writing could offer students a way to "express themselves" in math.

Their rationales were based implicitly on an epistemology that calls for a teacher to tell knowledge to a student. Such an epistemology does not admit the possibility for student discovery. In fact, in repeated interview sessions, all three of these math majors stated emphatically that the nature of math *requires* that teachers tell it to students.

The fact that these preservice teachers were able to find rationales for deciding that course ideas were valuable is encouraging. The fact that they adopted so few of Barnett's rationales and arguments is worth extended attention.

Looking at Our Assumptions and Objectives

Did Barnett's students get it right or wrong? They reported an enthusiasm for many of the instructional strategies they encountered through the course (for reports of strategies they dismissed, see Holt-Reynolds, 1991b, 1992). They left the course ready to defend journals, prereading activities, writing-to-learn assignments, and small-group discussions as valuable instructional options. They also left the course talking about how those options would be interesting to students, make them comfortable, allow them freedom of expression, and help them see the limitations of authorities. If they incorporated any of Barnett's principles for how teachers can foster either independence in learners or metacognitive awareness, they did not discuss them with me.

What are we to conclude from these data? The answer to that question depends in large part on how we understand and frame our assumptions about the activity we call teacher education and the activity we call learning to teach and on our objectives for each.

Assumptions

"Turning theory into practice" is a slogan that seems to capture one set of assumptions we might make about the activity of teaching new teachers. We could think of teacher education as a planned series of courses and experiences designed to pass the professional, pedagogical knowledge (Shulman, 1986) that expert teachers have on to novices. "Knowledge that" becomes "knowledge of" (Berliner, 1985) through exposure to that knowledge followed by practice implementing it. This way of understanding what it means to learn teaching helps teacher educators think about the nature of the professional knowledge base and about the sequence we might follow as we expose novices to that knowledge base. It offers us less help as we struggle to understand the affects of a lay knowledge base.

We might frame our task as teacher educators in another way. Let's assume that preservice teachers arrive with implicit theories and beliefs based on personal history. Many of us involved in exploring life histories, biographies, and other forms of personal histories would argue for such an assumption. We might go on to assume a lay, personal history-based knowledge of teaching accompanied by practical argument-like (see Fenstermacher, 1979) constructions and therefore expect that preservice teachers will check that knowledge, those beliefs, and previously established goals against the research-based, professional knowledge we offer through coursework.

In either case, we will find ourselves enmeshed in an implicit theory of our own. Both these sets of assumptions imply that research-based theories about teaching, learning, students, and classrooms will naturally and automatically receive preference in the minds of preservice teachers over the personal history-based beliefs they brought with them into the course. Both imply that we believe preservice teachers will (a) identify their own lay beliefs; (b) recognize that these beliefs differ from the principles we are inviting them to explore; (c) elect to temporarily suspend their beliefs and try ours on; and (d) replace, inform, expand, or tailor their beliefs to accommodate ours as any one or all of these actions becomes necessary.

Somewhere there may indeed be preservice teachers who act in these ways. I have yet to encounter any of them. The nine who spoke with me formally and whose responses are documented here represent the kinds of reactions I overhear informally across the coursework I teach. Preservice teachers report testing our principles against their own experiences as students and comparing our attributions for desired student outcomes with their own. They report a decided preference for their own, lived experiences as data upon which to build professional conclusions. They treat their personal histories as prototypic and generalize from the conclusions based on them to develop predictions about how other students will react to teacher actions. I have reported their internal dialogues (Holt-Reynolds, 1991a) and their processes for converting personal experiences as students into prescriptions for themselves as teachers (Knowles & Holt-Reynolds, 1991) in some detail elsewhere. Suffice it to say here that the conclusions preservice teachers have already reached about what teacher actions were causal in their own positive or negative experiences as students act as givens against which they judge the validity, value, and potential of the principles and strategies we advocate in coursework. Any assumptions we might harbor about preservice teachers adjusting their personal history-based beliefs as a natural, spontaneous part of engaging in coursework are ill founded (see Ball, 1988, 1989; McDiarmid, 1989).

The data represented here suggest quite a different picture. These nine preservice teachers gave no indication that they *rejected* any of Barnett's rationales; they talked as if their own were *the same* as his. Only Jane noted that she disagreed with Barnett, and she noted this on only one occasion. In over 8 hours of interview conversations with each of nine individuals, only one said that her view of teaching differed even a little from her professor's.

Does this suggest a profound conspiracy of impression management (Shipman, 1967)? That seems doubtful as I was not a part of the assessment of these individuals. In fact, I regularly invited them to take issue with Barnett—as he did himself through the interactive journals. These nine seem to have been, quite simply, unaware that their own beliefs and rationales differed from Barnett's. Are other preservice teachers similarly unaware? If so, then our assumption that they can and do distinguish between the beliefs they currently hold and the principles we ask them to consider is unfounded.

These preservice teachers acted as if Barnett's goals for good teaching matched their own. They proceeded to use those goals—without questioning, reshaping, informing, or enlarging them—as a framework around which to hang instructional strategies as they found them useful.

Objectives

If we hope that preservice teachers will leave our courses carrying a fat bag of teacher tricks that they can adapt to the contexts in which they find themselves in the years ahead, then we may not want to pursue these questions further. We may feel satisfied when preservice teachers adopt the particular teacher actions we advocate and worry ourselves very little about whether they also develop a professionally informed rationale in support of those actions. If by "teacher education" we mean that we want preservice teachers to develop technical expertise at setting up cooperative learning tasks, writing clear lesson plans, imagining clever schema activation prereading activities, crafting interesting and authentic writing tasks, and setting up and evaluating journals, then the rationales they develop for defending these actions are not important. We can continue to operate programs of teacher education in which teacher educators like Barnett are faced with students they know little or nothing about; "teach" them for a term; and evaluate their "progress" using decontextualized, amorphous projects like a series of imaginary lessons that illustrate course ideas. We can continue to count this activity as getting it right—as learning to teach.

If, however, we hope that preservice teachers leave our courses more aware of their personal history-based beliefs and habits of making sense out of classrooms, able to consciously choose to frame classroom events in new ways, and ready to select from among an array of instructional practices using a variety of rationales, then we need to craft programs of teacher education in which teacher educators like Barnett have ample opportunity to develop personal knowledge of the lay beliefs of the preservice teachers with whom they work. We need ways to invite preservice teachers explicitly to monitor their progress toward metacognitive control over their decisions as students of teaching, and we need ways to evaluate that progress. We need to consider carefully what kinds of coursework experiences can invite preservice teachers to focus attention on *how they evaluate* new pedagogical principles rather than exclusively on *what they can do* with new instructional ideas. We need to shift resources from exclusive support of technical skills to include support of rationale building. We need to confess that often preservice teachers can get it technically right while on other levels getting it wrong.

We also need to consider the relationship between coursework and field experiences. This chapter does not extend to the field. None of these nine were followed into student teaching or their first years in a classroom. Consequently, I cannot speculate about knowledge they developed in practice (Schön, 1983) or how the values they placed on these strategies played out in actual practice. Neither can these data shed much light on the relationship between rationales that preservice teachers can articulate and practice they can produce without an accompanying explanation. Intuitive ways of knowing (Arnheim, 1985) and acting lie beyond this study.

Conclusion

Hawkins (1974) writes about the relationship of teacher, student, and some third thing—"it"—that they explore and create together. In teacher education coursework settings, we too interact with students around some third thing—learning to teach. Together, we construct a persona called Teacher that our students will bring to life in classrooms with students of their own. I suspect we are far more conscious of how we hope they interact with students around a subject matter—it—than we are about how we should or could interact with them around the it they have come to us to study. We seem far more sure about what "good teaching" looks like in elementary and secondary settings than we are about what "good teacher education" looks like in university classrooms.

Our models of good elementary and secondary teaching have been built from a knowledge base about how young people learn. Might we build a model of good teacher education out of a similar data base reflecting how preservice teachers learn across contexts including home, school, and community, where the learning is frequently informal and unintended; university classrooms where the learning is more formal and experiential; and practical settings where we expect emerging professionals to transfer learning into action? What are the processes preservice teachers invoke in these contexts? How do they learn? It is time to identify our assumptions, check them against preservice teachers' experiences, and point our programs of teacher education in the direction those data suggest. Only then will we be able to imagine how to judge whether the preservice teachers we teach are getting it right or wrong.

References

Arnheim, R. (1985). The double-edged mind: Intuition and the intellect. In E. Eisner (Ed.), *Learning and teaching the ways of knowing: Eighty-fourth yearbook of the national society for the study of education* (pp. 77-96). Chicago: University of Chicago Press.

Ball, D. L. (1988). *Unlearning to teach mathematics* (Issue Paper No. 88-1). East Lansing: Michigan State University, National Center for Research on Teacher Education.

Ball, D. L. (1989). *Breaking with experience in learning to teach mathematics: The role of a preservice methods course* (Issue Paper No. 89-10). East

Lansing: Michigan State University, National Center for Research on Teacher Education.

Barritt, L., Beekman, T., Bleeker, H., & Mulderij, K. (1985). *Researching educational practice* (Monograph from the North Dakota Study Group on Evaluation). Grand Forks: University of North Dakota, Center for teaching and Learning.

Berliner, D. C. (1985). In pursuit of the expert pedagogue. *Educational Researcher, 15*(7), 5-13.

Bullough, R. V., Jr. (1989). *First year teacher: A case study.* New York: Teachers College Press.

Bullough, R. V., Jr. (1990). *Personal history and teaching metaphors in preservice teacher education.* Paper presented at the annual meeting of the American Educational Research Association, Boston.

Bullough, R. V., Jr. (in press). Personal history and teaching metaphors: A self study of teaching as conversation. *Teacher Education Quarterly.*

Clark, C. M. (1988). Asking the right questions about teacher preparation: Contributions of research on teacher thinking. *Educational Researcher, 17*(2), 5-12.

Fenstermacher, G. (1979). A philosophical consideration of recent research on teacher effectiveness. In L. S. Shulman (Ed.), *Review of research in education: VI* (pp. 12-36). Itasca, IL: F. E. Peacock.

Hawkins, D. (1974). I, thou, and it. In *The informed vision: Essays on learning and human nature* (pp. 92-127). New York: Agathon.

Hollingsworth, S. (1989). Prior beliefs and cognitive change in learning to teach. *American Educational Research Journal, 26*(2), 160-190.

Holt-Reynolds, D. (1991a). *The dialogues of teacher education: Entering and influencing preservice teachers' internal conversations* (Research Report No. 91-4). East Lansing: Michigan State University, National Center for Research on Teacher Learning.

Holt-Reynolds, D. (1991b). *Directed reading strategies and how preservice teachers decide they are unnecessary: Exploring the effects of personal histories.* Paper presented at the National Reading Conference, Palm Springs, CA.

Holt-Reynolds, D. (1992). Personal histories as relevant prior knowledge in coursework: Can we practice what we teach? *American Educational Research Journal, 29*(2), 325-349.

Hoy, W. (1968). The influence of experience on the beginning teacher. *School Review,* pp. 312-323.

Knowles, J. G. (1988, April). *"For whom the bell tolls": The failure of a student teacher and insights into self, teaching, and teacher education.*

Paper presented at the annual meeting of the American Educational Research Association, New Orleans, LA.

Knowles, J. G. (1990, February). *Launching the professional development of second-career beginning teachers: Boomerangs and barriers.* Paper presented at the Annual Meeting of the Association for Teacher Educators, Las Vegas, NV.

Knowles, J. G., & Hoefler, V. R. (1989). The student teacher who wouldn't go away: Learning from failure. *Journal of Experiential Education, 12*(2), 97-132.

Knowles, J. G., & Holt-Reynolds, D. (1991). Shaping pedagogies through personal histories in preservice teacher education. *Teachers College Record 93*(1), 87-113.

Lortie, D. (1975). *Schoolteacher: A sociological study.* Chicago: University of Chicago Press.

Macrorie, K. (1988). *The I-Search paper: Revised edition of research in writing.* Portsmouth, NH: Heinemann.

McDiarmid, G. W. (1989). *Tilting at webs of belief: Field experiences as a means of breaking with experience* (Research Report No. 89-8). East Lansing: Michigan State University, National Center for Research on Teacher Education.

Schön, D. A. (1983). *The reflective practitioner: How professionals think in action.* New York: Basic Books.

Shipman, M. (1967). Theory and practice in the education of teachers. *Educational Research, 9,* 208-212.

Shulman, L. S. (1986, Spring). Those who understand: Knowledge growth in teaching. *Educational Researcher, 15*(2), 4-14.

Zeichner, K. M. (1983). Individual and institutional factors related to the socialization of beginning teachers. In G. A. Griffin & H. Hukill (Eds.), *First years of teaching: What are the pertinent issues?* (pp. 1058-1099). Austin: University of Texas, Research and Development Center for Teacher Education.

Zeichner, K. M., & Tabachnick, B. R. (1981). Are the effects of university education "washed out" by school experience? *Journal of Teacher Education, 32*(3), 7-11.

Processes:
Reflections and Implications

Kenneth Zeichner

Bernadette Baker

The Three Studies and
Urban Teacher Preparation

The three chapters in this division of the yearbook address the task of preparing teachers for urban schools in different ways. Two of the three chapters (Carter & Larke; Ponticell, Olson, & Charlier) are directly concerned with one of the most important tasks facing U.S. teacher education for the foreseeable future, preparing teachers for urban schools. Carter and Larke in Chapter 4 are concerned with the preservice preparation of teachers for urban schools; Ponticell et al. in Chapter 5 are concerned with inservice teacher education for experienced teachers of mathematics and science already working in urban high schools. Chapter 6 by Holt-Reynolds is not explicitly focused on urban teacher preparation issues but has important implications for the urban context. Consequently, we will react to all three chapters in terms of their implications for helping teacher educators improve the very dismal record of U.S. teacher education institutions with regard to the preparation of teachers for urban schools.

Carter and Larke

Carter and Larke in Chapter 4 present a case study of 45 students at a midwestern state university who volunteered over a three-semester period to participate in urban field experiences and seminars and a course, School Community Involvement. All of these students, not unlike their peers across the United States, had initially expressed a preference for teaching in suburban schools, but by the end of their program, 9 of the 45 (20%) applied for teaching positions in urban areas and were hired.

Carter and Larke argue that more teacher education students could be persuaded to seek employment in urban schools if teacher education programs provided courses and field experiences that prepared them to do so. Like many teacher education programs across the country, this midwestern university had provided few opportunities for its students to observe or work in urban schools. The reconceptualization of the program described by Carter and Larke involved the introduction of a requirement that all teacher education students spend a minimum period of time in culturally diverse classrooms and the offering of courses that dealt with teaching and learning in urban schools. New urban field placements were also recruited for an optional urban student teaching experience and supervisors were hired who had successful teaching experience in urban schools.

Most of the chapter describes a case study of 45 students who completed this reconceptualized program. The reactions of the 9 students who eventually chose to work in urban schools (pursuers) are compared to those of the 36 students who did not choose urban teaching (nonpursuers). Several specific attitudes and behaviors distinguished the pursuers from the nonpursuers. For example, those who chose to teach in urban schools had prior positive experiences in urban schools whereas the nonpursuers lacked such experience. The pursuers and nonpursuers also reacted quite differently to the cultural conflicts they experienced in urban schools. Specifically, the nonpursuers reacted with anger and frustration to such things as an emphasis on the African American experience in the curriculum, whereas the pursuers reacted to this emphasis as an opportunity for them to learn more about African American history.

From the description of the reactions of the nonpursuers, it seems that urban schools are better off without their services. They tended to have negative attitudes about cultural diversity and cities, and they seemed to elect the urban student teaching experience mainly because they thought it would look good on their resumes. Carter and Larke argue that unless program selection becomes an important issue, urban schools will not benefit from efforts within teacher education programs to make their preparation programs more relevant to urban contexts. Despite the reconceptualized program, the majority of the students were not persuaded to seek teaching careers in urban schools. Carter and Larke also argue that the characteristics that they identify for the pursuers could be used as criteria for the selection of students into teacher education programs focusing on urban teacher preparation.

Carter and Larke's focus on the issue of selection is a welcome addition to a teacher education literature that often implies that urban teacher preparation is a simple task to be solved by courses in multicultural education and field placements in urban schools. Their study underlines the danger that what teacher educators see as innovations sometimes serve to strengthen and reinforce the very attitudes and practices that they are designed to combat.

Although nine students were persuaded through their experiences in this program to seek teaching positions in urban schools, it is not clear what capabilities they bring to these jobs. It is asserted in the chapter that all of the students were deemed by their supervisors to have had successful teaching experiences during their student teaching semester. However, the specific criteria that are used to define success in this instance are not revealed. This issue of criteria is critical with regard to urban schools. For a long time, a fragmented, skills-based, and sequentially ordered curriculum was defined as "effective practice" in urban schools. Recent work has challenged this emphasis on teacher-directed instruction of a skills-based curriculum because of the failure of this approach to develop students' analytic and conceptual skills or ability to express themselves in writing, and because of its failure to provide a larger meaning or purpose for learning (Knapp & Shields, 1990). Recent definitions of effective practice in urban classrooms have stressed highly interactive and collaborative classrooms that emphasize cultural congruency between home and school and an integrated thematic approach to instruction focusing on meaning (Zeichner, 1994). What exactly does the "success" of Carter and Larke's student teachers mean in relation to these two very different views of effectiveness? What kinds of instruction were being encouraged in the new courses in the program and by the practices in the schools recruited for urban placements? Some helpful clues are given in this chapter about the kinds of program components that together with attention to selection could help teacher educators better address urban teacher preparation, but what goes on inside these components is critical. Field experiences, multicultural education courses, and student teaching seminars are not necessarily helpful in preparing teachers for urban schools even if more teachers choose urban teaching careers as a result of them. We need to know more about the kind of teaching engaged in by the nine pursuers in this study before embracing Carter and Larke's specific suggestions for program reform.

Ponticell, Olson, and Charlier

Chapter 5 focuses on the important task of inservice teacher education and the teacher's work context in urban schools. Although it is important, as Carter and Larke suggest, for college and university teacher educators to make special efforts to address the preparation of teachers for urban contexts, no preservice teacher education program, however good it may be, will be adequate for improving the quality of teaching in urban schools without corresponding changes in the systemic aspects of urban schools (Weiner, 1993).

Despite a growing consensus about curricular and instructional practices that if implemented would help to narrow the achievement gap in urban schools between poor students of color and their middle-class peers, it is very clear that cultural congruence in instruction, a culturally inclusive curriculum, and collaborative and interactive classrooms are not enough by themselves to overcome the effects of racism, language discrimination, social stratification, unequal resource distribution, and a history of discrimination against poor people of color (Carter & Goodwin, 1994; Villegas, 1988). As Weiner (1989) points out, although teacher education programs can educate teachers to teach diverse students with respect, creativity, and skill within their classrooms, they cannot prepare individual teachers to substitute for the political and social movements needed to alter the systemic deficiencies of schools and the societal problems these reflect.

It is very clear that at present, despite examples of urban schools where poor students of color are achieving at high standards (e.g., National Coalition of Advocates for Students, 1991), the working conditions for teachers in urban schools in general are inadequate for implementing the kind of complex and demanding teaching that research has identified as necessary for teaching all students to high academic standards (Corcoran, Walker, & White, 1988). Efforts to influence the ways that teachers interact with students within classrooms must be accompanied by or preceded by changes in the context of teachers' work.

Ponticell et al. describe a 3-year staff development effort involving 80 teachers of mathematics and science in 10 Chicago high schools. The inservice project consisted of workshops and seminars in "effective teaching" strategies, individual teacher consultations with university and school supervisors, and a peer coaching component. The goal of the project was to provide a climate in these urban high schools in which teacher collaboration, risk taking, and experimentation were valued, supported, and practiced.

At the beginning of the project, the situation seemed bleak, not unlike that in many urban schools across the United States (Weiner, 1993). Teacher morale was low and classrooms were routine and dull with very low expectations for student accomplishment. Teachers generally held negative views of their students and deficit views of students' families. The staff development these teachers had experienced before this project consisted of mainly one-shot "hit-and-run" sessions, which are also characteristic of urban school systems. Teachers were very much isolated from their colleagues and had generally lost the belief in their students' ability to learn.

The authors used a series of surveys, interviews, and observations of program activities to assess the impact of the staff development program on 35 of the 80 teachers. They argue that as a result of the collaborative culture that was established within these high schools by the staff development initiative, there were significant changes in both classrooms and staff rooms. Within classrooms the researchers detected a clear movement away from the teacher-directed, dull classrooms evident at the beginning of the study toward more student-centered, exciting classrooms in which high expectations were developing for student learning. Teachers reported a higher participation rate by their students in lessons, more questions asked by students, more positive interactions between teachers and students, and a greater concern with student thinking by teachers.

It is not clear whether these changes in classroom instruction were congruent with the "effective teaching" practices stressed and modeled in the workshops attended by teachers. Given the different definitions that have been held by researchers about effective teaching practices for urban schools (see above) it is important for Ponticell et al. to be clearer about the content of the workshops that teachers experienced. There is a long history in U.S. urban schools of the adoption of so-called effective teaching practices that have failed to narrow the achievement gap between poor and middle-class students (Bastian, Fruchter, Gittel, Greer, & Haskings, 1985).

It is also important for the authors to say something about the content of the curriculum in these classrooms. More active student participation in the kind of narrow skills-based curriculum that is alien to students' worlds and fails to build upon the cultural resources that students bring to school—a type of curriculum not uncommon in urban schools—is hardly an improvement. The nature of instruction (teacher directed or student centered) is only one aspect of what needs to be considered. Nothing at all is said in the chapter about what was being taught within these more student-centered classrooms.

The authors claim that the major impact of Project MASTER came in its influence on breaking down the isolation among teachers and in influencing teachers' conceptions of their work. They argue that the peer coaching component of the project helped teachers develop a greater receptivity to collaboration as a part of teaching and a greater openness to examine critically the impact of their work with their students. Importantly, they also claim that the collegiality that developed among teachers rekindled teachers' beliefs in their ability to help their students learn.

It has become very clear that the kind of teacher-directed, collaborative, and ongoing staff development that is illustrated by Project MASTER must become the norm rather than the exception if the ambitious visions of teaching so evident in current urban school reform efforts are to be realized (Little, 1993). Peer coaching, teacher study groups, action research groups, cross visitation programs, and similar grassroots efforts to connect teachers with each other and to draw upon teacher expertise are beginning to become more widespread, and this is good (Hollingsworth & Sockett, 1994).

As much as we support the direction suggested by Project MASTER, we also worry about the message that this study could send regarding staff development in urban schools. The implementation of peer coaching in this particular instance seems to have helped raise teachers' expectations for their ability to promote the learning of their students and to have produced some concrete classroom changes away from teacher directedness and toward student centeredness, but whatever changes resulted in this instance had a lot to do with what went on within the structures that this program established in the 10 high schools. One cannot conclude from this study that if urban schools would only run effective teaching workshops for their teachers and set up peer coaching programs that their problems will go away.

In fact, although recognizing the changes that took place in this study, we must also question the extent to which deep-seated changes in teachers' attitudes and beliefs were actually realized. Specifically, it seems hard to believe that the very negative views of teachers about students and their families and communities so prevalent at the beginning of the study (attitudes that developed over teachers' lifetimes) were completely turned around at the end of this project. For example, did the teachers' views change about parents not caring about their children's education? We are not told in the chapter. Were the teachers more open at the end of the study to listening to what parents had to say and in recognizing the funds of knowledge existing in the community? Despite the important accomplishments that were achieved regarding teachers' views of collaboration and their greater willingness to examine their practice, there are many questions to be addressed. Racism, language discrimination, classism, and structural inequalities are difficult problems to deal with and require much in addition to peer coaching groups. What Project MASTER was able to accomplish should be recognized and appreciated, but it represents only a beginning in what needs to become a major effort to restructure the context of teachers' work in urban schools.

Finally, there is an interesting contrast in the progression of teacher learning evident in this study and in the study by Carter and Larke. Carter and Larke took as their starting point their need to change their students' attitudes about teaching in urban schools. The changes in attitudes that were then achieved led to changes in behavior, such as the choice to student-teach in urban schools. In the Ponticell et al. study, it appears that changes in behavior (e.g., experiences in teacher collaboration) served as the stimulus for changes in attitudes about collaboration and about student learning. In the final analysis, changes in teachers' attitudes and practices will be involved in teaching learning, but the starting place may differ.

Holt-Reynolds

Chapter 6, by Holt-Reynolds, is not explicitly concerned with preparing teachers for urban schools, but it has important implications for doing so. The author describes a study of nine preservice students enrolled in a Content Area Reading course at Michigan State University. Holt-Reynolds closely studied the course itself, its impact on students' learning to be teachers, and how the prospective teachers constructed meaning from the course. She discovered, consistent with the literature on teacher learning, that the beliefs based on personal history that the prospective teachers brought to the course were strong determiners of how students interpreted the course material. The students came to support most of the teaching strategies and practices advocated in the course, but because of their entering beliefs, they supported the teaching practices for reasons different from those held by the instructor. In fact, in one case, some of the students actually valued a strategy advocated in the course because they perceived its ability to serve a goal that the instructor had explicitly stated he hoped to eradicate. For the most part, the students were not aware that their support of the teaching strategies rested on beliefs different from those of their instructor.

This study underlines how very difficult it is to achieve an influence on students at a deeper level in teacher education programs. We may achieve changes in the ways in which teacher education students behave in classrooms (and often we are not able to do even that), but how prospective teachers think about their actions is often not addressed. When we think about the kinds of changes needed for preparing teachers for urban schools, which result in part from the culturally encapsulated nature of prospective teacher cohorts, the task seems large indeed. If it is as difficult as Holt-Reynolds suggests to change student teachers' beliefs about reading instruction, what does this say about our ability to enable the fundamental transformation of prospective teachers' worldviews that seems to be needed in preparing teachers for urban schools (Nieto, 1992)? Holt-Reynolds raises an important caution for teacher educators with regard to the practices advocated by Carter and Larke and Ponticell et al. Although these two studies stress the value of such things as urban field experiences for prospective teachers and peer coaching groups for experienced teachers, Holt-Reynolds urges us to examine very closely the level of impact we have actually achieved. Are we merely helping to strengthen and reinforce the attitudes and beliefs that prospective teachers and teachers bring to our programs? If we do not look beyond the behaviors of teachers to their underlying reasons and rationales, we may never know.

Holt-Reynolds presents us with a vision of teacher leadership for urban schools that is ambitious. It requires that teachers be aware of the various rationales underlying the use of particular teaching practices and curriculum approaches. The focus in both preservice and inservice teacher education has been on skill training, on merely trying to get teachers to use particular practices. This has especially been the case with regard to teaching in urban schools. Holt-Reynolds suggests that preservice and inservice teacher education programs need to uncover and deal with the conceptions, attitudes, and assumptions that teachers bring to them. A literature is now emerging that is beginning to articulate how we can achieve this process of conceptual change in teacher education (e.g., Wubbels, 1992). Holt-Reynolds also underlines the importance of establishing the kind of collaborative, ongoing, teacher-initiated staff development networks advocated by Ponticell et al. to support the ambitious vision of teacher leadership that is proposed.

Conclusion

The concept of teacher leadership advocated in this set of three studies is an attractive one that should largely be supported by teacher educators. A collaborative teacher culture within schools that supports and sustains teacher learning and a commitment to the teaching of all students to high academic standards are absolute preconditions for any serious change in the current condition of our urban schools. Despite our support for this general direction, we want to leave readers with two cautions about this course for urban teacher education.

First, although teacher leadership and empowerment must replace the efforts to change teaching by remote control and to entice teachers by "snake oil" staff development programs that have dominated urban schools for so long, we must give serious attention to what we are empowering teachers to do. The emphasis in these three studies has been on the processes and structures of teacher leadership. The structures advocated by these authors, such as urban student teaching and peer coaching, can be used to accomplish a variety of purposes, some of which could be antithetical to the idea of all students achieving at high academic standards. The curriculum in the urban classrooms of student teachers and teachers did not receive any attention at all in these three studies. What are these empowered teachers doing in their classrooms? How is what they are doing affecting the academic and personal development and the life chances of their students?

Another aspect of teacher leadership that needs to be addressed and that was not mentioned in these studies is the limitations on teacher leadership that are posed by the idea of a democratic schooling process in which a variety of participants play important roles in defining and sustaining school programs (Gutmann, 1987). For example, teacher empowerment is generally viewed in this set of studies as an end in itself unconnected to any concern with how the legitimate rights of parents and communities are to be addressed. The literature on urban schooling shows very clearly that despite its importance, there is also an underside to teacher leadership and teacher empowerment. It has been argued, for example, that in some cases, teacher empowerment serves to undermine important connections between schools and communities (Zeichner, 1991). An uncritical celebration of teacher leadership without attention to the need for teachers to become more community conscious and responsive to community needs and concerns will not lead to an improvement of schooling in urban areas.

Finally, the idea of teacher leadership as a central component of a program for the improvement of schooling in urban areas must be accompanied by efforts to deal directly with the whole host of "rotten outcomes" that plague urban areas, such as poverty, violence, drug abuse, and teenage pregnancy. These problems, which along with the educational problems in urban schools are a reflection of a crisis in the economic, social, and political structures of our society, can only be ameliorated by a broad-based approach to reform that includes but also goes beyond school reform projects. Advocating educational reforms for urban schools such as teacher leadership without also explicitly calling for a broader social reconstruction serves to strengthen the mistaken view that schools are largely responsible for the whole host of problems that confront students in urban areas. It also creates false expectations for what can be accomplished by educational reform alone. The kinds of changes for teacher education and the work environment for teachers advocated in these three studies are important and should be pursued, but only as part of a comprehensive effort to deal with societal reform.

References

Bastian, A., Fruchter, N., Gittel, M., Greer, C., & Haskings, K. (1985). *Choosing equality: The case for democratic schooling.* Philadelphia, PA: Temple University Press.

Carter, R. T., & Goodwin, A. L. (1994). Racial identity and education. In L. Darling-Hammond (Ed.), *Review of research in education* (Vol. 20, pp. 291-336). Washington, DC: AERA.

Corcoran, T., Walker, L., & White, J. L. (1988). *Working in urban schools.* Washington, DC: Institute for Educational Leadership.

Gutmann, A. (1987). *Democratic education.* Princeton, NJ: Princeton University Press.

Hollingsworth, S., & Sockett, H. (1994). *Teacher research and educational reform.* Chicago: University of Chicago Press.

Knapp, M. S., & Shields, P. M. (1990). Reconceiving academic instruction for children of poverty. *Phi Delta Kappan, 71*, 752-758.

Little, J. W. (1993). Teachers' professional development in a climate of educational reform. *Educational Evaluation and Policy Analysis, 15*(2), 129-152.

National Coalition of Advocates for Students. (1991). *The good common school: Making the vision work for all students.* Boston, MA: Author.

Nieto, S. (1992). *Affirming diversity: The sociopolitical context of multicultural education.* New York: Longman.

Villegas, A. M. (1988). School failures and cultural mismatch: Another view. *Urban Review, 20*(4), 253-265.

Weiner, L. (1989). Asking the right questions: An analytic framework for reform of urban teacher education. *Urban Review, 21*(3), 151-161.

Weiner, L. (1993). *Preparing teachers for urban schools.* New York: Teachers College Press.

Wubbels, T. (1992). Taking account of student teachers' preconceptions. *Teaching and Teacher Education, 8*(2), 137-150.

Zeichner, K. (1991). Contradictions and tensions in the professionalization of teaching and the democratization of schools. *Teachers College Record, 92*(3), 363-379.

Zeichner, K. (1994). *Defining the achievement gap: Issues of pedagogy, definition of knowledge and the teaching-learning process.* Philadelphia, PA: Research for Better Schools.

DIVISION III

Communicating Leadership and Change

COMMUNICATION:
OVERVIEW AND FRAMEWORK

Cassandra L. Book

Cassandra L. Book is Associate Dean of the College of Education, Professor of Teacher Education, and Adjunct Professor of Communication at Michigan State University. She has authored or co-authored 7 books and over 40 chapters and articles in communication and teacher education. She is the past Chairperson of the Educational Policy Board of the Speech Communication Association, past Chairperson of ATE's Research Committee, Executive Secretary of the Michigan Association of Colleges for Teacher Education, and past President of the Michigan Association of Speech Communication. She has been recognized for outstanding teaching by MSU, Central States Speech Association, and the Speech Communication Association.

The topic of communication is extremely important in a volume intended to address the topic of educating teachers for leadership and change, for the very act of teaching requires communication in one form or another, and the ability to lead others or to bring about change similarly requires effective communication. An understanding of the concept of communication is important for both teachers and teacher educators, for not all talk is communication, nor is all communication effective. In recent times, communication has been viewed as a dynamic process in which the participants influence and are influenced by each other through the use of verbal or nonverbal symbols. The functions of communication have been broadly identified to include persuading, informing, sharing feelings, participating in ritualized behaviors, and imagining. Competent communicators have been defined as those with a repertoire of communication strategies from which to draw and the ability to use criteria to select the appropriate strategies given the audience and context, to implement the strategies effectively, and finally to evaluate the success or failure of the communication attempt and to remedy the communication as needed. In effect, the teacher, the leader, and/or the change agent should benefit from considering the discipline of communication and the research that has contributed to understanding effective classroom communication.

The Nature of Communication

Communication is a complex interaction among participants to which each person brings a set of understandings; expectations; language skills; and attitudes toward the situation, the speaker, the topic, and him- or herself. Although the initiator of the communication exchange usually has certain outcomes he or she wishes to accomplish (e.g., to be understood by the receiver[s], to be liked by the receiver[s], to get the receiver[s] to do something), the receiver(s) may also have desired outcomes for the exchange. Communication requires the use of symbols, either in the form of language or nonverbal gestures or expressions, and each participant brings meaning to those symbols. The goal of communication is to ensure that all participants gain a similar understanding or meaning for those symbols, even if they do not agree on the conclusion. The complexity of negotiating both meaning and desired outcome cannot be underestimated, especially when there are multiple communicators in the exchange.

Communicators usually receive some sort of feedback about how the message was received, but the interpretation of that feedback can also be filled with errors or misunderstandings. In addition, the speaker or initiator of the message may not always be able to attend to all of the feedback given, such as when a classroom full of students provides everything from head nods to raised hands to dazed looks. Because each person tries to make sense of the message using his or her own interpretation of the symbols, each interpretation is likely to vary from the others and the communication usually proceeds without the opportunity to fine-tune the meanings.

The dynamic nature of communication is such that the meanings are constantly changing as the participants seek more information and greater clarity of the messages. In addition, as one participant adds insights to the exchange, the understandings of the others are likely to change, too. Because communication is transactional, all participants have the opportunity to influence and be influenced by the exchange. Communication is ongoing and evolutionary.

The complexity of communication in the classroom is compounded by the multiple participants, their unique backgrounds and understandings, the pressures of the context in which teachers are required to teach certain curricula and meet particular educational goals, and the many interferences in the setting. In the classroom, teachers who understand the transactional, dynamic nature of communication work to engage learners in revealing their understandings of the messages so that together the students and teacher can work to gain clarity about the concepts being taught (as well as to understand the feelings and attitudes that may be interfering with the students' abilities to attend to the matter at hand). Rather than merely asking students if they understand, to which the answer is certain to be yes, teachers who understand the complexity of communication ask students *what* they understand. By having students interact with the concepts presented and allowing students to interact with each other about the concepts, the teacher not only maximizes communication in the classroom but also maximizes the opportunity for students to make sense of the messages and to obtain multiple sources for gaining clarity. The old model of teachers talking and students listening violates the understanding of communication both as a transactional, dynamic process and as a model of effective instruction.

This understanding of communication as a transactional, dynamic process also facilitates one's role as a leader. For a leader to engage others in solving a problem or participating in a task, it is to the leader's advantage to allow the participants the opportunity to clearly understand the task to be done or problem to be solved. The more the participants can discuss the situation, the more clarity they bring to the situation. Also, the more the participants are able to "own" the problem as their own, the more likely they are to follow through on the task to its completion. On the other hand, if people have different perceptions of the problem or task that have not been clarified, they may work in opposition to each other or may even work in a way that precludes reaching the desired outcome. The more people can reach a consensus on the nature of the problem they seek to solve and a mutual desire to affect the outcome, the more likely they will be to fulfill the task and take pride in its completion. Communication that engages people in fully describing their perceptions, apprehensions, mode of doing things, and understanding is particularly beneficial when trying to get people to change their behaviors. The teacher as change agent has the best chance of bringing about change when he or she fully understands the resistance to change and ensures that both parties are talking about a similar understanding of the behavior to be changed. The risk for the change agent, however, is that his or her own understandings and beliefs may be challenged and possibly changed.

Communication Functions

Communication can be used to fulfill many goals. In general, communication functions to inform others; to persuade or control the behaviors, beliefs, or attitudes of others; to participate in ritualized behaviors such as greeting behaviors or other patterns of socially expected norms; to express feelings; and to imagine or hypothesize about something (including dramatizing). These communication purposes can be evident or subliminal and often one communication exchange will fulfill multiple purposes. However, in any communication act, it can be confusing if the message being sent verbally conflicts with another message being sent verbally or nonverbally. For example, a person may be saying words that appear to be concerned for another's feelings while at the same time sending a very controlling message that is attempting to get the person to do something. It is generally in the best interest of a communicator to be clear about the intended outcome of the message he or she is sending and to try to match the goal of the message with verbal and nonverbal messages chosen. If the receiver of the message misinterprets the goal of the message, it can lead to as much confusion and disruption as if the content of the message was not understood.

Communication Competence

The phrase "communication competence" was used by Wood (1977) to refer to a "person's knowledge of how to use language appropriately in all kinds of communication situations" (p. 5). Wood (1977) claimed that effective communicators need to be flexible in their abilities to employ a range of communication strategies that can be selected and adapted for the situation and audience. She describes four stages of communication competency. First, flexible communicators "must be able to perform a range of communication acts required by the conversation, the people, the setting, and the task-at-hand" (p. 5); communication competency requires a repertoire of communication acts being available to draw upon.

Second, Wood (1977) argued that "communication effectiveness is based on the appropriateness of what is stated ... [and that] the competent communicator carefully weighs the factors of the communication situation" (p. 5). The effective communicator considers the audience, the situation, the specific goal to be reached, the function of the communication, and the relationship of him- or herself with the audience before engaging in the communication. Determining the criteria on which to make a selection from one's repertoire of possible communication strategies is a characteristic of a competent communicator.

Third, competent communicators must be able to implement the communication strategy selected and do so effectively. The skills to enact the selection may include vocabulary, articulation, delivery, timing, compatible verbal and nonverbal messages, building a credible message, clarity, dynamism, and other factors that demonstrate competent implementation.

Fourth, the communicator must be able to judge the appropriateness of his or her communication to the situation and to the audience. The communicator should be able to determine if the message was received as intended and if the receiver is likely to respond in the desired way. The communicator should be sensitive to both the intellectual response to the message and the affective response. Both evaluations are important for the competent communicator to assess. With such evaluation, the communicator may need to create a follow-up message to verify the receiver's understanding or acceptance of the message or to correct any misinterpretation.

Although these four steps of competent communication appear to be linear, an evaluation may take place at each iteration such that the communicator may cycle back and draw a different communication strategy from his or her repertoire or may adjust the message throughout the exchange given new interpretations of the situation or audience. Effective communication requires an awareness of the interacting factors of the communication exchange; a willingness to adapt to the situation; and a disposition toward communication that takes into account the transactional, dynamic process.

This model of a competent communicator can be useful for the teacher. Assessment of the effectiveness of one's classroom communication may lead a teacher to conclude that, for example, more strategies, examples, relevant cases, or current vocabulary need to be added to his or her communication repertoire. The teacher may conclude that he or she has misinterpreted the knowledge base, communication skills, attitudes, or background of the students and that the criteria he or she used in constructing the message (lesson) was not well suited for the students. Or the teacher may have neglected to consider competing events in the students' lives that interfere with their ability to concentrate on the topic being presented. In essence, the teacher may need to assess the criteria he or she used to select from his or her repertoire. In addition, the teacher's implementation of the communication may not have been effective. Use of audio or video recordings can sometimes be helpful in examining the effectiveness of one's delivery, but feedback from students can also be a direct means of correcting the delivery. Finally, the teacher may need to verify with the students his or her assessment of the communication exchange. Sometimes teachers are more critical of their own communication than the students are, or teachers miss key elements that students would like to see altered. Such assessment of one's communication is often referred to as reflection. This model of competent communication could also be a model for reflection on one's communication.

Adapting to the context and the particular audience is a critical factor for a competent communicator and the effective teacher. This is particularly important for teachers in a multicultural classroom. Building on research on gender characteristics and other personality measures related to communication behavior in the classroom, researchers in communication have begun to examine the willingness of demographically different groups of students to interact in the classroom (Daly, Kreiser, & Roghaar, 1994). These researchers investigated data drawn from the National Educational Longitudinal Study of 1988. Demographic characteristics, personality measures, family influences, academic factors, and perceptions of teachers' responsiveness were correlated with comfort in asking questions in class. "Thirty-seven percent of the thousands of eighth grade students who participated in this study report feeling uncomfortable asking questions in at least one class" (p. 36). As these researchers point out, "To the extent that question-asking comfort translates into question-asking and, ultimately, learning, these findings raise important issues about classroom education in America today. Thus, understanding correlates of this willingness to participate in questioning becomes a key concern for instructional communication research" (p. 36). Among the correlates with question-asking comfort, males were more comfortable overall, particularly in math, science, and social studies, although females were slightly more comfortable asking questions in English than males were. Self-esteem seems to be a mitigating factor. Also, comfort in asking questions in the classroom significantly differed by region; home language background; and self-reported English language proficiency in reading, writing, understanding, and speaking. "Minority students were somewhat less comfortable asking questions than white students even when the influence of socio-economic status and income were covaried. Older students exhibited more hesitancy than younger students. Students from backgrounds of lower socio-economic status and family income were significantly less comfortable in question-asking than students from higher status and wealthier families" (p. 38). In essence, this study raises significant concerns about the influence of sociological characteristics on students' communication competence and willingness to communicate in the classroom. To the extent that a teacher tries to engage students in interaction in the classroom, he or she should attend to these intervening factors that may be interfering with the students' abilities and propensities to communicate. It would seem that more needs to be understood about the characteristics of the teacher in interacting with students from different sociological and cultural backgrounds.

When it comes to hiring decisions, communication is rated by principals as the most important skill a teacher can possess (Johnson, 1994). In a survey of 1,000 public, secondary school principals in the United States, "the six top-rated items were 'Enthusiasm,' 'Oral Communication Skills,' 'Competence in Area of Specialization,' 'Interpersonal Communication Skills,' 'Listening Skills,' and 'Writing Skills' " (p. 9). Although the perception of principals is that "communication skills are at least as important as other pedagogical skills in a repertoire of skills and factors needed for effective classroom performance" (p. 13), it is important to keep in mind that effective communication is context specific. In fact, there is much more to effective instructional communication than the generic communication characteristics that are generally considered by principals in hiring teachers. What appears to make a difference in the classroom are more sophisticated communication concepts.

Classroom Communication

Researchers from the field of education have focused on a number of teaching behaviors that make a difference in student learning. Brophy and Good (1986) summarized a large number of studies that demonstrated the relationships between teacher behaviors and student achievement. In general these studies focused on the quantity and pacing of instruction, whole-class versus small-group versus individualized instruction, giving information, questioning students, reacting to students, and the assignment of seatwork and homework. Brophy and Good (1986) summarized that "many findings must be qualified by reference to grade level, student characteristics, or teaching objectives. This reflects the fact that effective instruction involves selecting (from a larger repertoire) and orchestrating those teaching behaviors that are appropriate to the classroom context and to the teacher's goals, rather than mastering and consistently applying a few 'generic' teaching skills" (p. 360). These qualifications are useful because they point to the context-specific nature of communication in the classroom and the importance of teachers having a repertoire of communication skills from which to select those they perceive to be most appropriate for the context and desired outcome.

Nussbaum (1992) reviewed studies appearing in education literature from 1983 to 1990 that examined effective teaching behaviors. He cited studies that examined (a) the mutual behavioral influence between teacher and students, (b) the differential praise and criticism given by teachers of different races to male and female students of different races, (c) the variation in the level of dogmatism of teachers in different grade levels, (d) communication of teachers in different socioeconomic classrooms, (e) the effect of clarity of instruction on student achievement, (f) the impact of wait time on the quality of student-teacher interaction and student achievement, (g) the kind of interaction based on class size, (h) the relationship between race and gender of student with positive or negative feedback and opportunity to respond in the classroom, (i) the effect of teacher enthusiasm on student performance and on-task behavior, and (j) the effect of types of teacher inservice training on teachers' in-class behavior. Again, these studies reflected the context-specific nature of the effectiveness of types of communication in the classroom, but in many cases were based on a linear, rather than interactive, conception of the communication between students and teachers.

Communication and Student Learning

Researchers from the field of communication have also examined behaviors that make a difference in student learning and students' perceptions of effective teachers. Effective classroom communication skills include nonverbal and verbal teacher immediacy, willingness to communicate, specific verbal classroom behaviors, clarity, and communication style. Teacher immediacy is defined by Mehrabian (1969, p. 203) as communicative behaviors that enhance closeness to another and is related to affective (Andersen & Andersen, 1982; Gorham, 1988) and cognitive (Kelley & Gorham, 1988) learning. Citing the work of Andersen and Andersen (1987), which focused on nonverbal immediacy, Nussbaum (1992) indicated that

> Teacher immediacy behaviors [were] found to be positively related to effective teaching. Immediate teachers, in comparison to non-immediate teachers, communicate at physically closer distances, use touch in more socially appropriate ways, are more vocally expressive, smile more, utilize an open body position, use more eye contact, and more often arrange the classroom for interaction. (p 173)

More positive affective response to the teachers, content, and school, as well as more learning, occurred for students with more immediate teachers.

Gorham (1988) also found a positive relationship of verbal and nonverbal immediacy behaviors with student learning and noted the variation in the teachers' use of these behaviors based upon the class size. In this study, verbal immediacy behaviors were generated from students' descriptions of effective teacher verbal behaviors and included such behaviors as using personal examples, encouraging student talk, using humor, addressing students by name, initiating conversations with students inside and outside of class, praising students' work, asking questions that solicit student opinion, using inclusive language, following up on student-initiated topics, and giving feedback on students' work. In a study that examined the effect of teacher immediacy on different ethnic groups of students (Sanders & Wiseman, 1990), differences were found in the relationship of cognitive learning, behavioral learning, and affective response with specific immediacy behaviors for different ethnic groups. "For White, Asian, and Hispanic students, immediacy was more highly related to affective learning than to behavioral learning . . . but for all ethnic groups seven immediacy behaviors were positively associated with cognitive learning" (p. 350).

The importance of recognizing the different impact of immediacy behaviors on different students reinforces the nature of the transactional, context-specific nature of communication and the need for teachers to understand the importance of selecting communication behaviors appropriate for the classroom context. In fact, a study by Gorham and Zakahi (1990) demonstrated that "teachers are highly aware of their use of immediacy behaviors, and that their perceptions of learning agree with their students' perceptions" (p. 365). These authors indicate that teachers "are able to effectively monitor both the behaviors and outcomes central to the process-product model suggested in the immediacy literature" (p. 365).

Other studies of teacher immediacy examined the relationship of student motivation and immediacy (Christophel, 1990) and the relationship of verbal and nonverbal immediacy to teacher clarity across ethnic groups (Powell & Harville, 1990). This study by Powell and Harville (1990) is important in that it brings together two significant communication concepts showing that "nonverbal and verbal immediacy were significantly related to teacher clarity for each of the ethnic groups . . . [although] varied across ethnic groups (p. 374) . . . [and that] teacher clarity accounted for the greatest proportion of variance in two of the four outcome measures, evaluations of the class and evaluations of the instructor" (p. 375). Clarity, which is generally considered the quality of being comprehensible, including defining concepts, using examples, checking students understanding, and using specific language, has consistently been shown to be related to cognitive achievement and satisfaction (Book & McCaleb, 1985; Hines, Cruickshank, & Kennedy, 1985; Smith & Land, 1980).

Nussbaum (1992) summarized research about teachers' communication styles, including use of humor, self-disclosure, and narratives, particularly comparing teachers who have won teaching awards with those who have not. In some cases, these strategies seem to be avenues for clarifying the course content.

Nussbaum (1992) summarized the work of Rubin and Feezel (1986), who found that "a teacher's ability to obtain information, describe another's viewpoint, recognize non-understanding, pronounce clearly, understand suggestions, persuade, identify oral assignments, use topic order, use appropriate facial expressions and tone of voice, summarize, describe differences of opinion, and answer questions are positively correlated to perceptions of teaching effectiveness" (p. 173). Many of these communication behaviors are assessed by means of the Communication Competency Assessment Instrument (CCAI) (Rubin, 1982b) available from the Speech Communication Association. Studies validating the CCAI with college students have been conducted (Rubin, 1982a, 1985; Rubin & Graham, 1988; Rubin, Graham, & Mignerey, 1990; Rubin & Henzl, 1984; Rubin & Roberts, 1987).

In essence, there are communication behaviors that seem to make a difference in students' cognitive and behavioral learning and affective response to the class and the teacher. Verbal and nonverbal immediacy; clarity; communication behaviors such as delivery, organization, persuasion, and information gaining and providing; and interaction with learners, as well as use of humor, self-disclosure, and narratives, can make a difference in students' learning and perception of the course and the instructor. These communication behaviors are among the skills that should be within a teacher's repertoire to be implemented effectively in the classroom for specific students and goals to be reached. Also, teachers need to be aware of these skills and their use of them by working to monitor their effectiveness and by modifying their use as appropriate.

The Three Chapters

What follows are three chapters about communication. They take totally different approaches to the question of teachers communicating leadership and change. In Chapter 7, Jacobs takes a theoretical approach to understanding the nature of communication in the classroom and school. Hess and Short, in Chapter 8, talk about assessing specific communication skills of prospective teachers, notably those focused on empathy, listening, and interpersonal engagement with learners. Last, in Chapter 9, Darling and Dewey examine how senior-level graduate teaching assistants evolve into leaders of beginning teaching assistants.

A commentary on each of the chapters concludes the division, but it may be useful in this introduction to propose some perspectives from which to examine the chapters. First, the authors of all three chapters suggest that communication can be learned. This contrasts with the commonly held perspective that people communicate naturally and thus are not in need of learning about communication or about how to improve their communication. Second, the very fact that these authors look at different communication situations adds to the importance of communication being adapted to the specific context in which it is occurring. Third, these authors recognize communication as a dynamic, transactional process. Fourth, these authors suggest that reflection about one's communication skill is valued. Finally, these authors are all concerned about the development of teacher communication skills. Jacobs believes that a theoretical understanding of communication positions a teacher to better interact with students and to understand the context in which learning is to occur in the classroom and the school. He encourages teacher educators to include the study of communication in the teacher preparation program. Hess and Short demonstrate that specific communication skills can be improved for prospective teachers through a university course in communication. Darling and Dewey focus on the evolution of senior teaching assistants in their understanding and enactment in a role as leader of less experienced teaching assistants. The reader might wish to integrate the various aspects of these chapters into a whole vision of communication for teachers, recognizing the value of a theoretical understanding or philosophy of communication to undergird the attitudes, dispositions, and skills one uses when communicating with others and reflecting on the impact of one's communication.

References

Andersen, J. F., & Andersen, P. (1987). Never smile until Christmas? Casting doubt on old myth. *Journal of Thought, 22,* 57-61.

Andersen, P., & Andersen, J. F. (1982). Nonverbal immediacy in instruction. In L. Barker (Ed.), *Communication in the classroom* (pp. 98-120). Englewood Cliffs, NJ: Prentice-Hall.

Book, C. L., & McCaleb, J. (1985). *Teacher clarity and student awareness and achievement.* Paper presented at the annual meeting of the Speech Communication Association, Denver.

Brophy, J. E., & Good, T. L. (1986). Teacher behavior and student achievement. In M. C. Wittrock (Ed.), *Handbook of research on teaching* (3rd ed., pp. 328-375). New York: Macmillan.

Christophel, D. M. (1990). The relationships among teacher immediacy behaviors, student motivation, and learning. *Communication Education, 39,* 323-340.

Daly, J. A., Kreiser, P. O., & Roghaar, L. A. (1994). Question-asking comfort: Explorations of the demography of communication in the eighth grade classroom. *Communication Education, 43,* 27-41.

Gorham, J. (1988). The relationship between verbal teacher immediacy behaviors and student learning. *Communication Education, 37,* 40-53.

Gorham, J., & Zakahi, W. R. (1990). A comparison of teacher and student perceptions of immediacy and learning: Monitoring process and product. *Communication Education, 39,* 354-368.

Hines, C., Cruickshank, D., & Kennedy, J. (1985). Teacher clarity and its relationship to student achievement and satisfaction. *American Educational Research Journal, 22,* 87-99.

Johnson, S. D. (1994). A national assessment of secondary-school principals' perceptions of teaching-effectiveness criteria. *Communication Education, 43,* 1-16.

Kelley, D. H., & Gorham, J. (1988). Effects of immediacy on recall of information. *Communication Education, 37,* 198-207.

Mehrabian, A. (1969). Some referents and measures of nonverbal behavior. *Behavioral Research Methods and Instruments, 1,* 213-217.

Nussbaum, J. F. (1992). Effective teacher behaviors. *Communication Education, 41,* 167-180.

Powell, R. G., & Harville, B. (1990). The effects of teacher immediacy and clarity on instructional outcomes: An intercultural assessment. *Communication Education, 39,* 369-379.

Rubin, R. B. (1982a). Assessing speaking and listening competence at the college level: The communication competency assessment instrument. *Communication Education, 31,* 19-32.

Rubin, R. B. (1982b). *Communication Competency Assessment Instrument.* Annandale, VA: Speech Communication Association.

Rubin, R. B. (1985). Validity of the communication competency assessment instrument. *Communication Monographs, 52,* 173-185.

Rubin, R. B., & Feezel, J. D. (1986). Elements of teacher communication competence. *Communication Education, 35*(3), 254-268.

Rubin, R. B., & Graham, E. E. (1988). Communication correlates of college success: An exploratory investigation. *Communication Education, 37,* 14-27.

Rubin, R. B., Graham, E. E., & Mignerey, J. (1990). A longitudinal study of college students' communication competence. *Communication Education, 38,* 1-13.

Rubin, R. B., & Henzl, S. A. (1984). Cognitive complexity, communication competence, and verbal ability. *Communication Quarterly, 32,* 263-270.

Rubin, R. B., & Roberts, C. V. (1987). A comparative examination and analysis of three listening tests. *Communication Education, 36*, 142-153.

Sanders, J. A., & Wiseman, R. L. (1990). The effects of verbal and nonverbal teacher immediacy on perceived cognitive, affective, and behavioral learning in the multicultural classroom. *Communication Education, 39*, 341-353.

Smith, L. R., & Land, M. L. (1980). *Student perceptions of teacher clarity* (ERIC Document Reproduction Service No. Ed 183 105).

Wood, B. S. (Ed.). (1977). *Development of functional communication competencies: Grades 7-12*. Annandale, VA: Speech Communication Association.

7 Communicating and Teaching: Applied Communication Theory for Teacher Educators

Richard M. Jacobs

Richard M. Jacobs is Assistant Professor in the Department of Education and Human Services at Villanova University and Director of the Educational Administration Program. As well as authoring articles and papers integrating his interests in educational leadership and communication theory, he serves as guest editor for the *Journal of Management Systems*. He received his Ph.D. in Educational Administration from the University of Tulsa (1990).

ABSTRACT

During the 20th century, some theorists have hinted at, but accorded scant attention to, the discipline of communication as a resource to further the aim of school reform. In this chapter, I expand the parameters for training the next generation's teachers to include the study of communication. One approach to this discipline is offered as an avenue to promote thinking about communication in schools and classrooms. Then two communication theories, hermeneutics and the analysis of metaphors, are applied to show how this discipline's tools can encourage preservice teachers to reconceive schools and classrooms, reformulate their roles as teachers, and thus participate in the development of self-managing schools.

Communication in Schools and Classrooms

The most common behavior in schools and classrooms is communication. Just about everyone in schools wants to communicate with someone else. Students especially spend a great deal of their school day communicating with one another. As impossible as it seems to conceive of schools and classrooms devoid of communication (Jacobs, 1992), it is not difficult to conceive of schools and classrooms where *what* teachers communicate stimulates neither interest nor enthusiasm on their students' part. Where there is little or no time available for educators to engage in extended conversation with students or colleagues, Burlingame and Sergiovanni (1993) have noted that educational decision making becomes a decidedly rote, immediate activity in contrast to an authentic, deliberative activity. Early in this century, Dewey (1916) noted that one outcome of rote, educational decision making, one-way classroom communication, presents a threat to an authentic educative process:

> Why is it, in spite of the fact that teaching by pouring in, learning by a passive absorption, are universally condemned, that they are still so intrenched [*sic*] in practice? That education is not an affair of "telling" and being told, but an active and constructive process, is a principle almost as generally violated in practice as conceded in theory. Is not this deplorable situation due to the fact that the doctrine is itself merely told? It is preached; it is lectured; it is written about. But its enactment into practice requires that the school environment be equipped with agencies for doing. . . . Not that the use of language as an educational resource should lessen; but that its use should be more vital and fruitful by having its normal connection with shared activities. (p. 38)

For teachers to connect experience and learning and to make authentic, deliberative educational decisions, some have suggested that teacher growth and development must be explicitly linked to the relations, interactions, and conversations teachers have with one another as well as with their students. Barth (1990), for example, argued: "The relationships among the adults in schools are the basis, the precondition, the *sine qua non* that allow, energize, and sustain all other attempts at school improvement. Unless adults talk with one another, observe one another, and help one another, very little will change" (p. 32). From a supervisory perspective, Pajak (1992) contends that the primary obstacle to teacher growth and development is the lack of communication evidencing itself in schools. Others suggest that the primary bureaucratic structure for teacher growth, staff development programs, might provide a link to couple teacher communication with school improvement, especially in the areas of instruction, learning, and teacher identity (e.g., Bentzen, 1974; Evertson, Emmer, Sanford, & Clements, 1982; Glatthorn, 1987; Good, 1981; Gray & Gray, 1985; Joyce & McKibbin, 1982; Joyce & Showers, 1980; Sparks, 1983; Wood & Thompson, 1993). And from a diverging vantage, Davis (1994) argues that educators actually "teach through listening," that is, evidence a visible orienting to the subject of discussion through conversation with students. In contrast, Davis (1994) contends, traditional teaching "might best be characterized as an act of *telling* that demands little *listening*" (p. 271).

The case of Kerrie Baughman sustains these observations positing that teachers need to engage in conversation to make authentic, deliberative decisions about their pedagogical practice. In *First Year Teacher*, Bullough (1989) chronicled Kerrie's early challenges as a seventh-grade teacher at Rocky Mountain Junior High School. His case study portrayed Kerrie's not-so-unusual problems as well as how she dealt with a turbulent pedagogical context, especially as teacher accountability and curriculum standardization were being mandated by the state legislature.

Five years later, Bullough revisited Kerrie. In "Continuity and Change in Teacher Development," Bullough and Baughman (1993) narrate the significant challenges Kerrie encountered along the way to becoming a veteran teacher, the persistent patterns that emerged in her teaching and thinking about teaching, as well as Kerrie's transition from "modeling things that were modeled for me" (p. 88) to learning to be attentive to her students' needs. Kerrie reflected:

> I look over there and see [the students] are engaged. They feel pleased, they are so happy when they come up and we've conferenced. They are just thrilled with their progress. Now I'm looking to include the lost sheep. (p. 90)

In this follow-up report, the authors recount how Kerrie successfully acquired a teacher's identity, but only after she reflected upon what being a teacher meant and changed the metaphor guiding how she viewed teaching. In addition, the authors describe how Kerrie developed principles representing her pedagogical theory. Kerrie now solves pedagogical challenges by reflecting upon her practice.

> I solve the small problems as I go. You know, reflection comes on the way to and from school, and that has always been the case. I've done a lot of reflecting, but you can't [always pause to think while teaching], that can't happen in the classroom. You are way too busy [for it]; it happens at the quiet times. [Much of my problem solving] is [done] in my subconscious. All of a sudden [an idea] will come to me. (p. 91)

Kerrie has taken charge of her professional growth and development. She knows what is being communicated in her classroom and now seeks an "on-going conversation about teaching, views of self-as-teacher, and the context of teaching and of the value of extending that conversation" (p. 94). As a veteran teacher and in contrast to 4 years previously as a beginning teacher, Kerrie seems to want to understand better and to respond more appropriately to what her experiences communicate to her. To achieve this goal, Kerrie has created a support group for first-year teachers at Rocky Mountain Junior High School. Bullough opines, however, a "significant challenge facing teacher educators and others concerned with teacher development is to discover ways of extending this conversation" (p. 91).

In this chapter, I propose that *conversation*, more properly understood as human communication in its broadest sense, is the essential activity driving schools and classrooms, and that teacher growth and development, in particular, are linked to the quality of communication in schools and classrooms. To illuminate how educational practice and communication are related, I offer a definition of communication. Then I explore two communication theories, hermeneutics and the analysis of metaphors, to apply the discipline of communication to educational practice. This effort will help teacher educators to conceptualize how preservice teachers might use these tools to get beyond being solely concerned with themselves and to become more concerned with their students. It will also help them to move away from being solely concerned with procedural matters to being more concerned with understanding what is being communicated. This path through the discipline of communication is charted so as to guide teacher educators to understand how they can influence the next generation's teachers to reform schools by cementing the relationship linking education with communication in schools and classrooms.

Human Communication as Understanding

Theorists offer various definitions of what communication is (e.g., Dance, 1970; Griffin, 1991; Littlejohn, 1989; Trenholm, 1986), but it remains an abstract notion, or as Dance (1970) has written, a "family of concepts" that can be used in many ways. Dance (1970) asserts that human communication is a "process by which we understand others and in turn endeavor to be understood by them. It is dynamic, constantly changing and shifting in response to the total situation" (p. 204).

Dance's (1970) definition deftly captures the educational reality teachers confront daily in their schools and classrooms. Here, people and events are more fluid than static, dependent upon a constellation of factors that interact and react to one another, frequently beyond the control of any individual human being. More important, Dance observes, the tools associated with this discipline can help people reduce uncertainty, link and bind themselves with others, duplicate memories, and exert power in the midst of this process whereby human beings seek to understand what transpires about and within them. If this is true, teachers who use these tools would be in a better position to interpret and respond to what is communicated in their schools and classrooms and to improve communication within them.

In this chapter, I argue that preservice teachers, practiced and skilled in this discipline's concepts throughout the course of their professional training programs, can learn to extend the conversation Kerrie Baughman seeks, particularly as they endeavor to know, understand, and respond to what is being communicated in the dynamic and fluid context characterizing the schools and classrooms where communication transpires. Utilizing communication theory might also assist these educators to function as transformational school leaders (Leithwood, 1992), whose leadership role would foster the development of self-managing schools (Caldwell & Spinks, 1992) through reflective practice (Schön, 1990). More important, exposing preservice teachers to communication theory may provide them a foundation to facilitate understanding better what Hansen (1993) posits is the "moral layeredness" of what will, one day, be their professional practice.

Understanding Classroom Communication

Research pertaining to preservice and novice teachers suggests that teachers really learn how to teach as they modify and reconstruct their behaviors, knowledge, images, beliefs, and perceptions about teaching through reflective practice (Kagan, 1992). This notion contrasts with those more conventional teacher education programs that oversimplify the reality of teaching and ignore the many social and pedagogical variables (what Kagan, 1992, calls "the contexts") affecting instructional decisions. In this sense, novice "teachers" gradually become veteran "educators" once they have developed and refined a basic repertoire of experiences and information that will help them to interpret accurately the events transpiring within classrooms (Hargreaves & Fullan, 1992). Novice teachers remain overwhelmed by the many demands imposed upon them and understand classroom communication as they did when they were students until they develop that basic repertoire. And if they fail to develop their repertoire, they limit their conception of classroom communication to unidirectional information dissemination. Rather than encouraging this narrow conception of communication and the rote, immediate educational decision-making process encouraged by it, teacher educators might foster a more inclusive vision in their preservice students by turning their attention to Hermes, a demigod of Greek mythology. For the ancient Greeks, Hermes' characteristic audacity and wit enabled him to interpret accurately what the Fates were communicating through various omens.

Hermeneutical Theory: Knowing, Understanding, and Responding to Communication in Schools and Classrooms

Hermeneutics is a discipline of communication positing a three-dimensional framework to examine communication content. The first dimension, *knowing* what others communicate (Figure 7.1), requires being aware of the literal facts regarding what another has said or done.

These literal facts provide a framework through which one can examine communication content at a second level: *understanding* what the words and actions used actually mean (Figure 7.2). Knowing and understanding what others do and say is the basis of successfully translating and interpreting what other human beings seek to communicate.

Hermeneutics does not end with successful translation and interpretation. It pushes matters further toward a vital third dimension of human

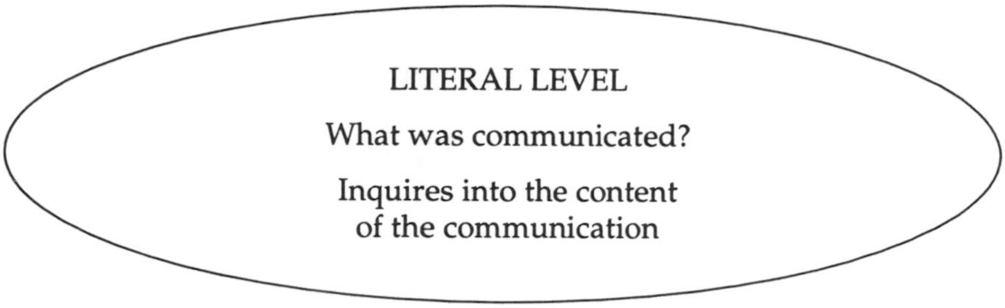

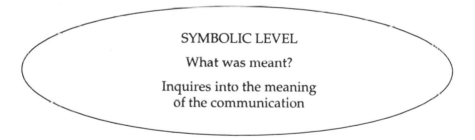

LITERAL LEVEL

What was communicated?

Inquires into the content
of the communication

The Literal Interpretation: To know how another human being experiences reality, one must know what the other communicates

- intention: to derive an accurate interpretation of what was said
- focus upon: the literal words and actions (whether verbal or non-verbal)

Figure 7.1. The Literal Level

SYMBOLIC LEVEL

What was meant?

Inquires into the meaning
of the communication

The Symbolic Understanding: To translate accurately the immaterial meanings conveyed within the communication content, one must understand what the other meant

- intention: to understand what was meant
- focus upon: the implicit meanings (the "symbols") obscured within communication content (the "signs")

Figure 7.2. The Symbolic Level

ETHICAL LEVEL

What am I to do about it?

Inquires into the response
to the communication

The Ethical Response: To respond appropriately to what was communicated and what was meant

- intention: to respond ethically
- focus upon: what one ought to do in response to the communication content and its meaning

Figure 7.3. The Ethical Level

communication, that of *responding* to communication content (Figure 7.3). How human beings respond to what others do and say as well as to what they mean is most significant if notions about human responsibility and ethics are to be discussed.

Hermeneutics, then, is a communications tool that can help human beings reflect upon and make more objective assessments of their subjective experiences as receivers of communication content (Hyde, 1982).

The communicative process, as it is understood hermeneutically, bears a striking resemblance to those cognitive activities teachers use as they struggle to reflect upon their practice. Palmer (1969) alluded to this ideal when he wrote: "Teachers . . . need to become experts in 'translation' more than 'analysis'; their task is to bring what is strange, unfamiliar, and obscure in its meaning into something meaningful that 'speaks our language' " (p. 29). He argues that without effective translation those who receive communication content (e.g., teachers and students) fail to respond appropriately to each other because of a mutual failure to interpret accurately the symbols intended to convey the content's meaning. For teachers to translate what students are communicating, it is important that teachers keep in mind what the content of classroom communication means to their students—what it describes about their experience. Then, as a result of this reflective process whereby teachers consciously link student experience with content, teachers may respond more appropriately to their students' communications by extending the pedagogical conversation with them.

Philosophers have labeled this reflective, intellectual exercise the "hermeneutical circle." This metaphor depicts interpretation as progressing in a cyclical pattern; that is, interpretation moves from general ideas to specific ideas and vice versa until the mind consciously modifies each idea based upon closer scrutiny of the other (Ricoeur, 1981). Eventually, an adequate and satisfying interpretation is made (Bauman, 1978) as human beings develop empathy and recreate and relive the experience being communicated; that is, they respond as human beings who possess increased understanding about what another person has communicated (Dilthey, 1989). Seven decades earlier, Dewey (1916) expressed a similar notion:

> Not only is social life identical with communication, but all communication (and hence all genuine social life) is educative. To be a recipient of a communication is to have an enlarged and changed experience. One shares in what another has thought and felt and in so far, meagerly or amply, has his own attitude modified. Nor is the one who communicates left unaffected. (p. 5)

As an applied communications tool, hermeneutical theory posits that teacher educators must assist preservice teachers to understand classroom communication phenomena. They need to inculcate the notion that successful teaching does not begin and end with the teacher transmitting and students receiving communication content, that is, communicating at the literal level. Hermeneutics is also dynamic, a tool that can help teachers to reclaim what their students and colleagues express, assert, say, or announce and to explore what has been conveyed, realized, and understood in the proclamation (Palmer, 1969).

Preservice Hermeneutical Practice: Reconceiving Classroom Instruction

Teachers who refine their communicative competence tend to concentrate more upon assisting their students to clarify and explore various problem-solving alternatives than upon procedural matters, a development that corresponds roughly to the stages of teacher growth posited by Berliner (1986). Conversely, proficient students who refine their communicative competence might help their teachers to clarify and explore their mode of communication—causing their teachers to experience that momentary reflective pause that helps them to engage in authentic, deliberative educational decision making and to explore other ways, for example, to converse with their students about a lesson's content.

Focusing upon classroom instruction provides a useful analogy to clarify how hermeneutical theory can help preservice teachers reconceptualize the process of classroom instruction. First and foremost, hermeneutics posits that if teachers and students are to communicate so as to achieve understanding, the pattern must be interactive. Teachers and students become partners in an interactive process to understand the broad nature of the explicit and implicit educational material being encountered. Hermeneutics also helps teachers and students sharpen the understanding each has of the general nature of the educational challenges and the specific alternatives available. Technically, the hermeneutical circle involves this dialectic—that general and specific ideas are refined and interpreted so the words and actions of teachers and students respond to the literal and symbolic elements communicating what the other means. As a consequence, both teachers and students can learn how to respond more appropriately to one another through a heightened consciousness of this dialectical process manifesting itself in classrooms.

Teachers spend most of their time in classrooms engaged in communicative activities with their students. Therefore, it is advisable that preservice teachers practice and develop proficiency in deriving meaning from classroom communication. One way to achieve this goal would be through observing or viewing videotapes of a variety of teachers in diverse educational settings. Teacher educators might adapt the paradigm used by Fuchs, Fuchs, Bentz, Phillips, and Hamlett (1994) to examine the nature of student interactions during peer tutoring sessions. Having preservice teachers reflect upon multiple teacher-student interactions, whether as individuals (through journal entries), as a group (through critical appraisal of the communicative processes engaged), or a combination of both, would provide a context through which teacher educators could foster interpretive competence in preservice teachers. Veteran teachers who are observed and evaluated might also profit by becoming involved in this discourse. By interacting with these preservice teachers, these veteran teachers could develop a deeper appreciation of the subtle ways in which the pedagogical theories they espouse are sometimes malpracticed within the confines of their classrooms. Veteran teachers who are willing to form this type of learning community with preservice teachers might serve as mentors and form collaborative networks when these preservice teachers begin their professional practice.

In sum, this cursory investigation of hermeneutical theory has served two purposes. First, hermeneutics provides tools to understand communication in schools and classrooms. For teachers, knowing about communication content is one matter, understanding its multiple meanings is a more complicated exercise, and making professional judgments about how to respond to communication content so as to extend conversations is a very complicated matter. At the same time, this three-step process opens the doors to important discourse concerning educational ethics. Second, as Palmer (1969) notes, hermeneutical theory provides a corrective to a temptation that teachers frequently experience, that is, to know, understand, and act upon communication content by imposing unwarranted, allegedly rational categories upon it. Hermeneutics illuminates the process through which teachers can better communicate with their students about many important matters, not necessarily just the content associated with various subjects. For example, hermeneutical theory lends credence to the notion that schools and classrooms can function as places where adults communicate their care for students and facilitate a deeper understanding of a citizen's rights and responsibilities in a pluralistic, democratic society.

Hermeneutics is only one facet of the discipline of communication that serves to enlarge the parameters of teaching beyond traditional categories. By describing the practical relevance hermeneutical theory possesses for understanding classroom communication, this exploration posits that hermeneutics can function for teachers as a methodology for better perceiving, understanding, and bearing responsibility for their educational decisions. But most important, this exploration also suggests that communication theory in general provides a useful framework to expand the parameters for discourse about teaching, especially for preservice teachers. Were teacher educators to introduce aspiring teachers to Hermes, they would discover in him tools to know, understand, and act upon the omens portending the unclear and turbulent future realities their students will confront when they enter their classrooms as novice teachers.

And yet, lest enthusiasm outpace sober reason, Sergiovanni (1986) suggests a more deliberative and integrative approach, maintaining that "informed doing requires that one consider what is (descriptive science), what ought to be (normative science), and what events mean (interpretive or hermeneutical science)" (p. 288). Introducing hermeneutics into teacher education curricula brings into balance those curriculum strands that stress descriptive theories about what teaching effectiveness is and normative theories about what teaching effectiveness ought to be.

Shifting Metaphors:
Understanding the Educational System

Lakoff and Johnson (1980) examined human communication from a very different vantage from that afforded by the study of hermeneutics. For these two scholars, the meaning embedded in human experience is not clearly evident in the experience itself. As a consequence, humans invoke metaphors to convey their experience more concretely. Metaphors, then, are imaginative concepts that define (or structure) human thought and action by providing a linguistic tool to communicate what humans comprehend partially but not totally. Feelings, aesthetic experiences, moral practices, and spiritual awareness, for example, are not devoid of rationality, as strict empiricists would maintain; rather, Lakoff and Johnson (1980) argue, human beings employ an imaginative rationality, a metaphor, to describe these abstract experiences. This notion is evident in Kerrie Baughman's self-reported discovery: to make sense of what her teaching experiences were communicating to her, she first had to shed the "mother" metaphor guiding her practice.

To orient preservice teachers to metaphors and how they might function as a tool to understand communication in schools and classrooms, teacher educators might ask their students to think about two metaphors that can be invoked to describe schooling, the "custodial" metaphor and the "covenant" metaphor. This effort would help preservice teachers conceptualize how different metaphors convey concrete schooling realities. Teacher educators can also ask their students to juxtapose metaphors to compare and contrast the realities evoked (as well as masked) by each metaphor. Preservice teachers would discover how schools and classrooms have been organized and evaluated around the images people use to describe educational reality as they perceive it; they would also discover that they can communicate alternate school and classroom realities that challenge other stakeholders (e.g., administrators, parents, students) to move beyond traditional metaphors that convey concrete meanings and at the same time constrain that reality.

Metaphorical Practice: Juxtaposing "In Loco Parentis" and "Educational Covenant"

During this century, one metaphor, in loco parentis, has conveyed a concrete image concerning the custodial functions associated with schooling, namely how teachers function as in-school surrogate parents. As part of their professional preparation, it would be helpful for preservice teachers to reflect critically upon the in loco parentis metaphor and how it conveys what many today now take for granted, particularly the bureaucratic and functional aspects of the educational system (Cusick, 1992).

It would also be instructive for preservice teachers to reflect critically upon other metaphors to understand alternative views of the educational system. Sergiovanni (1987) offers the surrogate metaphor of an educational covenant to describe the educational system. For Sergiovanni (1987), the educational covenant concretizes the shared values defining what is right and good, points to the school's mission, specifies obligations and duties, and spells out what must be done to meet commitments. In short, the educational covenant provides a fundamental raison d'être, a purpose, for teachers and students to engage in school and classroom activities.

Sergiovanni (1990) uses this metaphor to cast schools in decidedly different terms from those conveyed by in loco parentis and shifts the focus of discourse away from the morally neutral, traditional, secular metaphor, in loco parentis, to a morally positive metaphor, one connoting sacred purposes, the educational covenant. By so doing, Sergiovanni (1990) validates Lakoff and Johnson's (1980) assertion that metaphors possess power—not only do metaphors describe something we do not fully understand (e.g., schooling), they also illuminate other perspectives not conveyed by other metaphors. What perspectives does the educational covenant metaphor communicate? How might these perspectives foster an educational culture conducive to educational reform? How might metaphors help teachers to communicate and to shape alternative realities of stakeholders in the educational system?

One aspect of classroom organization reconceived by the covenant metaphor is the roles assumed by parents, teachers, and students. Because covenants are built upon the foundation of mutual respect and trust, a covenant envisions parents as entrusting their children to teachers who in turn bear a professional responsibility to make important educational decisions about what ought to be done in the process of educating children, in much the same way that doctors make medical decisions for patients. Teachers do not provide instruction, a commodity, but diagnose learning problems and prescribe individualized programs (a needed service). Thus, personal, subjective, intrinsic norms become the foundation for the professional judgments teachers make. And in classrooms where learning is less uniform and predictable, students must become active agents who engage in purposeful learning. In the dynamic classroom environment shaped by an educational covenant, unequivocal standards of assessment and a clearly delineated division of labor recede as parents, teachers, and students fulfill their responsibilities.

Invoking the covenant metaphor also leads to a fundamental reconception of educational authority. No longer can educational administrators, donning the garments of power, authority, and prestige, be isolated from the labor pool, the faculty. By necessity, the covenant metaphor conveys the notion that principals and teachers need to communicate because power within schools and classrooms can be determined by the quality of conversation. What becomes important is not what a school district's policy manual dictates but "who says what to whom and with what effect" (Rosengren, 1964, p. 73). In place of the normative bureaucratic hierarchy, the covenant metaphor conveys the notion of a professional *staff*. In this model, all staff members stand on much the same footing, busying themselves as they fulfill their obligations. But to do so, the entire staff needs to collaborate frequently about common concerns, educational issues, and simple problems as well. In a covenant-based school organization, for example, instructional programs would be developed through practice; trial-and-error methods would be encouraged, evaluated, and recognized as integral to innovation. The daily routine would involve responding to the unforeseen and changing. Positive peer pressure would engage the staff's creative capacities, challenging them to pursue new avenues to resolve problems as they emerge. Staff communication would certainly increase the potential for conflict, but teachers would find themselves challenged by this conflict to integrate their personal character with their professional role. Thus, teachers could no longer function as "artificial persons," that is, people whose roles are neatly detached from their personal character (Wolgast, 1992). They would have to be open and receptive human beings who respond, with due *regard* (vs. due *process*), to shifting and sometimes conflicting demands (Sockett, 1991).

The covenant metaphor also affects notions about how local educational reform is constructed. Staff communication would provide an informal means to devise, to test, and to implement new educational methods. Teachers would freely trade information about what works and discard what fails. Through their conversation, what Glatthorn (1987) has called "professional dialogue" (p. 31), teachers would initiate change, alter their attitudes and relationships based on shifting contingencies, evaluate progress, and ultimately develop new courses of action. Communication could also become the primary means for generating policy and ultimately for transforming schools. If educators communicated effectively, local educational reform could be constructed upon a body of information that would be equally dispersed among all members of the staff regardless of their status in the school.

Conceptions about educational policy making are also affected by this change of metaphors. No longer would policy making be understood to be the exclusive domain of recognized officials who set agendas and preside at meetings. Instead, an educational covenant suggests that educational policy would be given shape and formulated throughout the process of communication among teachers, parents, and school administrators, as well as elected officials (Caldwell & Spinks, 1992).

If preservice teachers were to study language carefully, in particular, metaphors, then they would examine the importance and power that metaphors possess, understand how they could use metaphors to reconceive reality by making it more ambiguous, and learn how metaphors enable factions with dissimilar interpretations about reality to organize toward similar goals (Donnellon, Gray, & Bougon, 1986). A theoretical basis for reforming classrooms could then be established before politicians and well-meaning citizens promulgate new metaphors that concretize some important educational realities but mask other severe limitations that would ultimately debilitate the schools and classrooms intended to promote the education of youth.

Teacher educators who take seriously the task of preparing teachers for the American nation could benefit by expanding their curriculum's parameters to include the discipline of communication, particularly the analysis of metaphors. By studying metaphorical conceptions about the educational system, teacher educators will help preservice teachers to identify differences in how they understand educational reality, to bring their conflicting visions into full public view, and to forge a tentative consensus. Of course, resolutions will not be easy to achieve. Teacher education will become messier, not neater. There will be no simple answers. But teacher educators will be engaging their students in a more democratic experience of educational policy making, particularly as it might occur in the culture of a self-managing school.

Weiss, Cambone, and Wyeth (1992) name the central problem confronting educators who practice their craft in a democratic nation: "Teachers often have a difficult time dealing with each other in a decision-oriented context. They are used to the old norms of live and let live. Now they have to *engage* with each other, take stands, confront conflict, negotiate differences. Very little in their background or training prepared them for this kind of democratic politics" (p. 356). Maxey (1993) sounds the same note:

> Although neither a singular nor a noncontradictory view, "democratic education," in at least one version, has attached to it at least three process values: communication, shared intelligence, and community. Within all organizational life, the democratic value of communication is essential. Those affected by decisions should be free to discuss the issues needing resolution and the means thought best for resolving them. A second process value is shared intelligence. Here, in the school setting, principal, teachers, parents, and students must exercise a kind of group "practical intelligence" and, finally school leaders and followers must form a community. . . . Democracy as a way of life entails commonalty. While recognizing that consensus is rarely permanent, and conflict is typically our condition, nonetheless democracy is pledged to the value of sharing with others. (pp. 49-50)

Although Weiss et al. (1992) and Maxey (1993) define the problem at the heart of educating youth in a pluralistic democracy, Sergiovanni (1987, 1990) uses a metaphor that can assist teacher educators to point the way toward a resolution, namely, that with persistence and authentic communication, teachers can develop a consensus and forge an educational covenant. It might not be the best of all covenants, educationally speaking. It will, however, be steeped in a lived experience of educational decision making in a democratic context and in truths that the majority of participants can uphold. This exercise would help preservice teachers to recognize the power metaphors exercise in shaping how humans conceptualize ambiguous and only partially understood ideas and also help them to comprehend schooling as the complex activity it is. They might learn, then, to appreciate the deep structures of the personal and interpersonal dimensions of what will, one day in the not too distant future, be their work in classrooms (Beck & Murphy, 1992).

Communication, Teacher Education,
and School Reform

The Association of Teacher Educators' (ATE) *Teacher Education Year-book I* featured an overview and framework that initiated a discussion concerning diverse perspectives on communication and its relationship to teacher education (Richmond & McCroskey, 1993). In *Teacher Education Yearbook II*, Glickman, McLaughlin, and Miller (1993) provided an introduction to the discipline of communication, noting: "The 'what' being communicated between teachers, teacher educators, and students should not be about organizations or competitive products, but rather about how school interactions can help or hinder the development of all students toward taking their rightful and responsible places in society" (pp. 150-151).

Given the proportion of each work day that teachers spend communicating this "what," or purpose of public education, with their students and colleagues, this chapter has extended the previous two *Yearbook* discussions by explicitly linking two disciplines, education and communication. Further, I argued that by focusing preservice teachers upon what communication is as well as how they might respond to it, a common protocol and language could result. In the end, the ultimate beneficiary of this conceptual link would be students in those schools and classrooms where teachers extend their conversations with one another and their students.

In contrast to communication courses and workshops emphasizing public relations gimmicks, preservice teachers exposed to the discipline of communication would uncover Dance's (1970) family of concepts that would involve them in a serious and scholarly effort to understand what is at the heart of education: human beings who share knowledge and skills about important things. Because education is an *interactive* process (Davis, 1994), exposing preservice teachers to the discipline of communication could help them envision, practice, and integrate ways to understand their experience as well as improve their professional practice once they enter the nation's schools.

This suggestion, however, is not novel. Dorsey (1957) suggested this notion well over three decades ago. In the intervening years, some theorists have taken heed (Lysaught, 1984). Yet, there are many other members of Dance's family of concepts requiring careful scrutiny by teacher educators. For example, Goffman's (1963) analysis of human behavior in public places can be applied, in particular, to the symbolic dimensions of teacher-student and principal-teacher interactions (Florio-Ruane, 1987; Floyd, 1993; Harper and Hughey, 1986; Martin, 1971; May & Devault, 1967; McCaleb, 1984; Powell & Arthur, 1985). Rhetoric and persuasion theory have broad applicability to teaching, as does semiotics (Everhart, 1991). Each adds a depth of richness to the portrait of teaching excellence and can provide preservice teachers with an array of perspectives illuminating the educational reality they will confront and shape through their responses to the conversations that will take place in their schools and classrooms.

If the ideas advocated in this chapter are actualized, preservice teachers will enter their classrooms trained in theories that would enable them to reflect upon, to communicate about, and to collaborate with others in the process of educating youth. Preservice teachers will also be trained to think about applying various communication theories to overcome some of the traditional entanglements (for example, those bureaucratic roadblocks and conflicts) that currently are perceived as inherent in the educational system (Cusick, 1992). Finally, preservice teachers will understand an educational ethic that stresses caring, trust, friendship, integrity, honesty, constancy, and fidelity in the sense Sockett (1991) has described it. Ultimately, preservice teachers will be trained to understand their responsibility to lead others to engage in a fundamental *reform*, not a *reinvention*, of U.S. schooling.[1] At the very least, preservice teachers must be exposed to the discipline of communication as previously described. As a result, they will learn how to allow dissimilar ideas to coexist as part of an overall quest to realize highly effective schools and classrooms. As Pajak (1992) aptly notes, "Communication is inclusive, allowing all involved to participate, understand, and commit themselves to the mission" (p. 129).

My thesis has extended Glickman et al.'s (1993) first step into uncharted territory, at least for teacher educators. "How far we need to go!" Glickman et al. wrote (1993, p. 214). Indeed, much work remains. As suggested earlier, other communication theories need to be examined to ascertain their applicability to educational organizations. Research also needs to be conducted to assess whether and to what degree communication tools enhance pedagogical processes. Rather than utilizing only empirical and quasi-empirical methodological approaches to explain and predict educational phenomena, the study of selected communication theories affords teacher educators the opportunity to expand beyond these methods. Teachers can then seize the opportunity to utilize what Corey (1953) introduced four decades ago as "action research to improve school practices" and Byron (1989) has termed "derivative" and "conjunctive" research methodologies. Ross and Regan (1993) initiated an important first step in this direction in demonstrating that professional sharing (i.e., teacher communication) has a weak effect upon teacher development unless their conversations are punctuated by metacognitions or challenged by other teachers. Waite (1993) has utilized ethnographic methods and conversation analysis to examine teacher-supervisor conferences and their contexts. Noting that supervision can no longer be viewed as a one-way phenomenon, he argues that supervisors need to model communicative skills, particularly active listening and incorporating what the other speaker says in one's own talk, to effect improved pedagogical practice and student learning through supervisory practice. Roberts (1994) has used one qualitative method, discourse analysis, to examine supervisory conversation and communicative competence. Her analysis suggests that communicative competence is a critical factor to effect change in teachers. Each of these methodological approaches offers new vantages to illuminate the omnipresent but elusive educational variable, school communication (Jacobs, 1993).

Although I disagree with some aspects of Dewey's (1916) pedagogical theory, I do believe that he was right on target when he linked education with communication and argued that schools are critical to the intergenerational progress of a pluralistic democracy. As the nation struggles to reform its schools and the 21st century dawns, teachers need to learn to communicate with their students, just as the nation's teachers needed to communicate with their students 100 years ago as the 20th century was dawning. School communication is the intergenerational issue for educators who are serious about educational reform.

Note

1. By reform, I mean to imagine anew, to conceive of possibilities and challenges, and to respond to reality. I use this term in contrast to the federal government's notion of "reinvent" by which former President Bush (1991) meant to "break the mold . . . literally start from scratch and reinvent the American school. No question should be off limits, no answers automatically assumed" (p. 55).

References

Barth, R. S. (1990). *Improving schools from within: Teachers, parents, and principals can make a difference.* San Francisco: Jossey-Bass.

Bauman, Z. (1978). *Hermeneutics and social science.* New York: Columbia University Press.

Beck, L. G., & Murphy, J. (1992). Searching for a robust understanding of the principalship. *Educational Administration Quarterly, 28*(3), 387-396.

Bentzen, M. (1974). *Changing schools: The magic feather principle.* New York: D. Appleton.

Berliner, D. C. (1986). In pursuit of the expert pedagogue. *Educational Researcher, 15*(7), 5-13.

Bullough, R. V. (1989). *First year teacher: A case study.* New York: Teachers College Press.

Bullough, R. V., & Baughman, K. (1993). Continuity and change in teacher development: First year teacher after five years. *Journal of Teacher Education, 44*(2), 86-95.

Burlingame, M., & Sergiovanni, T. J. (1993). Some questions about school leadership and communication theory. *Journal of Management Systems, 5*(2), 51-61.

Bush, G. (1991). Remarks by the president announcing America 2000, the White House, April 18, 1991. In U.S. Department of Education, *America 2000: An education strategy* (Appendix 2). Washington, DC: U.S. Department of Education.

Byron, W. J. (1989). *Quadrangle considerations.* Chicago: Loyola University Press.

Caldwell, B., & Spinks, J. (1992). *Leading the self-managing school.* Bristol, PA: Falmer.

Corey, S. M. (1953). *Action research to improve school practices.* New York: Teachers College Press.

Cusick, P. A. (1992). *The educational system: Its nature and logic.* New York: McGraw-Hill.

Dance, F.E.X. (1970). The "concept" of communication. *Journal of Communication, 2,* 201-210.

Davis, B. A. (1994). Mathematics teaching: Moving from telling to listening. *Journal of Curriculum and Supervision, 9*(3), 267-283.

Dewey, J. (1916). *Democracy and education.* New York: Free Press.

Dilthey, W. (1989). The hermeneutics of the human sciences. In K. Mueller-Vollmer (Ed.), *The hermeneutics reader* (pp. 148-164). New York: Continuum.

Donnellon, A., Gray, B., & Bougon, M. G. (1986). Communication, meaning, and organized action. *Administrative Science Quarterly, 31,* 43-55.

Dorsey, J. T., Jr. (1957). A communication model for administration. *Administrative Science Quarterly, 2,* 307-324.

Everhart, R. B. (1991). Semiotics as an orientation to administrative practice. *Educational Administration Quarterly, 27,* 358-377.

Evertson, C., Emmer, E., Sanford, J., & Clements, B. (1982). *Improving classroom management: An experiment in elementary classrooms.* Paper presented at the annual meeting of the American Educational Research Association, New York.

Florio-Ruane, S. (1987). Sociolinguistics for educational researchers. *American Educational Research Journal, 24,* 185-192.

Floyd, K. (1993). Symbolic interactionism: Some reflections about leadership and school organization. *Journal of Management Systems, 5*(2), 32-38.

Fuchs, L. S., Fuchs, D., Bentz, J., Phillips, N. B., & Hamlett, C. L. (1994). The nature of student interactions during peer tutoring with and without prior training and experience. *American Educational Research Journal, 31*(1), 75-103.

Glatthorn, A. A. (1987, November). Cooperative professional development: Peer-centered options for professional growth. *Educational Leadership, 45*(3), 31-35.

Glickman, C. D., McLaughlin, H. J., & Miller, V. (1993). Communication: Overview and framework. In M. J. O'Hair & S. J. Odell (Eds.), *Partnerships in education: Teacher education yearbook II* (pp. 149-156). Fort Worth, TX: Harcourt Brace Jovanovich.

Goffman, E. (1963). *Behavior in public places.* New York: Free Press.

Good, T. (1981, February). Teacher expectations and student perceptions: A decade of research. *Educational Leadership, 38,* 415-422.

Gray, W. A., & Gray, M. M. (1985, November). Synthesis of research on mentoring beginning teachers. *Educational Leadership, 43*(3), 37-43.

Griffin, E. M. (1991). *A first look at communication theory.* New York: McGraw-Hill.

Hansen, D. T. (1993, Winter). From role to person: The moral layeredness of classroom teaching. *American Educational Research Journal, 30*(4), 651-674.

Hargreaves, A., & Fullan, M. G. (1992). *Understanding teacher development.* London: Cassells.

Harper, B. H., & Hughey, J. D. (1986). Effects of communication responsiveness upon instructor judgment grading and student cognitive learning. *Communication Education, 35,* 147-156.

Hyde, M. J. (1982). Transcendental philosophy and human communication. In J. J. Pilotta (Ed.), *Interpersonal communication* (pp. 15-34). Washington, DC: Center for Advanced Research in Phenomenology.

Jacobs, R. M. (1992). Hermeneutics: Probing the nature and logic of school communication. *Association of Management Proceedings Education, 10*(1), 102-108.

Jacobs, R. M. (1993). Road maps to understand school communication. *Journal of Management Systems, 5*(1), 1-15.

Joyce, B., & McKibbin, M. (1982, November). Teacher growth states and school environments. *Educational Leadership, 40,* 36-41.

Joyce, B., & Showers, B. (1980, February). Improving inservice training: The messages of research. *Educational Leadership, 37,* 379-385.

Kagan, D. M. (1992). Professional growth among preservice and beginning teachers. *Review of Educational Research, 62*(2), 129-169.

Lakoff, G., & Johnson, M. (1980). *Metaphors we live by.* Chicago: University of Chicago Press.

Leithwood, K. A. (1992). The move toward transformational leadership. *Educational Leadership, 49*(5), 8-12.

Littlejohn, S. W. (1989). *Theories of human communication* (3rd ed.). Belmont, CA: Wadsworth.

Lysaught, J. P. (1984). Toward a comprehensive theory of communication: A review of selected contributions. *Educational Administration Quarterly, 20*(3), 101-27.

Martin, R. G. (1971). Communication and the act of teaching: A footnote to models of teaching. *Journal of Teacher Education, 22,* 418-425.

Maxey, S. J. (1993, January). Democracy, design, and the new reflective practice. *NASSP Bulletin, 78*(558), 46-50.

May, F. B., & Devault, M. V. (1967). Hypothetical dimensions of teachers' communication. *American Educational Research Journal, 4,* 271-278.

McCaleb, J. (1984). Selecting a measure of oral communication as a predictor of teaching performance. *Journal of Teacher Education, 35,* 33-38.

Pajak, E. F. (1992). A view from the central office. In C. D. Glickman (Ed.), *Supervision in transition* (pp. 126-138). Alexandria, VA: Association for Supervision and Curriculum Development.

Palmer, R. E. (1969). *Hermeneutics: Interpretation theory in Schleiermacher, Dilthey, Heidegger, and Gadamer.* Evanston, IL: Northwestern University Press.

Powell, R. G., & Arthur, R. (1985). Perceptions of affective communication and teaching effectiveness at different times in the semester. *Communication Quarterly, 4,* 254-261.

Richmond, V. P., & McCroskey, J. C. (1993). Communication: Overview and framework. In M. J. O'Hair & S. J. Odell (Eds.), *Diversity and teaching: Teacher education yearbook I* (pp. 165-174). Fort Worth, TX: Harcourt Brace Jovanovich.

Ricoeur, P. (1981). *Hermeneutics and the human sciences: Essays on language, action, and interpretation* (J. B. Thompson, Trans.). Cambridge, UK: Cambridge University Press.

Roberts, J. (1994, Winter). Discourse analysis of supervisory conferences: An exploration. *Journal of Supervision and Curriculum Development, 9*(2), 136-154.

Rosengren, W. R. (1964). Communication, organization, and conduct in the "therapeutic milieu." *Administrative Science Quarterly, 9*, 70-90.

Ross, J. A., & Regan, E. M. (1993). Sharing professional experience: Its impact on professional development. *Teaching and Teacher Education, 9*(1), 91-106.

Schön, D. A. (1990). *Educating the reflective practitioner.* San Francisco: Jossey-Bass.

Sergiovanni, T. J. (1986). Developing a relevant theory of administration. In T. J. Sergiovanni & J. E. Corbally (Eds.), *Leadership and organizational culture* (pp. 275-291). Urbana: University of Illinois Press.

Sergiovanni, T. J. (1987). *The principalship: A reflective practice perspective* (2nd ed.). Boston: Allyn & Bacon.

Sergiovanni, T. J. (1990). *Value-added leadership: How to get extraordinary performance in schools.* San Diego, CA: Harcourt Brace Jovanovich.

Sockett, H. (1991). Accountability, trust, and ethical codes of practice. In J. I. Goodlad, R. Soder, & K. A. Sirotnik (Eds.), *The moral dimensions of teaching* (pp. 224-250). San Francisco: Jossey-Bass.

Sparks, G. M. (1983, November). Synthesis of research on staff development for effective teaching. *Educational Leadership, 41*, 63-72.

Trenholm, S. (1986). *Human communication theory.* Englewood Cliffs, NJ: Prentice-Hall.

Waite, D. (1993). Teachers in conference: A qualitative study of teacher-supervisor face-to-face interactions. *American Educational Research Journal, 30*(4), 675-702.

Weiss, C. H., Cambone, J., & Wyeth, A. (1992). Trouble in paradise: Teacher conflicts in shared decision making. *Educational Administration Quarterly, 28*(3), 350-367.

Wolgast, E. (1992). *Ethics of an artificial person: Lost responsibility in professions and organizations.* Stanford, CA: Stanford University Press.

Wood, F. H., & Thompson, S. R. (1993). Assumptions about staff development based on research and best practice. *Journal of Staff Development, 14,* 52-57.

8 Evaluating Communication Skills of Students in Teacher Education

Gretchen C. Hess

Robert H. Short

Gretchen C. Hess is Associate Professor in the Department of Educational Psychology at the University of Alberta, Edmonton. Her research interests include teacher education, adolescence, learning and development, and professional communication among educators and health professionals.

Robert H. Short is Professor in the Department of Educational Psychology at the University of Alberta, Edmonton. His research interests include learning and cognition, brain/behavioral relations, and developmental psychology.

ABSTRACT

To facilitate the teaching of communication skills to students in teacher education programs, an instrument has been designed to assess their communication skills before and after an optional course in communication. The Communication Skills Inventory (CSI) includes multiple-choice and open-ended questions designed to measure listening and attending skills. Results from the data gathered from over 150 university students showed a significant change in test scores from the pre- to the posttest and suggest that communication skills can be taught in a large lecture-style course. However, the results suggest that several assumptions made about communication may be unfounded. Descriptive data including age, gender, educational/ language background, and self-ratings were used to compare subgroups. No significant differences between subgroups were found. Results of the study raise the questions of how and when the communication skills and accompanying attitudes can be taught most effectively.

It has long been accepted that good communication skills are of vital importance to psychologists and counselors, following the contributions of Carkhuff (1969, 1980), Ivey (e.g., Ivey & Gluckstern, 1982), and Gazda (e.g., Gazda, Asbury, Balzer, Childers, & Walters, 1984), among others. Many educators believe such skills are of equal importance to teachers. Moore (1989) states that without effective communication between the teacher and the student, learning cannot take place. Parkay and Hardcastle (1990) list being a counselor as one of the five main roles of a teacher. Jones and Jones (1990) state that "the importance of using effective communication skills cannot be overemphasized. They are the foundation for good classroom management" (p. 79). Hart (1993) goes even further and offers the thesis that "communication will be the most important subject taught in the latter part of the twentieth century" (p. 101). He believes that teaching communication will always be with us as the ultimate "people-making discipline" (p. 101). These authors see communication skills as important for different reasons—to increase student learning, to counsel students about their lives, and to motivate students by effective classroom management—but all agree that effective communication is important.

It seems to us that communication is becoming increasingly important as the role of teachers changes in the 1990s. In Canada we have witnessed more and more students with special needs being mainstreamed into regular classrooms. We have seen counseling and psychological services being cut back in several school systems. In addition, teachers are being forced to become more accountable for the academic performance of their students with the introduction of provincial examinations and several recent worldwide comparisons of student performance. At the same time teachers are urged to become student centered in their perspectives. Although good communication will not alone solve the problems caused by these changes, it is vital to the process of educating students more effectively. Numerous studies (e.g., McCroskey, Beatty, Kearney, & Plax, 1985; Rubin & Graham, 1988; Rubin, Graham, & Mignerey, 1990) have demonstrated a clear positive relationship between communication competence and academic achievement, scholastic aptitudes, and self-esteem.

Students who are apprehensive about their ability to communicate effectively typically withdraw from interpersonal situations and consequently limit the opportunity to demonstrate their knowledge, aptitudes, and skills in social settings. It seems to us, as educational psychologists, that school counselors and psychologists have a vital role to play in encouraging effective communication within the classroom—by modeling, by coaching teachers, and by setting an atmosphere in the schools that encourages good communication.

One way to further effective communication in the schools is through ensuring that new teachers recognize the importance of communication and have some expertise in the needed skills. A variety of approaches to help teach and develop such skills have been proposed. For example, some researchers in communication studies strongly recommend interpersonal communication courses for college students (e.g., Cronin & Glenn, 1990; Cronin & Grice, 1993; Morreale, Shockley-Zalabak, & Whitney, 1993). Their recommendations vary and include brief single-episode workshops, full-term courses, and fully integrated approaches with a variety of techniques taught across the college curriculum.

Undergraduates in the Faculty of Education at the University of Alberta have the option to take a communication course in the last year of their program. Teaching communication courses is rather different from teaching those primarily aimed at learning specific content, understanding theory, or evaluating research. Good communication is a process requiring judgment and timing as well as knowledge and comprehension of the ideas involved. In addition, it can probably be assumed that students start the course with varied levels of skill given their different family and social backgrounds.

The primary purpose of this study, therefore, was to administer an inventory to assess generic communication skills as a pre- and posttest to determine if the needed skills can be taught in a large-group lecture situation within the university setting. Further, we wanted to examine the relationship between performance on the inventory and certain demographic variables that might be relevant: age, gender, and English-language background of the students.

Philosophy of the Communication Course

We believe that effective teaching requires the skill to communicate with children in a compassionate and empathic manner. The importance of a child-centered approach to communication skill training has been recognized by educators since the publication of Rogers's (1961) landmark book, *On Becoming a Person*. Teachers can make better use of their teaching knowledge and teach more effectively when they are aware of the emotions, thoughts, and internal frames of reference of their pupils. This awareness can help teachers reformulate instructions and restructure teaching materials in ways that improve pupil learning, help overcome pupil fears, and motivate and encourage pupils.

The communication skills needed by teachers can be divided into four types: (a) *nonverbal skills* (Barnard, Barr, & Schumacher, 1985), for example, physical environment, personal space, facial expressions, gestures, vocal qualities, and personal style; (b) *attending or understanding skills* (adapted from Ivey & Gluckstern, 1982), for example, open and closed questioning, checking perceptions, and paraphrasing; (c) *responding or influencing skills* (also adapted from Ivey & Gluckstern, 1984), for example, reflecting feelings, focusing, self-disclosing, providing feedback, confronting); and (d) *crisis intervention skills* (adapted from Kuypers, 1979), for example, crisis defusing, providing a supportive atmosphere, fueling the crisis, planning, teaching a needed skill, giving facts and information, using positive reinforcement, and referral.

In the interpersonal communication course taught at the University of Alberta, the skills of communication listed above are explained in a large-group, lecture-style setting taught over of period of 6 weeks (80 minutes each week). Students also attend weekly seminars (80 minutes each) to practice the skills. In addition to learning the communication skills, students are introduced to various programs that encourage effective communication, good classroom management, or effective education in the classroom. This second part of the course is not tested in the pre- or posttest of this study.

The Communication Skills Inventory

To facilitate the teaching of these skills to students in teacher education programs, the Communication Skills Inventory (CSI) (Hess, 1990) was developed to assess generic communication skills of undergraduate students in a teacher education program. The term "generic" is used because it is intended that the skills being assessed are nontheoretical, nonspecific practical skills that do not require technical jargon or specific vocabulary. In other words, the inventory was designed to measure students' skills rather than their knowledge of communication as a discipline.

The inventory itself was created over a 10-year period. Instructors teaching the communications course also lead the seminars for small groups of the students. At the end of the term, a version of the current inventory was administered to students. Seminar leaders were asked to rank-order their students according to the communication skills they displayed during the seminars. The right and wrong answers of those students who were rated highest or lowest by their instructors were analyzed in depth. In many cases students were asked to give verbal feedback in an interview after the completion of the course as to why they chose a specific correct or incorrect item. Comprehensive item analysis was undertaken at the end of every term using the LERTAP program. Adjustments were made in the wording of the questions after each term. Gradually the instructors came to trust the inventory. At the time of the last piloting, all of the students who had been rated by the instructors to be in the top quarter through seminar ratings received scores of 80% or more on the inventory. The students who were rated as the least effective (the bottom five students) all received poor or failing (below 50%) scores on the inventory. At that point the questions were judged to be fairly accurate and appropriate. Although it was believed that no simple paper-and-pencil inventory could truly test all the myriad skills needed in good communication, it was felt that the instrument had reasonable content and construct validity.

Part I: Multiple-Choice Responses in a Listening Test

The CSI has three parts. Part I of the inventory, which is designed to assess the ability of students to listen and interpret the intended meaning of brief phrases, includes 10 multiple-choice questions from the Jones Mohr Listening Test (Jones & Mohr, 1976). Brief spoken statements are presented by means of an audiotaped recording, and subjects are required to circle the multiple-choice alternative that best corresponds to the speaker's intended meaning. All answers to this part of the inventory are keyed to a single correct response. Some sample items are shown in Table 8.1.

Part II: General Multiple-Choice Responses

Part II of the inventory involves seven multiple-choice questions designed to assess students' ability to select a response to a statement made by one person to another, one that would best reflect the facilitation

Table 8.1   Sample Questions From Communication Skills Inventory
(CSI) (Education Form), Part III

Part I: Listening Test

An audiotape will be played to accompany the following questions.
Circle the letter beside the response that best corresponds to the
speaker's intended meaning.

1. Let's go see him again.
   - a. I just can't wait.
   - b. I'd like to get something from him.
   - c. I never want to see him again.
   - d. I really enjoy seeing him.

2. Ah, I just can't seem to get involved.
   - a. I wish I were different.
   - b. I don't want to get involved.
   - c. . . . but I want to get involved.
   - d. I'm really kind of bored.

3. Gee! It's good to see you again.
   - a. I really don't enjoy this.
   - b. I'm happy to see you.
   - c. I like you.
   - d. It's about time. . . .

4. It's nice to be together again.
   - a. I've missed you so much.
   - b. It makes me feel at peace.
   - c. . . . but I liked it better without you.
   - d. I'm glad you're home.

---

in communication between the two of them. These have been adapted
from Carkhuff's (Carkhuff, 1980; Carkhuff, Berenson, & Pierce, 1977) and
Gazda's (Gazda et al., 1984) empathy and communication training scales.
The questions in this part of the inventory are keyed to a best and
second-best response. Table 8.2 illustrates the questions of this part.

Table 8.2 Sample Questions From Communication Skills Inventory (CSI) (Education Form), Part II

Part II: Discrimination of Helper Responses

For each of the following introductory statements, indicate the letter of the response that would best facilitate communication.

1. Student Teacher to another Student Teacher: "If I had done what I thought was best instead of listening to my co-operating teacher, that child's mother wouldn't be mad at me right now."

    a. "You're feeling bad about the child and her mother. Are you also worried about what the co-operating teacher will write on your evaluation about the whole incident?"

    b. "What did you do?"

    c. "Sounds like you are having the same problems with your co-operating teacher as Sarah Johnson is having with hers. Maybe you should go talk with Sarah?"

    d. "By not doing what you thought best, you're in a mess. But what else could you have done?"

    e. "And now you're kicking yourself. I would have done the same. I guess we have to learn to stand up for ourselves when it comes to dealing with the parents. Hard way to learn, isn't it?"

2. Teenage Student in a school to Student Teacher: "It seems like everybody has plans for my future; my parents, my girlfriend, my friends, everybody—but I don't know what to do. I don't know whether to go to university or not."

    a. "Well, it's easier to go to university right after high school than it ever will be again, especially if your parents are willing to pay for it. There are also more jobs open to you with a university education. Anyway, you could always quit if you hated it after a term or two."

    b. "Perhaps you could try standing up for yourself and asserting your own wishes."

    c. "I know how you feel, I have thirty people who all want different things from me. Frustrating, isn't it?"

    d. "You resent having other people make plans for you, and yet you are feeling lost about your own directions."

    e. "Uh . . . so what do you think you should do?"

Table 8.3   Sample Questions From Communication Skills Inventory
(CSI) (Education Form), Part III

Part III: Open Responses

In this part of the inventory you are to write your own responses to
statements rather than choosing a response from the multiple-choice
format. In response to each of the statements given, write a response
that best facilitates communication. Write on the answer sheet provided.

1. Education Student to Professor: "I don't know why I have to take all
    these theory and philosophy courses. I just want to graduate, so that
    I can go spend my time with kids in the classroom."

2. Parent to Teacher: "My daughter went to another school down the
    road and they didn't teach her anything. How do I know you are
    going to teach my daughter anything?"

Part III: Open-Ended Responses

Part III of the inventory involves two open-ended questions in which
students are required to generate their own response to a person's written
statement. Again the instructions ask for a response "that best facilitates
communication." These questions are scored on a scale of 0 to 2, indicating how well the responses reflect (a) the content, (b) the feelings of the
person speaking in the hypothetical situation, and (c) the amount of
empathy demonstrated in the response to that person. The best possible
score on each of the two questions is a 6. These questions are presented
in Table 8.3.

In addition to the assessment component of the inventory, students
are asked to supply descriptive data including age, gender, educational
history, and language background, plus self-ratings of communication
ability.

Method

The subjects used in this study, all students at the University of
Alberta, were either fourth-year education students enrolled in a 4-year
bachelor of education (B.Ed.) degree or students enrolled in a 2-year

program for teacher certification following a bachelor's degree in another discipline. The communication course is one of four optional educational psychology or educational foundations courses that are taken by students in the last year of their program of study. All students are required to have completed their required student teaching practica prior to selecting an option. Approximately one third of the student body elect this particular course in any year.

A total of 178 students took part in this study, participation being one of the course requirements. For some of the research analyses a number of students fewer than this total was used because of incomplete or missing data. The mean age of students was 26.4 years (standard deviation = 6.4 years) with a range from 20 years to 50 years. All were enrolled in the communication course between 1990 and 1992.

Results and Discussion

Pre- and Posttest Changes

One of the most important questions to be answered by this study was whether the experience and knowledge gained from a university-level interpersonal communication course for undergraduate students in teacher education would increase their performance on a test constructed to assess a variety of communication skills. Students completed the inventory at the beginning of the course and again later at its completion at the end of the term. The differences between pretest and posttest performance measures on the CSI were all statistically significant. Multiple t tests for comparing differences between the pairs of means on the pre- and post-tests were used in this part of the analysis. The results shown in Table 8.4 reveal that pre- and posttest differences occurred in all of the assessment parts of the inventory.

These results clearly indicate that students' communication skills did indeed improve, at least in terms of their performance on the CSI, as a result of taking an interpersonal communication course. The improvement in performance on the inventory as a whole was approximately 40%, with the biggest increases occurring in Parts II and III. The statistically significant, yet relatively small increase in Part I of the inventory may indicate that the "listening and interpretation of intended meaning" skill component may be of minimal value in the overall assessment of communication skills, particularly as it is currently constituted.

Table 8.4   Means, Standard Deviations, and *t* Test Values for the Differences Between Pre- and Posttest Scores on Parts I, II, III, and the Total, on the Communication Skills Inventory (CSI)

	n	*Mean*	*SD*	*t value*	*df*	*2-tail prob.*
Part I						
Pretest	178	6.00	1.57			
				−3.80	177	0.00
Posttest	178	6.52	1.71			
Part II						
Pretest	178	6.07	3.35			
				−8.60	177	0.00
Posttest	178	8.89	3.46			
Part III						
Pretest	152	4.78	3.08			
				−12.24	151	0.00
Posttest	152	8.11	2.65			
Total						
Pretest	152	16.95	5.73			
				−14.50	151	0.00
Posttest	152	24.10	4.61			

$p < .05$.

Students' Self-Rating of Communication Ability

There was a surprising absence of change in the students' ratings of their own ability to communicate with others considering their general improvement in communication skills reflected in performance on the inventory (see Table 8.5). It is not unreasonable to expect that the increase in knowledge and skill that typically accompanies a skill attainment course such as the one involved in this study would also result in an increase in self-ratings of ability. It seems intuitively correct that courses in what could be considered tangible skill attainment such as those involving physical abilities would normally result in an increase in self-confidence and self-rating of ability. However, an elevated sense of self-efficacy in communication ability is probably more likely to be determined

Table 8.5   Means, Standard Deviations, and *t* Test Values for the
Differences Between Pre- and Posttest Scores on Students'
Estimates of Their Own Ability to Communicate on the
Communication Skills Inventory (CSI)

	n	*Mean*	*SD*	*t value*	*df*	*2-tail prob.*
Pretest	160	3.84	0.63	0.26	159	0.79
Posttest	160	3.83	0.60			

p < .05.

by the subjects' prior history of interactions and successes with family,
friends, and acquaintances than with the attainment of knowledge within
the context of a university course, particularly in the short term. The
awareness of one's own communication ability is firmly ingrained and is
continually being confirmed in social situations. Knowledge such as that
acquired in an interpersonal communication course probably needs to be
put into practice over an extended period of time before demonstrable
changes in self efficacy are going to occur.

In addition to the *t*-test comparisons of the self-rating of communication ability, a series of Pearson product moment correlation coefficients
was computed comparing these self-ratings at both the pre- and posttest
administration times to the CSI pretest total score and the three subscale
scores (Parts I, II, and III) of the inventory. It was hypothesized that Part
III of the inventory in particular, requiring the generation of several
responses to open-ended, empathy-based questions, might reveal a relationship to self-ratings. None of these correlations proved to be statistically significant.

Student Factors Affecting Communication Skill Attainment

A second objective of this study was to see if student factors such as
age, gender, and language background would differentially affect performance on the CSI. Several societal stereotypes prevail about people's
facility to communicate effectively. Perhaps the most pervasive stereotype
concerns gender differences. Generally females are seen by society as
being better communicators. Their superior facility for attending, listening, understanding, and interpreting within the context of interpersonal

Table 8.6   Means and Standard Deviations of the Pre- and Posttest Scores by Gender on the Communication Skills Inventory (CSI)

	n	Mean	SD
Pretest			
Males	32	15.19	4.99
Females	119	17.49	5.82
Posttest			
Males	32	23.03	4.38
Females	119	24.39	4.66

NOTE: Neither the main effect for gender nor the interaction effect for gender × pre-/posttest differences was statistically significant (MANOVA).

communication is regarded by many as a societal given. The belief that women have been socialized to care more about affiliative concerns than men is widely accepted.

The results of this study show that there were minimal differences between males and females in communication skill as measured by the CSI (see Table 8.6). Females were slightly better than males in the pretest component of the inventory but this difference was partially diminished in the posttest. The results of the MANOVA show that there were no significant gender differences on the inventory. It should be noted that there was a disproportionately high number of females in the study sample (f = 119, m = 32), which may influence the degree of generalizability of these results.

A second factor that could potentially affect communication ability is the age of the individual. Clearly, differences in communication ability exist throughout childhood and are a direct result of growth, maturational, and socialization influences. Within an adult population, differences in communication ability are seen as primarily being the result of differences in experience or socialization. As a general rule it is believed that as people age their experiential background leads them to greater levels of interpersonal skills. Greater socialization equates with a higher level of communication skill. This belief, however, was not substantiated by the results of this study (see Table 8.7). Even with an age range of 30 years there were no differences in performance between any of the age groups.

The final factor that was investigated in this study was the influence of language and culture on interpersonal communication. Students whose

Table 8.7   Means and Standard Deviations of the Pre- and Posttest
Scores by Age on the Communication Skills Inventory (CSI)

	n	*Mean*	*SD*
Pretest			
Age groups			
20-21	35	16.60	5.28
22	28	17.82	6.31
23-24	26	15.96	4.91
25-30	27	17.52	6.77
31-50	36	16.95	5.73
Posttest			
Age groups			
20-21	35	24.43	4.65
22	28	23.54	4.95
23-24	26	24.80	5.27
25-30	27	25.11	4.20
31-50	36	22.97	4.00

NOTE: Neither the main effect for age nor the interaction effect for age × pre-/
posttest differences was statistically significant (MANOVA).

first language is other than English and whose cultural background is
other than Canadian may be at a clear disadvantage when attempting to
interpret communication cues generated within the Canadian context.
Language is an integral part of empathic communication, and the wide
variety of languages and cultures in a multicultural society such as Canada's may have a dramatic impact on communication ability and performance on a communication inventory such as the CSI. Although a
difference in both pre- and posttest performance was revealed with students who have English as a second language (i.e., performance was
slightly lower), the small number of these students in comparison to
students who have English as a first language limits the generalizability
of the findings (see Table 8.8).

In addition to the above analyses, a series of Pearson product moment
correlation coefficients was constructed comparing performance on both
the pre- and posttests of the CSI and the variables of gender, age, and
language background. No significant correlations were found to exist
among these variables.

Table 8.8 Means and Standard Deviations of the Pre- and Posttest Scores by Language Background (English as First or Second Language) on the Communication Skills Inventory (CSI)

	n	Mean	SD
Pretest			
EFL	136	17.37	5.66
ESL	11	14.54	5.31
Posttest			
EFL	136	24.45	4.34
ESL	11	21.18	6.03

NOTE: The main effect for language background was statistically significant ($p < .05$). The interaction effect for language background × pre-/posttest differences was not statistically significant (MANOVA).

Conclusions

The results of this study indicate that certain communication skills can be taught effectively in large expository lecture settings when combined with small groups that allow students to practice and receive feedback on the relevant skills. Student performance on the CSI indicates that a substantial gain in skill was acquired as a result of taking a communication course of this type, and its use is recommended for others involved in teaching similar courses. Although the results of this study show that student factors such as age, gender, and language background seem to play a minimal or nonexistent role in affecting the acquisition of communication skills, the relatively small number of subjects in some of the group difference analyses may warrant a further investigation of these student factors.

It is our belief that the role of the teacher, particularly in North America, is undergoing considerable change. This change is clearly reflecting the multitude of contemporary societal, political, and economic pressures being imposed upon education. The need for accountability, the influence of the human rights movement, and substantial budgetary restrictions are but a few of the influences on modern education. These often broadly determined influences have resulted in teachers being required to do more and more with fewer resources. Increasingly, teachers are expected to know about the special needs of the students in their care and to be capable of performing in the roles of counselor, special educator, and school psychologist as well as in their more traditional roles. It is only when special or extreme cases occur that specialists are brought in for direction. Once considered to be primarily the domain of specifically trained personnel, the wide range of special needs that children manifest is now being met at all levels and grades by regular classroom teachers who have received limited specialty training during their teacher education programs or on an inservice basis later in their careers. Courses in the needs of special students, psychometrics, student counseling, and communication skills are now being included as requirements in many teacher education programs. The demand for these courses also means that many of the courses need to be taught in a large lecture setting, which is not always conducive to the development of subtle interpersonal skills. This study was, in part, an endeavor to show that even within a traditional classroom setting (i.e., one that primarily uses expository teaching methods) substantial skill development can occur and that a test instrument such as the CSI can prove to be valuable in assessing these skills.

References

Barnard, D., Barr, J. T., & Schumacher, G. E. (1985). *Person to person: Nonverbal communication: The AACP-Lilly Pharmacy Communication Skills Project.* Bethesda, MD: American Association of Colleges of Pharmacy.

Carkhuff, R. R. (1969). *Helping and human relations: A primer for lay and professional helpers: Vol. 1. Selection and training.* New York: Holt, Rinehart & Winston.

Carkhuff, R. R. (1980). *The art of helping IV* (4th ed.). Amherst, MA: Human Resource Development Press.

Carkhuff, R. R., Berenson, D. H., & Pierce, R. M. (1977). *The skills of teaching: Interpersonal skills.* Amherst, MA: Human Resources Press.

Cronin, M. W., & Glenn, P. (1990, June). *Oral communication across the curriculum in higher education: Assessment, recommendations and implications for the speech communication discipline.* Paper presented at the meeting of the International Communication Association, Dublin, Ireland.

Cronin, M. W., & Grice, G. L. (1993). A comparative analysis of training models versus consulting/training models for implementing oral communication across the curriculum. *Communication Education, 42*(1), 1-9.

Gazda, G. M., Asbury, F. R., Balzer, F. J., Childers, W. C., & Walters, R. P. (1984). *Human relations development: A manual for educators* (3rd ed.). Newton, MA: Allyn & Bacon.

Hart, R. P. (1993). Why communication? Why education? Toward a politic of teaching. *Communication Education, 42*(2), 97-105.

Hess, G. C. (1990). *Communication Skills Inventory* [Unpublished inventory]. Edmonton, AB: University of Alberta.

Ivey, A. E., & Gluckstern, N. (1982). *Basic attending skills* (2nd ed.). North Amherst, MA: Microtraining Associates.

Ivey, A. E., & Gluckstern, N. (1984). *Basic influencing skills* (2nd ed.). North Amherst, MA: Microtraining Associates.

Jones, J. E., & Mohr, L. (1976). *The Jones Mohr Listening Test*. La Jolla, CA: University Associates.

Jones, V. F., & Jones, L. S. (1990). *Comprehensive classroom management: Motivating and managing students* (3rd ed.). Boston, MA: Allyn & Bacon.

Kuypers, J. (1979). *Process directions and traps in crisis intervention* [Unpublished presentation]. Winnipeg, MB: University of Manitoba.

McCroskey, J. C., Beatty, M. J., Kearney, P., & Plax, T. G. (1985). The content validity of the PRCA-24 as a measure of communication apprehension across communication contexts. *Communication Quarterly, 33*(2), 165-173.

Moore, K. D. (1989). *Classroom teaching skills: A primer*. New York: Random House.

Morreale, S., Shockley-Zalabak, P., & Whitney, P. (1993). The center for excellence in oral communication: Integrating communication across the curriculum. *Communication Education, 42*(1), 10-21.

Parkay, F. W., & Hardcastle, B. (1990). *Becoming a teacher: Accepting the challenge of a profession*. Boston: Allyn & Bacon.

Rogers, C. R. (1961). *On becoming a person*. Boston: Houghton Mifflin.

Rubin, R. B., & Graham, E. E. (1988). Communication correlates of college success: An exploratory investigation. *Communication Education, 37*(1), 14-27.

Rubin, R. B., Graham, E. E., & Mignerey, J. T. (1990). A longitudinal study of college students' communication competence. *Communication Education, 39*(1), 1-14.

9 Reflection in Leadership: An Examination of Peer Leader Role Development

Ann L. Darling

Martha L. Dewey

Ann L. Darling earned her Ph.D. at the University of Washington in 1987. She is currently Associate Professor in the Department of Communication at the University of Utah. She is also Director of the University Communication Skills Program there. Her research interests focus on teaching assistant socialization, communication pedagogy (especially public speaking instruction), and communication skill development.

Martha L. Dewey earned her M.A. at Yale University School of Divinity and is completing her Ph.D. at the University of Illinois. She is currently Director of the Cornell Interactive Theatre Ensemble at Cornell University's Department of Theatre Arts. Her research interests are in history and theory of rhetoric and its application to public communication pedagogy, performance studies, and the intersection of religion and the arts.

ABSTRACT

In this chapter, we report the findings of a study that examined the process of learning how to enact a leadership role. Specifically, we employed Schön's (1983, 1987) model of reflection-in-action to discover and describe the communicative dimensions of peer leader role development. Three experienced teaching assistants assigned to assist with the training and development of groups of new teaching assistants provided the data for our investigation. Transcripts of weekly meetings and open-ended questionnaires were inductively analyzed. Results indicate that individual communicative strategies for experimenting with role enactment reveal tensions in the process of role development.

Although obviously disparate, research on teaching assistant (TA) training and TA role development share at least one common element: the recognition that experienced TAs play an important role in the preparation and development of new TAs. The role that experienced TAs play with new TAs is both formal and informal and pertains to both skill enhancement and identity development (Darling & Dewey, 1990; Staton & Darling, 1989). Regardless of the form or content of the influence, our research and experience document the fact that experienced TAs do participate in the process by which new TAs become the professoriate of tomorrow.

Despite this apparently uncontested fact, almost no research has been conducted to examine the influence that the experience of leadership, formal or informal, has on the individuals acting as leaders. As more and more recommendations about the merit and strength of using experienced TAs in a leadership role are shared (e.g., Sprague & Nyquist, 1989), supervisors of TAs and researchers interested in TA training and development bear the responsibility of examining how these experienced TAs learn and enact their leadership role. The purpose of this chapter is to report the results of one such investigation. A case study approach was used to discover and describe the reflection-in-action in which new leaders engaged during the process of learning and doing the leadership role. Our work is grounded in a perspective of the TA role emphasizing the ongoing professional development of TAs as the "professoriate of tomorrow," and a conception of reflection-in-action that focuses upon communicative behaviors. On a more concrete level, we examined the merit of using experienced TAs as leaders for newer TAs.

TA Role Development

Sprague and Nyquist (1989) recently argued for the examination of TA training from a developmental perspective. TAs, they suggest, move through three phases as they progress toward a career in the academy. Initially, TAs may be usefully conceived of as "senior learners"; upon completion of an undergraduate degree, they are typically skilled and motivated in the arts of learning. For the most part, TAs at this level still identify positively with the student role and do not have as yet any concrete way to conceptualize the teaching role. The second phase occurs after some degree of experience in the TA role has enabled the individual to internalize an apparatus for thinking about teaching. At this level, the "colleague in training" is less likely to align her- or himself with students on a personal basis and is more likely to examine what she or he is doing as a teacher. In the final phase of professional role development, the individual functions as a "junior colleague," having amassed a wide range of experiences in and beliefs about teaching.

Sprague and Nyquist (1989) go on to identify, for each level of an individual's development in the role, the types of relationships with supervisors and other TAs, the types of teaching assignments, the types of training activities, and the functions of evaluation that might be most useful. For example, they suggest that senior learners need to receive information about what is to be done in the role and support and reassurance from more experienced TAs. Existing research on TA training and socialization confirms, at least from the perspective of the new TA, that experienced TAs *do* act as important agents in the role development process (Darling & Dewey, 1990; Staton & Darling, 1989). Research focused on skill development suggests that experienced TAs can be helpful in teaching particular tasks, such as grading and lecturing (Abbott, Wulff & Szego, 1989). Similarly, research on TA socialization indicates that experienced TAs act as important sources of information and support for new TAs in the process of assimilation to the TA role and to the academic department (Darling & Staton, 1989). In such instances as these, experienced TAs are functioning as junior colleagues according to Sprague and Nyquist (1989), because they are assisting in the initial role development of new TAs.

To nurture the formation of teaching skills and dispositions at any particular stage, TA trainers must structure experiences that are uniquely appropriate for that particular stage of development. Sprague and Nyquist (1989) advocate the use of Schön's (1987) "reflective practicum" as an appropriate training activity for the junior colleague whose responsibilities include the orientation, training, and development of new TAs. The reflective practicum features "a setting designed for the task of learning a practice" (p. 37). This setting can be characterized by simulated problems, as in case study analyses, or as Schön states, a reflective practicum can be characterized by "[TAs] taking on real-world projects under close supervision" (p. 37). In an ideal situation, the authors argue, with Schön, that the case study version of the reflective practicum is particularly useful because, "In a practicum with other reflective practitioners, TAs gain experience in articulating and supporting their positions on pedagogical issues" (Sprague & Nyquist, 1989, p. 50). In the real world of the academy, however, numerous investigations reveal that experienced TAs act as training and socialization agents without the benefit of this ideal reflective practicum. Instead, these experienced TAs operate in situations more like the alternative model that Schön describes, the reflective practicum characterized by real-world problems.

We agree with Sprague and Nyquist (1989) that the reflective practicum can function usefully to further the development of individual pedagogical beliefs within and among a group of junior colleagues. We contend, however, that attention primarily devoted to individual pedagogical *beliefs* is shortsighted. We believe it is essential that the reflective practicum attend, as well, to the *activities* in which experienced TAs engage as they strive to fulfill the role of trainer for new TAs. Further, we believe that if we are to understand the development of the junior colleague identity as critically as we have endeavored to understand the senior learner, we must examine naturally occurring concerns and concomitant behaviors that characterize enactment of the junior colleague role. Consequently, in our effort to develop a comprehensive educational experience for junior colleagues, we return to Schön's (1987) conceptualization of reflection as a fruitful place to unite both imperatives.

Reflection-in-Action

Schön (1987) presents a model of action recognizing first that our everyday behavior can and does reveal what we know. TAs, for example, reveal their knowledge of the TA role through behaviors they manifest as they enact that role. As MacKinnon (1987) suggests, such behaviors are often consistent with the TA's level of development. For example, a TA at the level of senior learner might respond to a grade contestation by identifying with the student's personal unhappiness and might strive to alleviate that unhappiness. Contrastingly, a junior colleague might respond to the grade contestation episode as an opportunity for further teaching and strive to provide some concrete assistance to a student who, for example, is having trouble making accurate distinctions or correct applications. Thus, a TA's particular level of development will influence the types of "knowing-in-action" that we might observe in his or her behavior. Put very simply, people do what they know.

When, however, we encounter a novel situation or challenge, such as taking on a new role or a new aspect of a role, our knowing-in-action is transformed into another kind of activity, which Schön (1987) labels "reflection-in-action" and defines as follows: "In *reflection-in-action*, the rethinking of some part of our knowing-in-action leads to on-the-spot experiment and further thinking that affects what we do" (p. 29). To deal with a new role, for which we have not yet developed a repertoire of behaviors and beliefs, we need to think about our actions, experiment with potentially satisfactory types of behaviors, and ultimately assimilate new behaviors and beliefs into our knowing-in-action. In such circumstances, we are engaging in what Schön calls reflection-in-action.

Further, Schön develops two types of reflection-in-action. Individuals might "reflect *on* action" by looking back at a particular performance in order to assess and understand that performance. Video critique of teaching is a tool that MacKinnon (1987) used to get new teachers to reflect on action. Individuals might also "reflect *in* action." In these instances individuals "reflect in the midst of action without interrupting it. In an *action-present* [italics in original] . . . our thinking serves to reshape what we are doing while we are doing it" (p. 26). Smyth (1987) concurs with Schön and suggests further that this reflective process occurs naturally as actors attempt to solve complex social problems such as role enactment. Making conscious attempts to conduct oneself in ways that are consistent with what one believes to be effective action might usefully be considered an example of how we reflect-*in*-action. Using Schön to understand how colleagues in training begin to take on the role of junior colleagues, then, the observer might note the occurrence of reflection-in-action as the TAs (a) identify problematic dimensions of the leadership role, (b) experiment with resolutions to those problems, and (c) establish a new repertoire of behaviors and beliefs for the role, including an ability to behave spontaneously rather than reflectively at the more advanced level of development.

The TA Training Model

The department examined in this research project is large (over 600 undergraduate majors) and part of a large land grant institution with a primary research mission. In this department a researcher/practitioner model was adopted to provide a comprehensive developmental program for the aspiring professoriate. The model embraces a research/practitioner stance in that individuals involved in training are concomitantly involved in research about the character and effectiveness of that training.

Within the department all formal TA training and development occurs within specific course organizations. In this particular report, we focus on research conducted in regard to training for TAs involved with the basic public speaking course. In that course, experienced TAs served in formal positions of leadership; as "peer leaders" (PL) these experienced TAs facilitated the training and development of new TAs. PLs were assigned to work with a specific group ("peer group") of three or four new TAs, meeting regularly throughout the first year of teaching. During the first semester peer groups met on a weekly basis to discuss instructional plans and any individual problems that had occurred or were continuing to occur.

In the process of fulfilling their responsibilities for the development of others, the PLs also experienced, and often attended to, their own development in the new leader role. During the first semester PLs attended weekly meetings with the course director and assistant course director to discuss what was going on in the peer groups and how they might best facilitate individual role development and positively influence instructional effectiveness. During the second semester PLs met with the course director and assistant course director twice a month to talk specifically about course development and revision. Thus, in their capacity as advisers to new TAs and as agents in a course revision process, the PLs in our project were engaging in activities consistent with the junior colleague level of development. The empirical questions guiding our research focused on the reflection-in-action revealed by each PL as he or she made the developmental transition from the role of colleague in training to the role of junior colleague.

Research Questions

Our research was stimulated by recognizing that when experienced TAs were given the title of peer leader, they were stepping into a brand-new role and thus entering a transitional phase of professional development. We were interested in discovering how, during the first semester, they handled the transition from colleague in training (experienced TA) to junior colleague (experienced peer leader).

It seemed appropriate to ask empirical questions about this transition using the reflection-in-action model because in the first semester of enacting the new leadership role, the PLs were likely to engage in reflection-in-action when surprised by novel situations and new challenges (Smyth, 1987). To discover and describe the process of learning and performing the leadership role, we expanded Schön's (1987) conception of reflection-in-action to include expressive communication behaviors. In essence, we examined peer leader reflection-in-action by attending to two particular kinds of leader communication: writing about the peer leader role and speaking within (i.e., while *enacting*) the peer leader role.

In addition, this project provides an examination of the effectiveness of a particular training model. As we examined reflection in the PL role, we were also in a position to examine the extent to which new PLs are in fact adequately prepared to handle the difficult tasks of TA supervision and support. Thus, although this research was primarily about the forms and uses of reflection in a role transition process, it also reveals telling information about how we might effectively, and even ethically, use experienced TAs as PLs.

The primary and general question that we posed was: How is reflection-in-action realized communicatively in the process of role development? To explore that general question we posed the following specific questions:

RQ 1: What does peer leader writing about the role reveal about role development?

RQ 2: What does peer leader speaking within the role reveal about role development?

Methods and Procedures

Data Collection

A qualitative case study (QCS) approach was used to gather the data for this project. As an approach to research, the QCS focuses attention on the collection and analysis of data from naturally occurring and ongoing social activity. The ongoing and naturally occurring experiences of three newly appointed PLs provided the material from which we extracted our data. The QCS also requires that the research be focused on a "specified class of phenomena" (Philipsen, 1982). In this case, the specified class of phenomena was the occurrence of and patterns in reflection-in-action used by new PLs.

Written responses to open-ended questionnaires constituted one source of data. Each PL completed two questionnaires that were used in the analysis.[1] The first questionnaire, completed after the first 6 weeks of enacting the PL role,[2] asked the PL to describe the role and what it meant to her or him. The first questionnaire also asked the PL to describe what was difficult about fulfilling the role and what she or he planned to do to resolve those difficulties. The final questionnaire, completed during the last week of the first semester (approximately 14 weeks into the role), asked the PL to again describe the role and what it meant to her or him. The comparison between the first and last role descriptions allowed us to describe any changes in individuals' conceptualization of the role.

Transcripts of peer group meetings provided a second source of data. Each PL met with her or his peer group once a week throughout the first semester of the academic year. These meetings (13 for each of three groups yielding a total of 39 transcriptions) were audiotaped and professionally transcribed. The transcriptions allowed us to observe, describe, and analyze patterned speaking during role enactment.

Data Analysis

Because the data were collected in the form of narratively written responses to open-ended questions and naturally occurring conversations, we needed appropriate methodological tools with which to identify, extract, and manipulate data from naturally produced discourse. Typological analysis, an analytical procedure developed specifically for the use of data gathered from naturally occurring behavior, was utilized in this investigation. Typological analysis involves the use and development of categories, identification of indicators of the categories, and exploration of relationships between categories (Goetz & LeCompte, 1984). This inductive data analytic technique allows for the use of a theoretically or empirically derived framework as well as the identification and description of new categories and characteristics of categories.

Typological analysis requires that the analyst scan data sources (in this case, narrative responses to questionnaires and tape transcriptions) to identify instances of categories and patterned regularities among categories that might form the basis for explanation. In the present investigation, the phenomena of interest were the occurrence of and the patterns in communicative manifestations of role development. We used the reflection-in-action model as a framework for extracting and codifying units of data from our corpus of material. The reflection model, in other words, provided the initial category scheme that we used to both extract and analyze data.

Descriptive Framework

Consistent with the tenets of typological analysis, then, we drew upon Schön's (1983) model of reflective activity to identify a useful descriptive framework. Schön's initial work on reflection includes a description of the structure of reflection. That structure, he suggests, comprises three distinct but interactive elements. These elements—problem setting, experimentation, and reframing—were used in the present investigation to identify and describe how new PLs reflected in action

Individuals set (or "frame") problems in response to something new or surprising about their situation that is making new demands on the current behavioral repertoire of their knowing-in-action. In other words, a problem is set by an individual based on that particular actor's level of development and unique response to situational demands. In this case, each of our actors was taking on a new role, that of a PL. The particular way that each described the role and problems in fulfilling the role constituted each PL's initial problem setting. They provided this information on the initial questionnaire.

We reviewed each individual response (describing the role and discussing difficulties in fulfilling the role) to establish the initial setting of the problem by each PL. We identified complete ideas (in the form of phrases, sentences, or paragraphs) that represented the PL's unique way of conceptualizing particular dimensions of the role. We summarized each individual's problem set (with its multiple role dimensions) and placed it grammatically in the form of a statement: "The problem of being a peer leader is . . ."

The second element in the reflection-in-action structure is "experimentation." According to Schön (1983), once a problem is set an individual experiments with various ways of acting toward resolution of the problem. We extracted evidence of experimentation in two ways. First, in the initial questionnaire we asked individuals to describe what was difficult about the role and what strategies they planned to use to resolve some of those difficulties. The strategies that PLs described were extracted from the questionnaires and used as templates for observing experimentation in action during peer group meetings. For example, when a PL responded that it was difficult to determine whether the peer group meetings were useful for everyone, that response constituted a statement about the PL's problem setting. When that same individual went on to say that to resolve the difficulty, she or he planned to ask for feedback about the utility of the meetings, that response constituted a strategy to be used as a template for observing the PL's experimentation; we extracted statements that indicated a request or desire for feedback about the usefulness of peer group meetings. In other words, a statement made by a PL during a peer group meeting *only* became data when it reflected a behavior that she or he indicated would be used to respond to the problem of being a PL.

Analyzing transcripts of peer group meetings comprised our second analytic move with regard to experimenting. Here we were interested specifically in identifying the ways in which individuals experimented with enacting the particular role dimensions and the related strategies they had identified in order to resolve problems. Using the individual PL's own description of role dimensions and strategies, we reviewed transcripts and extracted instances in which these were used.

The final structural element of reflection is "resolve," or "reframing" of the initial problem (Schön, 1983). Responses to the final questionnaire, in which individuals provided a second description of the role, constituted evidence that resolve had occurred. Here again, we identified complete and unique statements about the role, and summarized multiple role dimensions into a coherent statement in the form of: "The problem of being a peer leader is . . ."

Results

Our research reveals that reflection-in-action is indeed a useful tool for observing the process of role development. Further, our findings suggest that communicating plays an important role both in role development and in reflection. In this section, we describe the results of our investigation with regard to each of the two research questions.

RQ 1: What Does Peer Leader Writing About the Role Reveal About Role Development?

Sprague and Nyquist (1991), reviewing various models of role development, observe that differences between experts and relative novices in a particular role are often indicated by differences in the types of concerns and dimensions of the role upon which the individual may focus. As we collected and analyzed data in response to our first research question, we tended to concur with the general line of reasoning articulated by Sprague and Nyquist (1991), that is, evidence of role development is constituted by a shift in perspective regarding the role from one of relative simplicity to one of greater complexity.

The reflection-in-action model offers a concrete way to observe and document the types of shifts in perspective that were of interest to us. The reflection process begins with problem setting and ends with resolve (reframing) of the original problem. According to Schön (1987), individuals reframe problems based on new knowledge and/or different ways of thinking about the particular problem. In our project we were interested specifically in communicative evidence of role development. Consequently, we used messages about the problem of being a peer leader (written at the early stage of role enactment) as evidence of the initial level of development. We used the same type of message (written at the end of the semester) to extract data about role development over the course of the semester. Because problem setting and reframing are unique, individual processes, we describe each case separately as we discuss our findings in relation to the first research question.

Cathy. Cathy was a third-year graduate student working on her Ph.D. in organizational communication. Cathy's previous teaching experience included one year (her first year) in the basic public speaking course and one year in a persuasive speaking course. During her time in the department she had achieved recognition as a mature, responsible scholar who cared a great deal about both her teaching and her research. When asked to be a PL, Cathy felt both honored and concerned about whether she would be able to do the job well; before agreeing to take the appointment she requested an additional meeting with the course director to clarify the course director's expectations and the specific duties of the position.

Cathy's initial *problem setting* revealed her persistent concern with the specific tasks of the role. Identification and categorization of Cathy's description of the PL role resulted in three distinct dimensions of the role. According to Cathy, being a PL meant being a resource, a trainer, and a good administrator. Being a resource entailed providing information but at the same time demonstrating that she was "*not* an expert." Cathy was very concerned that as she was not an expert, she should not be perceived as such simply because she had been given a particular appointment and title. Describing herself as "a resource" helped her to set her problem as one of providing information while negating any implication of expertise.

As a trainer, Cathy indicated she was responsible for "allowing creativity within the guidelines" set by course content and policies. She also felt responsible for being a "good listener"; she wanted to listen to the new TAs "share their ideas and encourage them to develop their own ideas." Finally, Cathy described her role as involving administrative duties. Specifically, Cathy wrote about the need to prepare and conduct "well organized, useful meetings." Further, as an administrator she felt responsible for enforcing policies, but "not too strictly."

From her role description and her discussion of particular difficulties with role enactment, we were able to articulate a conclusion about the problem of being a PL for Cathy: *The problem of being a PL is figuring out what her job really entailed.* A closer examination of three dimensions of the role and the difficulties that she had with role enactment revealed that Cathy perceived tensions and opposition in the role that were difficult for her to balance. For example, as the trainer, Cathy saw herself primarily responsible for allowing creativity and listening to people develop their own ideas about how to teach the course. As a good administrator, however, Cathy felt compelled to make sure that everyone operated within the boundaries of legitimacy as set by course policies and content. In addition to these tensions, Cathy wanted to provide useful information without allowing herself to be defined as an expert. For Cathy, then, the initial problem of being a PL was that of figuring out which of these dimensions of the role she was supposed to enact in her role behavior. This dilemma seems very consistent with what we would expect new junior colleagues to experience (Sprague & Nyquist, 1989).

Later in the semester, Cathy's *reframing of the problem* presented a rather different description of PL role enactment. Whereas Cathy previously focused on isolated and opposing dimensions of the role, with an emphasis upon role tasks, she later described the role in a more integrated, holistic way. Cathy's later role description and discussion of enactment difficulties suggested that being a PL means *being a responsible participant in an organizational network* (the course structure and training system). She described the primary responsibilities of role enactment as "attending meetings" to "participate in the processes of course development and TA training." Cathy also described the PL as a "messenger of the course director." As a messenger, a PL is to some degree "caught in the middle"; the PL is responsible for making sure that new TAs learn how to deliver quality instruction to the undergraduates and at the same time needs to help new TAs develop in their own roles by allowing freedom and creativity.

Mary. Mary was also a third-year graduate student working on her Ph.D. in organizational communication. Mary had a great deal of teaching experience and had begun to describe herself as primarily a teacher. While supporting her graduate education, Mary held a teaching assistantship in our department and a part-time appointment in another unit on campus. In addition, Mary taught courses at a local community college. While involved with this research project Mary was job hunting and looking for positions in small liberal arts colleges with an expressed commitment to teaching. Unlike Cathy, Mary did not appear overly concerned about the tasks of the role, and she accepted the position without question.

Mary's *problem setting* revealed that she had concrete ideas about what the role should entail but experienced some difficulty meeting these expectations to her satisfaction. Identification and categorization of Mary's description of the PL role resulted in four dimensions: *facilitator, encourager, helper,* and *autocrat.* As a facilitator, Mary described her role in terms of "answering questions" and functioning as a "sounding board" for the new TAs. She wanted, specifically, to be "laid back" in her role enactment. Her difficulty with this dimension of the role was getting the new TAs to ask questions and articulate problems so that she *could* enact the role of "laid-back facilitator." As an encourager, Mary considered herself responsible for "encouraging new TAs to make their own decisions" about teaching and to recognize that a variety of methods and approaches exist and are worthy of consideration by both the new TAs and herself. Her difficulties with this dimension of the role were similar to those of the facilitator dimension: getting TAs to articulate a decision-making process and to bring a variety of teaching methods and approaches to the meetings.

Mary's description of the PL role also included acting as a "helper." In this dimension of her role, she wanted to answer concrete questions and provide concrete assistance. For example, she wanted to show people where the resources for copying were located and how to get along with the departmental secretaries. She articulated no specific difficulties with this dimension of the role. Finally, Mary described herself as an "autocrat." She stated further that the "autocratic" dimension of her role was necessary rather than desirable and was directly related to the difficulties she had with the dimensions of facilitator and encourager. For example, Mary explained that sometimes in the interest of "efficiency" (i.e., when something had to get done and there was little time to meander) she acted as an autocrat, taking charge of the meeting and agenda. Thus, the autocratic dimension came into play when she felt unable to get people to speak up and share their concerns, "when other means don't work." She stated further that in this dimension of the role she might occasionally be "a bit too brutal with people who want to be told what to do."

From her role description and her discussion of particular difficulties of role enactment, we were able to articulate a conclusion about the problem of being a PL for Mary: *The problem of being a peer leader is controlling the type of participation contributed by new TAs in the peer group.*

Mary's later description of the role and of particular difficulties in enactment is quite different. In *reframing the problem* Mary suggested only two dimensions of the role: *facilitator* and *agent of role development*. The facilitator dimension, as described by Mary, involved (a) providing new TAs with "information that they need, without being prescriptive" about the use of that information and (b) helping the new TAs "organize the different types of information that they receive." Mary also became more conscious of the dimension of her role concerned with the training and development of new TAs. The final phrase in Mary's later discussion of the role is "so, being a PL also is dealing with four other students in some ways." The later role description, then, focused less on the goals of answering new TAs' questions and getting them to ask questions, and focused more instead on her *responsibility for helping new TAs feel confident in their instructional role.*

James. James was a second-year graduate student working on his Ph.D. in cultural studies of communication. During his first year, James did not teach the basic public speaking course but did teach the basic course in speaking and writing. The director of that course recommended that James be appointed as a PL based on his expressed interest in and commitment to teaching. James was thus appointed as a PL for the basic public speaking course during the same semester that he would first teach the course. He accepted the position without seeking any additional information about the role, but he was concerned about his credibility as a PL because of his not actually having taught the public speaking course.

James's initial *problem setting* revealed a focus upon the specific types of activities in which a PL should engage. Our identification and categorization of James's data resulted in two specific dimensions of the role: *supporter* and *fellow learner*. As a supporter, James saw himself as a "friend to talk to" and a provider of "support for the new TAs experience." James's initial discussion of the difficulties of enacting his role revealed his interest in a particular kind of support: "I'm concerned about helping new TAs realize the need to 'speak' and to 'voice' their opinions."

The second dimension of James's role was that of "fellow learner." This dimension of his role was very important to him. For example, he stated emphatically that "I try to remain open to suggestions and opportunities to learn from their experience." He perceived this dimension of his role as somewhat problematic because he felt his belief that a leader could and should learn from group members was fundamentally contradictory to the conception many people had of leader-novice relationships. James's responses to the initial questionnaire indicated that power and culturally shared beliefs about power were important elements in his conceptualization and enactment of the role.

Taken together, James's initial role description and his discussion of difficulties in enacting the role manifested a deep concern with the issue of institutional indoctrination in the training process. Our statement of his problem in being a peer leader takes into account this concern: *The problem of being a PL is discovering how to shape and model a supportive and mutually enriching relationship with the new TAs in my group.*

James's *reframing of the problem* revealed his unique role development. His initial concern with power had evolved into a commitment to particular kinds of personal and professional growth. The reframing of the problem in the final role description focused on his *responsibility for facilitating TA professional development and personal empowerment.* James described how his own professional attitudes and beliefs had developed over the course of the semester such that he found himself "rethinking my own teaching from an administrator's perspective." He stated that he was now aware of the "heavy responsibility" of administering a large course with a training mandate. He also described the role in terms of a responsibility for "empowerment of new TAs." He wanted new TAs to learn how "to articulate their concerns and work to change the system."

RQ 2: What Does Peer Leader Speaking Within the Role Reveal About Role Development?

Our second research question concerned manifestations of the experimenting element of the reflection-in-action process. Experimenting necessarily involves a "reflexive interchange" between the individual and the problematic situation (Schön, 1983, 1987). In this case, the problematic situation involved enacting the PL role during peer group meetings. Our data analysis revealed that individuals developed and used different types of talk for experimenting with role enactment and that patterns in their talk suggested tensions in the role development process. Our initial strategy for data analysis with regard to the second research question was to examine communicative enactment of the particular role dimensions, *as these had been described by the individual actors,* and to look for patterns of transition from the early to the later dimensions. We planned to identify and categorize the different types of talk and organize them in a data matrix to track patterned shifts in the use of particular types of talk. However, early in the data analysis process we realized that our original strategy was flawed.

Initial examination of transcripts of meetings revealed that an individual PL *rarely* used a single type of talk consistent with only the early or only the later role description. We were immediately and profoundly aware of long units of leader monologue (speeches, in essence) in which the individual PL utilized a number of different types of talk, typically representing *both* the early and the later dimensions of the role. James, for example, had initially described one dimension of the role as fellow learner; in transcripts of his meetings, we did see isolated instances in which James explicitly indicated that he was learning (in situ) from members of his peer group (e.g., after sharing his own frustration with the evaluation of student outlines, James responded to a suggestion offered by a new TA: "That's a good idea because we aren't really required to grade their outlines ahead of time"). But it was far more common in the transcripts of all three PLs to observe in a single unit of discourse the use of multiple types of talk representing dimensions of the role from both problem setting (early role description) and reframing (later role description).

Consequently, we modified our strategy for data analysis to attend to (indeed, to embrace) this richly messy pattern of behavior, which appeared to be an important feature of how role development is revealed by *speaking within* a role. We continued the effort to identify single types of talk that revealed role enactment, but instead of extracting them from the context of dialogue in which they occurred, we left them intact and in context, and we turned our focus upon the *patterned use of multiple types of talk* as the phenomenon of interest. We used Lofland and Lofland's (1984) conception of a social practice to discover and describe experimenting with role enactment: "The smallest behavioral unit of a social setting may be envisioned as a social practice, a recurrent category of talk and/or action that the observer focuses on as having analytic significance" (p. 75).

Once particular types of talk had been identified within the discourse in which they were embedded, we began the process of examining how types of talk co-occurred (i.e., talk that always, sometimes, or never followed another type of talk; talk that always occurred in conjunction with another type of talk; talk that never occurred in conjunction with another type of talk). Thus, we used Lofland and Lofland's (1984) scheme for identifying the sequential characteristics of a social practice. The following is a discussion of the unique patterned use of multiple types of talk manifested by each of the three PLs.

Cathy. Analysis of Cathy's transcripts revealed two patterns of talk characteristic of experimenting her role enactment during peer group meetings: *entwining* and *kitchen-sinking*. Entwining was also the *primary* pattern revealed in James's discourse. Thus, in the interest of print space we reserve our discussion of this particular pattern for his case report. Cathy was the only individual who used the pattern we have labeled "kitchen-sinking," a label we borrow from some of the conflict-style literature in an effort to characterize the following pattern: "throwing it all in and hoping something works." As the following examples illustrate, Cathy had a habit of using (in the same unit of discourse) multiple types of talk that were consistent with a number of role dimensions from both of her role descriptions. Further, consistent with the metaphor of "throwing in the kitchen sink," we observed no pattern as to what types of talk would be thrown in when or in relation to what other types of talk.

In our first example, Cathy has chosen to talk with her group members about the probable change in course textbooks for the second semester. In the transcript of this discussion we observed that Cathy moved through a series of different types of talk, beginning with talk revealing the dimension of *resource* (in the capacity of "information provider"). Here Cathy first provided the new TAs with information they wouldn't otherwise know for several months: "Speaking of the book, don't tell this to your students or they will be very angry and I don't blame them . . . because it means they will not be able to sell their texts back." Cathy then moved immediately into talk consistent with the dimension of *good administrator*—with its particular emphasis upon being useful due to organization and preparation: "What I want to give you now is a summary of the changes so that you all don't have to reread the book." Then, immediately, Cathy moved to another type of talk, this time demonstrating (in accordance with her early description of the dimension of *resource*) that although she has provided information she "is *not* an expert": "I don't understand why we just can't change. We're changing textbooks in the middle of the year. I don't think we can change textbooks in the middle of the year. I would just change, but I don't know what the authority structure is here." In this move, Cathy revealed that she was not an expert with regard to two issues: how and when to select a textbook, and how the authority structure for the course was organized. Although both issues concern information that a PL might be expected to know, Cathy for some reason seems committed to revealing her *lack* of knowledge. Cathy's final move in this unit of discourse was to use talk once again consistent with the dimension of the prepared and organized *administrator*, this time systematically pointing out the strengths of the new edition: "Basically, this textbook is a little bit better. There is a section on critical thinking and the examples are better."

We observed several additional examples of kitchen-sinking in Cathy's enactment of the role. In the following lengthy example, as in the one above, Cathy applied multiple types of talk in one discourse unit devoted to a single issue. First, however, Cathy began the meeting with a rather long appeal for volunteers to help write test items that would become part of the course test bank (talk revealing the later dimension of *responsible participant in an organized network*). Immediately following this she introduced the next set of instructional procedures of the course; at this point, she "threw in the kitchen sink." Note especially that she drew from virtually every dimension revealed in her role descriptions, those described during the initial problem setting as well as during the later reframing:

> There's something on every lecture and in some cases there are chapters from books you can look at [*resource*]. . . . Keep in mind, for instance, that if you use these you will want to integrate your own material [*trainer*]. . . . What I'd like to have you do is to check here to indicate what you've got so that we can share [*responsible participant of an organizational network*]. . . . We really want to get people's comments. Like if you loved the listening chapter or if you think this was not good [*responsible messenger of the course director*]. . . . Another suggestion on how to use this, it's probably good to get these things in advance rather than wait until the last minute [*administrator*]. . . . When I copy my rendition I will give it to you and you can make your own rendition [*trainer*]. . . . How are things going for you and are you coming across any problems with the lecture or with the interaction in class? [*trainer*]

Cathy's pattern of kitchen-sinking was unique to her; we did not see evidence of this pattern in either James's or Mary's transcripts. We find the pattern of kitchen-sinking particularly intriguing given Cathy's initial setting of the problem of being a peer leader. Recall that Cathy's early writing about the PL role revealed her concern about the tasks of the role. She was concerned to discover exactly what she was supposed to *do* in the role so that she could enact the role successfully. Perhaps because she was initially unable to develop (to her satisfaction) a concrete "job description," she experimented by utilizing talk consistent with all of the various role dimensions she thought were important. This way of experimenting perhaps enabled her to enact a role that was, at the time, inherently ambiguous. Cathy's later reframing suggested that she was eventually able to tolerate the ambiguity of the role, integrate the various dimensions to some degree, and reconstitute a perspective in which ambiguity itself became an important part of the role—enabling the various members and components of the training network to work together, yet ensuring a measure of individual autonomy.

Mary. We label the predominant pattern in Mary's experimenting *punctuating.* By her own admission, Mary became autocratic when other means for getting the new TAs to talk about their problems (the *facilitator* dimension) or to make their own decisions (the *encourager* dimension) did not work. Our analysis of Mary's transcripts revealed that the dimension of *autocrat* appeared in her discourse as "punctuation"—following either a failed attempt at facilitation or a failed attempt at encouragement. We identified this pattern as punctuation because in the pattern, talk consistent with the dimension of *autocrat* was repeatedly used to bring some kind of closure to a discussion that was begun with talk consistent with two other role dimensions, the *encourager* or *facilitator.* We offer two examples in an effort to clarify this pattern.

In the first example Mary began with talk consistent with the role of the *encourager,* as she tried to get the group of new TAs to analyze a problem presented by one TA: "Think about this just in terms of managing why she was saying why were the grades so low and you respond this is how I grade. Is that really what she is asking?" Notice how Mary has not declared, in any authoritative manner, what should be done or what might be properly interpreted from the situation under discussion. Instead, she was trying to get the new TAs to make and examine their own decisions about what might be happening in the classroom. This talk fails to provoke TA decision making, however, and after one brief comment from a new

TA Mary falls back upon talk (consistent with the *autocrat* dimension) that she had described in her early writing about the role: "The first thing is, first of all I would have said in general I grade it and the grades were as low as you guys performed. If you want more information, you'll have to see me one-on-one. Never ever, ever try to justify your grading. I don't think you should ever justify your grading in front of the whole class." Here, Mary has stopped trying to get the new TAs to analyze the situation for themselves; instead, she presents her own definition, offers a plan of action, and provides a rationale for that plan—none of which appear open for further group discussion or debate.

We see the same pattern again in a later transcript. As before, Mary was unable to get the type of response that she wanted from talk consistent with the dimension of *encourager*. In this situation, Mary had wanted the new TAs to consider the inadequacy of the critique sheets. She had set up a discussion by directing their attention to (what was for her) a glaring deficiency. At several points in this leader monologue (a "speech" that continues for two pages in the transcript) she had tried to elicit a response from them (the dimension of *encourager*). Failing this, she gave up and concluded the discussion (in the dimension of *autocrat*) by directly mandating the task and warning of the consequences of failure to follow through: "Now if you look very closely at the criteria sheet there is no way you can use this criteria sheet to grade a panel presentation, right? . . . Look at the criteria sheet real carefully. . . . So make sure that you go over these criteria seriously before the group presentations and understand how you're going to grade the groups and things like that."

James. James's transcripts revealed not only relatively simple applications of types of talk (consistent with solitary dimensions of the role) like the one described earlier, but also complex applications in which multiple types of talk were present in a patterned way. We observed that James attempted to balance a few specific types of talk (consistent with particular role dimensions) by shifting from one to another during role enactment in a pattern of alternation (rather like the activity of weaving) that was repeated during the course of the semester. We label this pattern *entwining*. James's pattern of entwining incorporated talk consistent with one early role dimension (the *fellow learner*) and with both later role dimensions (*professional development* and *personal empowerment*).

In the middle of the fourth transcript James began a long "speech" with talk that was administrative in tone (revealing the later role dimension of *professional development*). Here James was setting forth, as if from some hierarchical position of authority, the way oral critiques "should be done" by the TAs (when in fact there was no such policy for any particular way to manage the oral critique of speeches): "So you can collect the cards and give the cards to the speaker on the same day and give your own critique sheet the following day. There might be discrepancies. . . . You can even talk about the discrepancies between your observation and the class's observation." At this point in the speech, we observed a sudden shift to a new type of talk consistent with a different role dimension, the thought-provoking voice of *personal empowerment*. The shift in "tone" was striking; whereas James was previously mandating policy (a policy that did not, in fact, exist), he was now *encouraging* the TAs to become intellectually engaged in the decision-making process: "It's one thing to say it's an advantage to know later on people will write about the speeches. . . . It's another thing to say that when you know you're critiquing other people ultimately you will be critiqued. . . . See what I'm trying to say? Obviously there will be a lot of overpraising, but then our aim is not to get expertise opinions from them just to engage them in the process." The speech is finally brought to a close through the voice of the *fellow learner:* "You know, *I've* done something like that before but it wasn't very successful . . . but that stuff happens."

In Transcript 9, the pattern of entwining was observed again, but this time the voice of the *fellow learner* is absent. As in the fourth transcript, James begins a rather long speech with the administrative voice (*professional development*): "That's really good and I think I'll let [the course director] know and reflect that." In the ensuing discussion of different types of teachers, James made a gradual shift to the encouraging (even proselytizing) voice of *personal empowerment:* "That is why I need your input to bring a different perspective." At this moment, James was trying to get the new TAs to voice their opinions; however, we observed no such sharing of opinions by the TAs. We did observe, instead, that James rapidly concluded the speech in the administrative voice: "Come up with one assignment that will help you achieve that goal. . . . Then I can let the course director see it too."

The pattern of entwining talk seemed interesting to us, given the emphasis upon power in James's problem setting. James's entwining of talk revealing an administrative tone (*professional development*) and talk consistent with either the *fellow learner* or with *personal empowerment* is intriguing for two reasons. First, given James's expressed concern about institutionalized power, it makes sense that he would be uncomfortable with a primarily administrative approach to the leadership role. In his experimenting, we might say that James drew upon a collection of role behaviors and played them off against each other in ways that he might consider both professionally responsible *and* personally palatable. We suspect that James achieved a satisfying balance in alternating (weaving in and out of) the authoritative voice of the administrator with the friendly voice of the fellow learner and/or the provocative voice of one who seeks to empower his listeners.

Second, we find the pattern of entwining interesting because during the course of the semester, we witnessed the gradual disappearance of talk consistent with the dimension of *fellow learner*. Thus, in the last transcript revealing James's experimenting, the pattern of entwining incorporated only the dimensions of *professional development* and *personal empowerment*, which were the only dimensions of the role described in his written reframing of the role.

Conclusions and Discussion

In this project we employed a QCS approach to discover and describe communicative manifestations of PL role development. We utilized Schön's (1983, 1987) model of reflection-in-action to facilitate the descriptive process. Our research suggests that PL *writing about* the role and *speaking within* the role revealed distinct patterns of role development. Consistent with Philipsen's (1982) two dimensions of a QCS, our work is both descriptive and analytical. We used descriptive data to "test the soundness of extant claims" (p. 11) and to "construct and test descriptive frameworks" (p. 13).

Two specific conclusions are warranted by this research. First, expansion of the reflection-in-action model to include expressive communicative behaviors was, indeed, useful. MacKinnon (1987) and Schön (1983, 1987) both tend to characterize reflection-in-action as primarily a cognitive process during which an individual *thinks* about what she or he has done or is planning to do. Although we would not disagree that thought plays an important role in the reflective process, our research suggests that the reflective process also occurs in expressive communication, both in describing to others what behaviors will or might be enacted in a role and in the actual enactment of the role through talk—through the *speaking within* the role. Therefore, one important conclusion of this project is that reflection is an expressive as well as cognitive process. This conclusion is supported by recent research on the cognitive development of children that suggests that learning is enhanced when individuals "have rich opportunities for reflective conversation" (Garner, 1990, p. 524).

A second conclusion of this research is that the reflection-in-action model provided a useful framework for discovering and describing the way that role development naturally occurred for three PLs. Using Schön's (1983, 1987) model of reflection, we were able to document specific dimensions of the role and to track role development over the course of the semester. Further, we were able to describe individual patterns in experimenting with particular role dimensions during role enactment, discovering that PL talk suggested tensions in the process of role development.

The specific patterns revealed in the enactment of the role are not as empirically interesting as the fact *of* the patterns—that is, we do not assert that kitchen-sinking, punctuating, or entwining represent a topology of the ways that experimentation occurs for new PLs. We do assert, however, that assimilating and accommodating new role behaviors are not linear processes of learning and applying new skills. Instead, these data suggest that as individuals invent new role behaviors for themselves they do so in the context of role tension; beliefs about what the role *is* pull against newly developed ideas about what the role *might be.* This tension is revealed in the fact that for each PL experimentation *always* involved combining behaviors consistent with early role description with behaviors consistent with the newer, more emergent role description. Such tension patterns are consistent with a constructivist approach to education in which individuals are encouraged to investigate, invent, and create their own problems and solutions (Fosnot, 1989).

Beyond the empirical contributions of this research lie some very pragmatic, and in some ways troubling, observations. Not at all surprising, new PLs do not always do or say the right things. They do not act in ways that we (the course supervisors) would consider to be consistent with effective supervision and support. In fact, in several instances (many of which were documented in this chapter; others were not) these PLs said and did things that were antithetical to good teaching as well as good supervision and support. Although we can agree philosophically with the effectiveness of a learning-by-doing approach to leadership training, we must also consider questions of cost. Is it "okay" for new TAs to be placed in the relatively unprepared hands of colleagues in training or junior colleagues? Or should we not use these individuals until they are well into the junior colleague level of their own role development? Can the junior colleague role be adequately developed without (i.e., prior to) such leadership experiences? These are questions that became very evident in the progress of analyzing these data. They are questions for which we have no answers.

This project suggests several directions for subsequent research. We became intrigued by the difference between the orderly reflection characteristic of written discourse and the more chaotic (but perhaps more interesting) reflection characteristic of oral discourse. We might benefit from examining this difference in more detail, posing questions about the consequences of using one type of communicative expression more than the other in our research and theorizing about the reflective process.

Notes

1. Six weeks into the semester the PLs were asked to respond in writing to the following questions: "Please describe yourself as a leader (e.g., What kind of leader are you? How do you approach your leadership role?)" and "Please list and describe the aspects of your role that have been most difficult to accomplish. Discuss what has made those things difficult and how you plan to resolve the difficulties." At the end of the semester the PLs were asked to respond in writing to the following question: "Imagine that a friend who is not a peer leader has just asked you to describe what being a peer leader means for you. What would you say to that person?"

2. We waited until the sixth week of semester to ensure a reflective and informed response to the question. Prior to the sixth week these individuals had been, quite literally, bombarded with meetings, paperwork, lessons to plan, meetings to plan, and so forth. We allowed time for that activity to subside and for them to have some relatively stable time in the role before asking them to describe their experiences and problems in the role.

References

Abbott, R. D., Wulff, D. H., & Szego, C. K. (1989). Review of research on TA training. In J. D. Nyquist, R. Abbott, & D. Wulff (Eds.), *Teaching assistant training in the 1990's* (pp. 111-124). San Francisco: Jossey-Bass.

Darling, A. L., & Dewey, M. L. (1990). Teaching assistant socialization: An examination of communication experiences with peer leaders. *Teaching and Teacher Education, 6,* 315-326.

Darling, A. L., & Staton, A. Q. (1989). Socialization of graduate teaching assistants: A case study in an American university. *International Journal of Qualitative Studies in Education, 2,* 221-235.

Fosnot, C. T. (1989). *Inquiring teachers, inquiring learners.* New York: Teachers College Press.

Garner, R. (1990). When children and adults do not use learning strategies: Toward a theory of settings. *Review of Educational Research, 60,* 517-529.

Goetz, J. P., & LeCompte, M. D. (1984). *Ethnography and qualitative design in educational research.* Orlando, FL: Academic Press.

Lofland, J., & Lofland, L. (1984). *Analyzing social settings: A guide to qualitative observation and analysis.* Belmont, CA: Wadsworth.

MacKinnon, A. M. (1987). Detecting reflection-in-action among preservice elementary science teachers. *Teaching and Teacher Education, 3,* 135-145.

Philipsen, G. (1982). The qualitative case study as a strategy in communication inquiry. *Communicator, 12,* 71-84.

Schön, D. A. (1983). *The reflective practitioner: How practitioners think in action.* New York: Basic Books.

Schön, D. A. (1987). *Educating the reflective practitioner.* San Francisco: Jossey-Bass.

Smyth, W. J. (1987). Cinderella syndrome: A philosophical view of supervision as a field of study. *Teachers College Record, 88,* 567-588.

Sprague, J., & Nyquist, J. D. (1989). TA supervision. In J. D. Nyquist, R. Abbott, & D. Wulff (Eds.), *Teaching assistant training in the 1990's* (pp. 15-22). San Francisco: Jossey-Bass.

Sprague, J., & Nyquist, J. D. (1991). A developmental perspective on the TA role. In J. D. Nyquist, R. D. Abbott, D. H. Wulff, & J. Sprague (Eds.), *Preparing the professoriate of tomorrow to teach* (pp. 295-312). Dubuque, IA: Kendall-Hunt.

Staton, A. Q., & Darling, A. L. (1989). Socialization of teaching assistants. In J. D. Nyquist, R. Abbott, & D. Wulff (Eds.), *Teaching assistant training in the 1990's* (pp. 15- 22). San Francisco: Jossey-Bass.

Communication:
Reflections and Implications

Cassandra L. Book

In the introduction to this division, I described communication as a dynamic process in which the participants have the opportunity to influence and be influenced by their interaction. I identified functions of communication that have implications for the goals of teacher and student interaction in the classroom. A model of communication competency suggested that teachers, like all communicators, need a repertoire of communication skills and strategies from which they choose, given the context, the audience (students), and the outcomes to be accomplished. I proposed that teachers as communicators need to be skillful in implementing and then assessing their communication, and I presented specific communication behaviors that have been linked to student achievement and behavioral change, as well as attitude and motivation. It is against this backdrop that I now examine the three chapters included in this division.

Communicating and Teaching:
Applied Communication Theory for Teacher Educators

Jacobs, in Chapter 7, is concerned about change in the schools and the impact a theory of communication can have on teachers' and administrators' abilities to bring about change. Although the chapter is targeted for teacher educators, the author argues that the inclusion of the study of communication is important for prospective teachers, especially as they try to make sense of the interactions in their classrooms. His characterization of communication is compatible with that proposed in the introduction to this division. He augments his analysis by incorporating Dewey's (1916) point that "To be a recipient of communication is to have an enlarged and changed experience. One shares in what another has thought and felt and in so far, meagerly or amply, has his own attitude modified. Nor is the one who communicates left unaffected" (p. 5). Thus, Jacobs amplifies the nature of communication as transactional and posits this as a theory for examining one's communication with students.

Jacobs also highlights the professional responsibility of teachers for understanding the theory and practice of communication and thus the importance of teachers taking responsibility for improving their communication. This point takes the communication competence model described in the introduction a step further by arguing for the ethical responsibility of the teacher to critically examine his or her communication.

The metaphors that Jacobs describes provide lenses for thinking about classrooms, school reform, and teaching. They are interesting and may broaden one's repertoire of frameworks for considering communication. However, it is unlikely that these metaphors would enhance one's communication skills. Nonetheless, Jacobs rightfully focuses the reader's attention on ways of examining communication and to that end enhances the probability that prospective teachers will think more carefully about the interactions among students, colleagues, and administrators in schools.

The value of this chapter rests in the author's commitment to the value of prospective teachers having and understanding at least one theory of communication and using that theory to examine the interactions with students and others in the school context. Although his description of hermeneutics and metaphors may seem ethereal, his characterization of the transactional, dynamic process called communication provides a sound basis against which to consider the complexity of communication in the classroom and the school reform effort.

Evaluating Communication Skills of Students in Teacher Education

Hess and Short, in Chapter 8, focus on the interpersonal communication skills they propose are useful for teachers and demonstrate that such skills can be taught, assessed, and improved through university coursework. They specifically indicate that teachers should "recognize the importance of communication and have some expertise in the needed skills." Thus, they share the perspective of the introduction and the point of view of Jacobs. They also recognize that "good communication is a process requiring judgment and timing as well as knowledge and comprehension of the ideas involved" and that the prospective teachers have "varied levels of skill given their different family and social backgrounds." This, too, demonstrates a consistency with the notion that communication is specific to the context and individuals involved, as well as with the idea that effective implementation of communication skills is dependent on making judgments based on analysis of the situation.

These authors seem to take a psychological approach to communication, particularly in their attention to empathy and listening skills. Although these skills are important and related to effective communication skills identified by Rubin and Feezel (1986) as cited in Nussbaum (1992) and some of the clarity literature, it would be useful to more fully examine the nature of the communication skills taught and assessed in the course offered by Hess and Short. It might be particularly valuable to determine the relationship between students' improvement on the communication skills measured in the Communication Skills Inventory (CSI) and those measured in the Communication Competency Assessment Instrument (CCAI) or communication skills that have been demonstrated to be related to cognitive and behavioral learning and affective response, such as teacher immediacy and clarity. Because the authors do not provide enough information about exactly what communication skills are taught in the interpersonal communication course or how they are practiced and assessed, it is difficult to know if the prospective teachers are given the opportunity to (a) build their communication repertoire, (b) establish and use criteria for making judgments about which strategies to use, (c) practice implementing their skills and receiving feedback on their effectiveness, and (d) evaluate their own perception of their effectiveness and propose means of modifying their communication behaviors in a subsequent event.

Finally, it is not surprising that the students in the study did not change their ratings of their own ability to communicate with others. It appears that this inventory assesses the students' knowledge of selected communication skills and their ability to choose from a series of options the best response to a question that would demonstrate empathy or ability to paraphrase what had been said. However, performance on such a paper-and-pencil test should not be perceived as a substitute for actual ability or inclination to effectively use such skills. Even if these students were successful in responding to the open-ended questions, writing a response is still a different skill from spontaneously providing an appropriate oral response. Once again, the limited skills attended to in this inventory may not extend students' confidence in their overall communication competence.

The value of this study is that it demonstrates a valuing for communication skills needed by teachers and models that university coursework can provide a salient vehicle for preparing prospective teachers. It may be useful to extend the nature of the communication skills studied in this course and subsequently assessed to include those demonstrated to be related to positive cognitive and behavioral learning as well as positive affective response. On the other hand, it may be that this study can provide the baseline data for comparing scores on the CSI with other inventories or measures of effective classroom communication. In addition, it may be useful for faculty in this communication course to examine the impact of the communication skills of the prospective teachers on various ethnic groups and to consider the context specific nature of communication within their instruction.

Reflection in Leadership:
An Examination of Peer Leader Role Development

Darling and Dewey, in Chapter 9, posit that experienced teaching assistants (TAs) play a significant role in the development of beginning TAs and that as the senior TAs take on this leadership role, their understanding of the role and their enactment of it evolves. By use of a qualitative case study method, these researchers provide insight into the role development of several senior TAs through their analysis of the TAs' written responses to open-ended questionnaires as well as transcripts of audiotaped conversations of the TAs' reflections about their roles. Schön's theoretical perspective on reflection-in-action provided the framework for examining the TAs' role development, but these authors went beyond Schön's concept of thinking about what one has done or plans to do to examining the TAs' written and oral expressions of what they have done or plan to do. They examined both the development of the TAs' repertoire of behaviors as well as their beliefs about what new behaviors were needed in their new roles.

This chapter is a wonderful illustration of the relationship of communication and leadership and how change occurs as one communicates about his or her experimentation with new behaviors. The questions raised about what writing about a role and speaking within a role can reveal about role development could be adapted to examining how experienced teachers take on the mentoring role with prospective or first-year teachers. In addition, these questions and the methodology could be used to help novice teachers explore their own development as teachers.

Clearly the perspective taken by Darling and Dewey is consistent with that described in the introduction to this division in that they recognize and value reflection on one's communication. They go further than the introduction to provide another theoretical perspective on reflection-in-action as distinct from reflection-on-action. This more sophisticated analysis provides a useful way of thinking and talking about role development and communication competence development. The authors' conclusion that "these data suggest that as individuals invent new role behaviors for themselves they do so in the context of role tension; beliefs about what the role *is* pull against newly developed ideas about what the role *might be*" also gives guidance for the novice teacher and the teacher mentor. It would be useful to examine how persons in these roles define the role tensions and how they expand their communication repertoires to accommodate the needs of the situations. This chapter has heuristic value for the conceptualization of other research questions pertinent to the use of communication in leadership and change.

Conclusion

Communication is pertinent, indeed critical, to the role of teachers at all levels. Attention to the communication behaviors that make a difference in the cognitive and behavioral learning and affective response of students is needed and should be incorporated into the preparation of preservice or beginning teachers. Teachers should be made aware of the impact of their communication behaviors on different ethnic groups and should work to enhance their communication competence by broadening their communication repertoire, considering criteria for selecting strategies and behaviors appropriate for the situation, effectively implementing their communication skills, and reflecting upon their communication during and after the event. Helping teachers to consider the functions their communication serves and the possible interferences with their messages being properly perceived is an important role of teacher education, along with facilitating the overall disposition to value communication as a transactional, dynamic process. Leadership of school reform, change in the way in which students are taught, and overall enhancement of the teaching-learning paradigm profits from an understanding of communication theory, positive attitude toward engaging in communication, and a willingness to improve communication skills.

References

Dewey, J. (1916). *Democracy and education.* New York: Free Press.

Nussbaum, J. F. (1992). Effective teacher behaviors. *Communication Education, 41,* 167-180.

Rubin, R. B., & Feezel, J. D. (1986). Elements of teacher communication competence. *Communication Education, 35*(3), 254-268.

DIVISION IV

Curriculum for Leadership and Change

CURRICULUM: OVERVIEW AND FRAMEWORK

Kenneth A. Sirotnik

Kenneth A. Sirotnik is Professor and Chair of Educational Leadership and Policy Studies in the College of Education at the University of Washington. His research, teaching, and other professional activities range widely over many issues, including measurement, statistics, evaluation, technology, educational policy, organizational change, and school improvement. Among his latest books are *The Moral Dimensions of Teaching* (co-edited with John Goodlad and Roger Soder) and *Understanding Educational Statistics* (co-authored with James Popham).

What do we mean by *leadership,* let alone *teacher* leadership? Is leadership any different in principle for teachers from what it is for administrators?

How realistic is the notion of teacher leadership given the conditions and circumstances that continue to prevail in most schools? Even if conditions were more favorable, would teachers want roles or responsibilities that extend beyond the doors of their classrooms? Notwithstanding the answers to (or, more likely, the debate on) these and other questions, what *should be* the role and responsibility of the teacher in today's and tomorrow's schools? What, then, are the implications of queries such as these for a curriculum of "teacher leadership"?

I can only briefly address these questions by way of setting a context for the several chapters to follow. At the end of these chapters, I will conclude with some reactions and further thoughts on the question of a leadership curriculum.

Leadership and Teacher Leadership

Several years ago, the faculty in educational leadership and policy studies in the College of Education at the University of Washington long deliberated on how to define or characterize "leadership." Many of us involved in these discussions were quite familiar with the previous decades of literature—which is still burgeoning—on leadership and organizational behavior. Yet, after all of our good scholarly debate and conversation, we were unable to come up with anything more creative, useful, or precise than this: Leadership is the exercise of significant and responsible influence. I suspect that this definition is as good as (or no worse than) any.

I also suspect that it is sensible not to define leadership in any more specific terms. It is an elusive concept at best, and it requires a good deal of contextual interpretation and constructed meanings in particular settings; at particular times; for particular purposes, issues, and actions. Yet the above definition, as vague as it might be, contains three key words: *exercise, significant,* and *responsible.* (*Influence* is also a key word, but ordinary dictionary definitions will do, e.g., the power to affect/sway/persuade people and/or direct/alter courses of events.) The word "exercise" is intended to convey a deliberate, decision-oriented, acting-taking concept of leadership (in contrast to a passive, laissez-faire type of notion). The word "significant" is meant to signal that leadership is not without substance, not without a content of importance. For example, although always a matter of judgment, influencing decisions about teachers' access to supply cabinets is arguably less significant than influencing decisions pertaining to students' access to knowledge and the structures and practices (e.g., tracking and ability grouping) that affect it. By "significant," therefore, I am also intending to convey the broader idea of *instructional* (or, even better, *pedagogical*) leadership.

Perhaps most important is the word "responsible." Embedded in this word is the moral core that derives from the tacit agreement entered into by educators by virtue of an occupation directed at significantly and profoundly influencing the lives of children and youth. In fact, it is this agreement (and the attendant moral obligations) that constitutes the essential warrant for arguing that the occupation is a *profession* (Soder, 1990). In other words, attempts to professionalize teaching by comparing it to medicine, law, and the like will never be persuasive. Rather, the argument must rest on the moral imperatives that flow directly from the responsibilities to care for and educate the young. And the impact of these responsibilities can increase substantially as leadership extends beyond the classroom.

A curriculum for educating teachers for leadership and change, therefore, must attend not only to definitions of leadership but also to the moral and ethical content and actions that ground the professional work of educators.

Coming Out of the Classroom

It has been my experience working in principal preparation programs and with educators involved in decentralized decision-making efforts and new leadership roles that the "we-they," "us versus them" syndrome is alive and well between teachers and administrators. Teachers preparing to be principals often report feelings/perceptions of estrangement from their colleagues once they move out of the classroom and into an internship role. Similar experiences have been reported by classroom teachers moving into structured school leadership roles (Wasley, 1991).

There are undoubtedly many possible explanations for the "we-they" attitudes: oppressive accountability frameworks, conflict of interests between "workers" and "management," different worldviews of academic and administrative domains, narrow conceptions and constructions of roles, and more. But whatever the reasons, little headway will be made in expanding leadership roles if leadership continues to be excessively role bound and the privilege of a few. To be sure, there will remain differentials in leadership domains between teachers and between teachers and administrators. Yet, in more fundamental respects, core issues and dilemmas in leadership in educational organizations will obtain in both domains.

A curriculum for educating teachers for leadership and change, therefore, must attend not only to the connections and conflicts in teaching and administrative roles—issues of *transactional* leadership—but also to the common values, purposes, and human interests that rise above organizational hierarchy—issues of *transformative* leadership (Burns, 1978).

The "Real World" of Today's Schools

So when and how does all this leadership and change take place? During what part of teachers' ordinary workdays do they "exercise significant and responsible influence" beyond that exercised as a matter of course in their classrooms—during 30-minute lunches, 7-minute passing periods between classes, monthly faculty meetings, yearly inservice days . . . ? Clearly, the conditions and circumstances of today's schools could not have been more deliberately designed to prevent expanded leadership opportunities. In the few evaluative studies of the few schools that have attempted significant restructuring of leadership and decision-making responsibilities, teachers routinely report two things: feelings of general satisfaction with expanded leadership roles, and feelings of specific frustration, stress, and strain due to the time demands of these roles and the time taken away from their first order of business—classroom teaching (Malen, 1993; Smylie, 1994).

Continuing this line of frustrating questions: What is the past record of success with efforts to fundamentally change and improve schools? To what extent has classroom teaching and learning changed substantially over the last 100 years? Will educators, policy makers, and others ever take heed of the lessons learned many times over from the history of educational change and school improvement? Whether we argue epistemologically (in relation to the nature and use of knowledge in action), organizationally (in relation to the impact of differing conceptions and metaphors that guide images of schools and schooling), or experientially (in relation to the findings from postmortems of past attempts at school reform), we are led to the same conclusion (Sirotnik, 1989): People who live and work in complex organizations like schools need to be thoroughly and continually involved as knowledge producing and using agents in their own improvement efforts, if significant and enduring organizational change is the purpose we have in mind.

A curriculum for educating teachers for leadership and change, therefore, must be realistic and frank, both with respect to the present arrangements of work in schools and to the fairly radical changes that would be necessary to overcome many of these organizational barriers. What I have in mind is a brutally honest yet sanguine curriculum that mirrors Sarason's (1990) critical yet hopeful analysis in his book *The Predictable Failure of Educational Reform: Can We Change Course Before It's Too Late?*

Leadership—Who Wants It?

I have a cartoon pinned on the wall in my office of a flock of geese in V-formation—except the head goose has smashed against the spire of a tall building, feathers flying everywhere. The caption reads: "The hazards of leadership."

These days, it seems, there are fewer people, or at least fewer capable people, who are willing to take on the role of administrator, particularly the principalship in secondary schools and the superintendency in the larger school districts. The increasingly litigious nature of schooling; the interesting but difficult problems of growing diversity and pluralism; the highly politicized climate created by few, but vocal, special interests; and the relatively resource-poor and/or resource-uneven environment are among the many factors that make a difficult job even more so.

But the "hazards of leadership" are even more complicated for class-room teachers. I suspect that Lortie's (1975) seminal analysis two decades ago holds true today for many (not all) teachers: "Conservatism, individualism, and presentism are significant components in the ethos of American classroom teachers" (p. 212). Teachers have been well socialized into the classroom domain of their responsibility by their own 13-year apprenticeships as K-12 students, their teacher education programs, and their first several years of experiences on the job. Although perhaps some are desirous for "more power," all teachers have tremendous autonomy behind the classroom door. Coming out of the classroom in visible and collaborative leadership roles and responsibilities presents the threat of, as well as the professional opportunity for, broader work and more public accountability.

One of my current doctoral students is completing a comparative case study of several schools involved in more and less intense restructuring efforts toward site-based decision making. The focus of her study is on power, particularly teachers' use (and nonuse) of power in their response to organizational changes requiring their participation outside of class-room teaching. Preliminary analyses suggest, among other things, that teachers who are able to build a sense of efficacy through collaborative work tend to participate in restructuring efforts; those who tend not to participate, or who deliberately undermine these efforts, find efficacy only in their individual authority and autonomy in the classroom (C. Reed, personal communication, April 27, 1994).

A curriculum for educating teachers for leadership and change, therefore, will have to deliberately challenge the parameters of power that teachers come to sense through the socialization processes of their work in schools. This curriculum will need to pay careful attention to the ways in which terms like "power" and "empowerment" are tossed around in these days of "restructuring," with particular focus not only on denotations and connotations, but also on the diverse assumptions underlying the advocacy of "teacher power" by various constituencies (Johnson, 1990).

From "Is" to "Ought"

Notwithstanding the above issues concerning the way things are for teachers in schools, what *should* the work of teachers be like? This is not a question that can be settled empirically. This is a question that compels us to return to the moral core of our business, that of public schooling in a constitutional democracy. Obviously, this introduction is not the place to thoroughly explicate this matter. I will necessarily be brief.

When my colleagues and I (Goodlad, Soder, & Sirotnik, 1990) explored what we called "the moral dimensions of teaching," we began by asking:

> What are public schools for in a democratic society? What *should* they be for, and for whom? Whose interests are served and whose *should be* served in a system of compulsory education? What is the nature of the relationship between the interests of the individual, the family, the community, the state, and society? Are there reasoned answers to these and like questions, or is there just an assortment of value positions, each as "good" as the other? Or, to put it another way, are there not fundamental normative positions derived from moral and ethical argument that serve to ground appropriate answers to crucial educational questions such as these? (p. ix)

Critical and constructive inquiry, and the willingness and skills to do it, would seem to be prerequisite to a participatory democracy; and among the oft-stated purposes of schooling is the enculturation or socialization of our future voting citizens so that they can make intelligent and responsible decisions. This may often involve challenging the status quo and asking hard questions like those above.

Embedded in the above sentences are the elements of leadership that I mentioned initially—the exercise of significant and responsible influence. It is hard for me to imagine a curriculum of critical inquiry for students constructed and delivered by educators unwilling or unable to engage in the process themselves. Sarason (1990) makes a similar point:

> Whatever factors, variables, and ambiance are conducive for the growth, development, and self-regard of a school's staff are precisely those that are crucial to obtaining the same consequences for students in a classroom. To focus on the latter and ignore or gloss over the former is an invitation to disillusionment. (p. 152)

A curriculum for educating teachers for leadership and change, therefore, should be a major part of the curriculum for teacher education generally. Whether in formal leadership roles or not, the exercise of significant influence over the lives of children carries with it the moral obligation to argue responsibly about how this influence will be manifested. Such argument will necessarily be rooted in tensions among values, beliefs, and human interests as they play out in our political democracy. One might think that such a curriculum was obvious and commonplace in teacher education programs. Unfortunately it is not (Sirotnik, 1990).

Three Research Reports

The chapters to follow are quite diverse and come at the idea of a leadership curriculum from very different angles. Taken together, they address and extend some of the questions and concerns that I have outlined above. In Chapter 10, Kowalski discusses the enduring conditions and circumstances of the workplace that present difficult obstacles to the whole idea of expanded leadership roles for teachers. He is optimistic, however, that a curriculum of "teacher professionalism," one that includes discussions of value tensions, knowledge bases, and teacher autonomy, can help break through these organizational barriers.

Ponzio and Fisher, in Chapter 11, use the disciplined ways of knowing embedded in a view of science curriculum as the window through which teacher leadership can be explored. Following the more recent trend (but certainly not a new idea) of viewing teaching and learning as a constructed process—knowing and reknowing as an interaction between discipline and experience—these authors extrapolate important implications for leadership: teachers as reflective practitioners and preparation that starts well before formal training.

Finally, in Chapter 12, Alley and Jung take us back to the future by reminding us that there is a future with which to be concerned and for which to be prepared. Their discussion illustrates how difficult it is to predict the future and the moral tension between merely predicting it and actively creating it.

References

Burns, J. M. (1978). *Leadership*. New York: Harper & Row.

Goodlad, J. I., Soder, R., & Sirotnik, K. A. (Eds.). (1990). *The moral dimensions of teaching*. San Francisco: Jossey-Bass.

Johnson, S. M. (1990). Teachers, power and school change. In W. H. Clune & J. F. Witte (Eds.), *Choice and control in American education* (Vol. 2, pp. 343-370). Philadelphia, PA: Falmer.

Lortie, D. (1975). *School teacher: A sociological study*. Chicago: University of Chicago Press.

Malen, B. (1993). "Professionalizing" teaching by expanding teachers' roles. In S. J. Jacobson & R. Berne (Eds.), *Reforming education: The emerging systemic approach* (pp. 43-65). Thousand Oaks, CA: Corwin.

Sarason, S. B. (1990). *The predictable failure of educational reform: Can we change course before it's too late?* San Francisco: Jossey-Bass.

Sirotnik, K. A. (1989). The school as the center of change. In T. J. Sergiovanni & J. H. Moore (Eds.), *Schooling for tomorrow: Directing reforms to issues that count* (pp. 89-113). Boston: Allyn & Bacon.

Sirotnik, K. A. (1990). On the eroding foundations of teacher education. *Phi Delta Kappan, 71*, 710-716.

Smylie, M. A. (1994). Redesigning teachers' work: Connections to the classroom. In L. Darling-Hammond (Ed.), *Review of Educational Research, 20*, 129-177.

Soder, R. (1990). The rhetoric of teacher professionalization. In J. I. Goodlad, R. Soder, & K. A. Sirotnik (Eds.), *The moral dimensions of teaching* (pp. 35-86). San Francisco: Jossey-Bass.

Wasley, P. A. (1991). *Teachers who lead: The rhetoric of reform and the realities of practice*. New York: Teachers College Press.

10 Preparing Teachers to Be Leaders: Barriers in the Workplace

Theodore J. Kowalski

Theodore J. Kowalski is Professor of Educational Leadership at Ball State University. He is the author of numerous articles and ten books, the most recent of which is *Contemporary School Administration* (1993). His research interests include organizational behavior and teacher-administrator relationships.

ABSTRACT

Efforts to prepare teachers to be leaders are often impeded by a number of barriers in society and schools. Obstacles in the workplace are largely products of organizational cultures and climates that place teachers in subordinate roles. The argument is made that consideration of these barriers must be incorporated into revisions of teacher education curricula.

Discussing reform efforts during the mid-1980s, Darling-Hammond (1988) observed that there were two very different streams of policy based on dissimilar ideas of teaching and learning. One led to the conclusion that schools needed better regulations and the other led to the conclusion that schools needed better teaching. After more than a decade of tinkering with strategies predicated largely on the notion that schools could be improved by simply requiring students and teachers to do more of what they were already doing, reformers are aiming their endeavors toward the structural dimensions of schools. This change in course has created a window of opportunity described by Little (1993): "State and local policy makers seem most readily disposed to support appeals to professionalization where they see it as (a) sustaining a reasonably well-prepared and stable teacher work force, and (b) coupled with assurances of local accountability for student outcomes" (p. 132). In shifting from intensification mandates to school restructuring as a primary strategy, reformers have given teacher educators an opportunity to shape a new generation of teacher leaders— practitioners who will be empowered to make critical decisions about the process and ends of education.

Unfortunately, the road to true professionalism is strewn with count-less obstructions, many of which fall outside the domains of preservice and inservice education. Some have a social foundation and are the products of long-standing public perceptions. Americans, for example, have not bestowed on elementary and secondary school teachers the same status and respect accorded to practitioners in better recognized profes-sions (e.g., physicians, architects). Others obstructions have an institu-tional base. Institutional obstructions, deeply rooted in the character and traditions of public education, are subtle and not readily recognized by either educators or the general public. Perhaps most important, social and institutional obstructions are not mutually exclusive; over time, they have fused to create an intricate set of requirements and expectations for teachers.

The objective here is to unravel those barriers to teacher professional-ism that are primarily ingrained in the organizational structure of schools. Historically, these impedimenta have been largely ignored by teacher education programs (Barr, 1987) even though they are sufficiently power-ful to abort any change effort that emanates from the university campus. The discussion of institutional barriers is preceded by brief reviews of the organizational dimension of schools and teacher socialization.

Schools as Social Organizations

Although organizations come in many forms and possess varying purposes, all are social units deliberately designed to achieve specific goals (Reitz, 1987). They are entities that develop distinctive cultures— values, belief systems, and norms that serve to direct the behavior of groups and individuals within them (Owens, 1991). In schools, such normative structures help teachers interpret everyday occurrences and sort out confusion, uncertainty, and ambiguity in their work life (Goens & Clover, 1991).

The value of understanding schools as social institutions is related to the fact that behavior in organizations is not random. Rather, there are fundamental consistencies influenced by a complex network of interactions among individuals and formal and informal groups within a cultural context (Robbins, 1986). In all social systems, workers and managers face sanctions designed to encourage their compliance with expected behavior. Teachers are no exception. Sanctions in schools may be imposed by the organization (e.g., by district or school administrators) or its subsystems (e.g., informal teacher groups); in both instances, sanctions constitute a potent mechanism for controlling teacher behavior. The degree to which teachers and administrators adhere to a common set of norms, beliefs, and values determines whether a school has a strong or weak culture.

Culture is but one characteristic of a school's total environment. There also are physical attributes (e.g., school building and equipment), organizational structures (e.g., calendars, schedules), social relationships (e.g., working relationships among teachers), and human elements (e.g., the needs, wants, and motivations of individuals who work in the school). Collectively, these characteristics constitute the school's climate—a comprehensive construct for understanding work-related behavior (Kowalski & Reitzug, 1993).

Even though individual behavior is a mix of institutional expectations and individual personality (Owens, 1991), there are two realities suggesting that culture and climate are especially potent forces in determining the behavior of teachers. First, schools as institutions have proven to be tremendously resistant to change. Although minor alterations have occurred from time to time, the basic institutional framework of most public schools has remained intact. To a great extent, this inflexibility is produced by traditional expectations that public education function as an agency of stability rather than as a social force to beget change (i.e., schools ought to protect existing values and practices of the majority) (Spring, 1990).

Second, teacher role expectations across most school districts have remained rather fixed. Despite new instructional paradigms, technology, and recent reform initiatives, many teachers still work in isolation, implementing prescribed curricula with predetermined materials. Clearly, teachers enjoy some independence when their classroom doors are closed; however, basic institutional expectations continue to place them in subordinate roles. There is little evidence to date that school reform efforts have changed this condition. A recent study found that nearly 60% of the teachers have yet to see any type of change in their individual schools (Harris & Wagner, 1993).

Teacher Socialization

Studies on teacher socialization offer insights into the relationship between teacher behavior and work environment. Historically, teacher educators have largely accepted the notion that exposure to institutional characteristics are a most powerful determinant of actual teacher roles (e.g., Etheridge, 1988; Larkin, 1973; Rosenholtz, 1989). This fact is especially cogent when one considers that school cultures are often shaped by external forces and not by teachers and administrators. Cooper (1988) described how educators passively accept their roles in many schools:

> School people have surely not prospered, or even benefited, from "received" culture and imposed wisdom. Yet school inhabitants have lived as though they were unsophisticated natives ministered to by well-meaning missionaries who exude paternalism. Practitioners have had their shortcomings and inadequacies catalogued and classified and, sadly, have come to accept the blueprint of their deficiencies as though they had drawn it themselves. They have become passive and dependent in pursuit of their own voices. (pp. 45-46)

In the last several years, the magnitude and strength of socialization have been challenged. Feiman-Nemser and Floden (1986), for example, asserted that recent studies raised questions as to whether "experienced teachers abide by a single set of norms, whether new teachers change significantly, and whether they are merely passive recipients of a teaching culture" (p. 520). Zeichner and Gore (1990) argued that functionalist studies (i.e., research that casts teachers as prisoners of either their pasts or their workplaces) failed to recognize (a) individual differences in teacher development by concentrating solely on descriptions of central tendencies and (b) that new teachers have the capacity to influence their work environments as well as being influenced by them. This latter observation is especially cogent to school restructuring.

Summaries of research on effective schools provide some evidence that the collective efforts of strong educators can produce work environments that are noticeably unique (e.g., Purkey & Smith, 1985). The most effective schools typically have strong cultures oriented toward operational flexibility. Yet, most schools do not exhibit such characteristics, and as a result, most teachers still are routed into traditional roles.

Several observations may prove helpful to understanding the importance of socialization. First, the strength of socialization varies from school to school and is dependent on whether a school has a strong or weak culture. Second, socialization can be either positive or negative, but because most socialization has been associated with traditional roles, it generally is perceived as a negative influence (Feiman-Nemser & Floden, 1986). Third, generalizations about socialization are made more difficult by the fact that much of the research on teacher socialization has focused more directly on professional socialization (e.g., the effects of teachers on each other, the effects of preservice education) than on organizational socialization (e.g., the effects of culture and climate on behavior)—and the two are clearly different.

Institutional Barriers to Teachers as Leaders

Institutional barriers are defined as those change obstacles stemming from organizational attributes of schools and school systems. Identifying all would be virtually impossible; rather, the intention here is to provide a summary of the most pervasive ones. These obstacles are basically manifestations of the normative dimensions of classical organizational theory (bureaucracy), and they have evolved in public education over the last 100 years.

Expectations of Efficiency

Underlying much of the criticism of elementary and secondary education is a perception that public education is not terribly efficient. Frequently, negative editorials point out that increased spending, especially in urban areas, has failed to yield improved outcomes. Concerns about public school productivity certainly are not new; demands for technical efficiency can be traced all the way back to the early development of urban school districts in the United States. Hierarchies of authority, divisions of labor, and reliance on rules and regulations reflect an industrial-management tradition that views organizations as essentially rational entities. The infusion of these values into public education nurtured the idea that institutional goals were more likely to be attained if workers were (a) closely supervised and (b) restricted to their work roles without unduly interfering in organizational planning and decisions (Hanson, 1991).

There has always been a level of tension between support for organizational efficiency and the ideals of democracy (Strike, 1993). For example, many taxpayers simultaneously support shared decision making and fiscal constraints even though these two objectives are incongruous and their coexistence is likely to generate conflict. Owens (1991) wrote that two conditions are necessary for conflict—divergent views and the incompatibility of those views. If teachers participate in governance decisions, if they are given latitude to make independent judgments in areas of instruction and curriculum, what level of efficiency must be sacrificed? If forced to choose between efficiency, a goal that is essentially economic, and democratic governance, a goal that is essentially philosophical and political, which will policy makers select?

Expectations of Control

Studies frequently show that teachers identify school culture as inhibiting their influence over their own practice (e.g., Wilson, 1993). In large measure, this complaint is related to excessive rules in most schools. The issue of control has three dimensions. The first is characterized by tensions between state legislatures and local school boards (state vs. local control); the second is characterized by tensions between school districts and individual schools (centralization vs. decentralization); and the third is characterized by tensions between administrators and teachers within a school (legitimate control vs. professionalism). Each contributes to the control mechanisms placed over teachers, and accordingly, each has some bearing on institutionalizing the concept of teacher leaders.

Contrary to popular opinion, organizational control does not stem solely from management-oriented administrators who refuse to share power. If this were true, the barrier of institutional control would be less complex. In reality, control over teacher behavior emanates from several conditions. Consider just three:

1. Legislatures and state departments of education frequently exercise control over public education in response to political pressures. They also do so because of state constitutional provisions.

2. School districts in the 1960s and 1970s drifted toward higher levels of centralization and control because of a growing compliance

orientation that made school board members and administrators wary of litigation and state-imposed sanctions (e.g., fear that the absence of control would result in employee noncompliance with new laws on discrimination) (Tyack, 1990).

3. Studies on site-based management have indicated that principals are concerned about sharing power and reducing control especially when school reform initiatives bring into question responsibilities in areas where they perceive themselves as having a low level of authority but a high level of responsibility (e.g., Kowalski, 1993; Lucas, Brown, & Markus, 1991).

Arguments in favor of teacher empowerment have frequently stressed the abilities of highly structured, centralized organizations by showing how tight controls prevent teachers from targeting their instruction to individual student needs. Clearly, this stance is defensible. But is it sufficiently convincing to reduce traditional control mechanisms imposed by the states, school districts, and administrators?

Teacher Autonomy and Decentralization

Closely related to control is the issue of teacher autonomy. It is inconceivable that teachers can become leaders without gaining greater degrees of freedom in their work. Even though many possess partial autonomy, few possess it at a level that would be associated with practice in more established professions. Corwin and Borman (1988) wrote: "In the final analysis, teachers are subordinate employees of school districts subject to districtwide and schoolwide policies, rules, and procedures. Hence, their autonomy is never absolute but always subject to negotiation" (p. 220). Influenced by societal expectations, limited autonomy is associated with a perspective that teachers are primarily responsible for implementing the decisions of others.

It is not insignificant that the initial responses to school reform, immediately following the publishing of the report *A Nation at Risk* in 1983 (National Commission on Excellence in Education [NCEE], 1983), were predicated on assumptions that the problems of education involved incompetent teachers and lazy students. Only after it became clear that intensification mandates would not produce excellence did reformers begin to consider school restructuring—and they did so largely at the urging of leaders in the education profession. Given the fact that earlier efforts to improve schools were essentially unsuccessful and arguments that education would be more effective if instructional decisions were decentralized, many political and business leaders moved to endorse initiatives calling for a new generation of U.S. schools. But does the advocacy of greater freedom for schools reflect a shift in public perceptions regarding teacher autonomy? Good and Brophy (1986) observed: "Ironically, many of those who argue most strongly for school autonomy are least interested in teacher autonomy" (p. 588). Sadly, there is little evidence that the advocacy of decentralization is associated with societal beliefs that teachers ought to have greater freedom in practicing their profession.

Teacher Autonomy and Unionism

Through much of the 20th century, there have been normative conflicts between educators who see themselves as professionals and the bureaucratic organizations in which they work. The resulting friction was a primary factor in the growth of unionism in public education. Lieberman (1986) explained that teacher unionism was advanced by feelings of helplessness; Newman (1990) characterized it as a justifiable quest for autonomy. But even though teachers have gained a greater voice in some organizational decisions, it has come at the price of reduced autonomy for individual teachers (Corwin & Borman, 1988). Even today, many teachers remain ambivalent about union membership.

Arguments promoting the coexistence of unionism and professionalism are usually based on the conviction that national organizations for educators (such as the National Education Association and the American Federation of Teachers) can function much like the American Medical Association—that is, they can serve to protect the interests of their members and members' clients without jeopardizing the professional status of their members (Newman, 1990). Such analogies, nevertheless, fail to address the most essential question. If teachers become leaders, if they are treated as true professionals, why do they need the collective power of a union? Noteworthy in this respect are indications that national union leaders may be reconsidering their support for decentralization (e.g., site-based management) as a primary reform strategy (Bradley, 1992).

Acceptance of a Knowledge Base

Strike (1993) argued that a knowledge base for the teaching profession would have to meet both social and epistemic tests before the public would recognize its existence. In the absence of such evidence, legislators, parents, and others are unable to identify the "real professionals." Consider consequences visible in the governance and policy mechanisms directing public education. Not only are most policies developed by elected officials at the state (governor and legislatures) and local (school boards) levels, but they are typically produced with specificity, in abundance, and without the counsel or direction of professional educators. Particularly revealing has been the behavior of policy makers in times of perceived crisis. Following the Soviet success in launching Sputnik in the late 1950s, the federal government encouraged scientists in various disciplines to develop packaged instructional materials for elementary and secondary schools to ensure that the curriculum would be "teacherproof" (Schubert, 1986). Reactions after the publication of *A Nation at Risk* (NCEE, 1983) were quite similar. A recent national study of teachers, for example, found that a majority continue to see themselves as the targets of reform, and only 37% felt they were agents of reform (Harris & Wagner, 1993).

Because the public does not recognize a body of esoteric knowledge establishing teaching as a true profession, efforts to distinguish between competent and incompetent teachers are judged to be subjective and self-serving. An example is found in the skepticism being voiced about current efforts to create a national system of certification. There also is incertitude as to whether teachers possess knowledge and skills that permit them to make decisions about the ends of education that will be equal or superior to those made by legislatures and school boards (Strike, 1993).

Role Definition

There has always been a degree of incongruity between the role teachers believe they should perform and the role established for them by society and school officials. Further, teacher roles are not constant within or among schools. This variance makes it more difficult to precisely define what is meant by the term "teacher leaders." A study by Smylie and Denny (1990) discovered that teachers tend to define teacher leaders "primarily around functions of helping and supporting their colleagues to fulfill classroom responsibilities and improve their practice" (p. 252). Yet, results from their research exhibited that the work of teacher leaders was primarily at the school or school district levels (e.g., program development, collaboration with administrators). The difference was largely explained on the basis of time parameters—that is, teachers tended to assume only those leadership functions not interfering with obligations expressed in their traditional teacher roles. These outcomes suggest that school structure and patterns of power, practice, and beliefs contribute to discrepancies between expected and actual roles.

The teacher's world of work is filled with ambiguity and conflicting goals (Griffin, 1985). Actual behavior is a combination of institutional role (work expectations defined by the school) and the personality of the role incumbent (Owens, 1991). Even if a uniform definition of teacher leader is accepted by both teacher educators and school administrators, individual differences in teacher beliefs, attitudes, needs, and motivations are likely to produce unique iterations of behavior. Until the concept of teacher leadership is defined sufficiently to account for societal, institutional, and individual dynamics, resistance to it is likely.

School and Community Relationships

Several authors (e.g., Strike, 1993; Zeichner, 1991) have explored the institutional implications of interfacing teacher professionalism with the goal of maintaining a symbiotic relationship between public schools and their environments (communities). The most cogent question emerging from their work pertains to balancing the benefits of decentralization and teacher empowerment (e.g., individualized instruction) and the benefits of maintaining local control of public education (e.g., democratic ideal of citizen involvement and role in policy development).

In advocating new conceptualizations of reform within a democratic context, Strike (1993) contended that parents and students ought not to be treated as clients, but rather as partners. His notion of teacher autonomy in a democratic context was predicated on two assertions: (a) that increased autonomy would mean teachers becoming firsts among equals in discourse about education, and (b) that tensions between bureaucratic organizations and communities would most likely be reduced if local decision making replaced the view of democracy that vests sovereignty in state legislatures.

Zeichner (1991) argued that no reform plan or degree of teacher autonomy is sufficient to deal with the institutional and structural inequalities in our society that spawn educational problems. Accordingly, he too rejected the idea that democratic control of public education should be sacrificed for professionalism. Clearly, educators ought not to frame the challenge as one of choosing between professionalism and democracy, but rather as one of refashioning organizational cultures and climates so the two may coexist.

Conclusion

In discussing school reform efforts, Louis and King (1992) likened the responsibility to that of Sisyphus—a mythical Greek figure who faced the task of pushing a boulder up a mountain only to have it roll down once he reached the top. Their analogy rings true for many educators who have become frustrated because their efforts to change practice are thwarted by the framework of controls and normative expectations embedded in their work environments. There is, however, new hope that schools can be transformed. This anticipation springs from a growing public awareness that education is most effective when content and instructional methods are targeted directly to the needs of individual learners by their teachers.

Despite widespread and urgent calls for school restructuring, socialization in the workplace continues to reinforce established teaching practices. In large measure, this may be a product of teachers not understanding organizational behavior and institutional change. Hence, they accept social pressures and tight administrative controls and feel helpless to change them.

In a positive vein, there is growing evidence that teachers and administrators can make a difference in reshaping schools and institutional roles. Studying change in schools, Prestine and Bowen (1993) noted that knowledge structures, beliefs, and accumulated wisdom of practice exert influence on and are influenced by changes in process and substance. They concluded, "It is the overall, shared organizational understandings that bond what is done and how it is done" (p. 316). Thus, the degree to which a community of educators comprehends decision making, organizational behavior, and institutional change appears critical to school restructuring.

One purpose here was to identify major institutional barriers that may prevent teachers from becoming true leaders. This was done not to suggest that reform is futile, but rather to recommend that teacher educators give ample consideration to such obstacles as they redesign curricula. Historically, education professors rarely have looked beyond the campus to determine if their curricular changes would be congruent with school practices (Mertens & Yarger, 1988). It would, indeed, be unfortunate to repeat this error.

If the quest to create a generation of teacher leaders is to succeed, an acceptable knowledge base must be developed—one that will be recognized by policy makers, the profession, and society. In attempting to create this knowledge base, teacher educators ought to give ample consideration to questions about the purpose of schools in society, policy development, tensions between efficiency and democracy, tensions between the collective power of unions and the individual autonomy of professionals, the validation of a professional knowledge base, and the compatibility of teacher professionalism and public education in a democracy.

In addition to creating programs that will be directed toward preparing a generation of teacher leaders, education professors ought to be concerned about overcoming the negative effects of socialization. At the very least, a small number of schools needs to be created that will permit aspiring practitioners to assume responsibility, test ideas, and practice leadership free from the traditional constraints of bureaucratic cultures and climates. These must be environments in which teacher education students can work with highly skilled practitioners who model leadership. It is more likely that educators will be empowered to change public schools if their initial socialization to practice is in an environment that is conducive to professionalization. In this regard, professional development schools—schools built on partnerships between teacher educators and public school officials—have proven to be especially promising ventures (Stallings & Kowalski, 1990).

References

Barr, R. D. (1987). The culture of the schools and teacher education. *Journal of Teacher Education, 29*(6), 80.

Bradley, A. (1992, December 9). School reforms bump up against unions' most cherished protections. *Education Week, 1,* 17-18.

Cooper, M. (1988). Whose culture is it, anyway? In A. Lieberman (Ed.), *Building professional culture in schools* (pp. 45-54). New York: Teachers College Press.

Corwin, R. G., & Borman, K. M. (1988). School as workplace: Structural constraints on administration. In N. Boyan (Ed.), *Handbook of research on educational administration* (pp. 209-237). New York: Longman.

Darling-Hammond, L. (1988). The futures of teaching. *Educational Leadership, 16*(3), 4-10.

Etheridge, C. P. (1988). *Socialization on the job: How beginning teachers move from university learnings to school-based practices* (ERIC Document Reproduction Service No. ED 302 538).

Feiman-Nemser, S., & Floden, R. E. (1986). The cultures of teaching. In M. Wittrock (Ed.), *Handbook of research on teaching* (3rd ed., pp. 505-526). New York: Macmillan.

Goens, G. A., & Clover, S. I. (1991). *Mastering school reform.* Boston: Allyn & Bacon.

Good, T. L., & Brophy, J. E. (1986). School effects. In M. Wittrock (Ed.), *Handbook of research on teaching* (3rd ed., pp. 570-604). New York: Macmillan.

Griffin, G. (1985). The school as a workplace and the master teacher concept. *Elementary School Journal, 86*(1), 1-16.

Hanson, E. M. (1991). *Educational administration and organizational behavior* (3rd ed.). Boston: Allyn & Bacon.

Harris, L., & Wagner, R. F. (1993). *Testing assumptions: A survey of teachers' attitudes toward the nation's school reform agenda.* New York: Ford Foundation.

Kowalski, T. J. (1993, February). *Site-based management, unionism, and teacher empowerment: Beliefs of suburban school principals.* Paper presented at the annual meeting of the American Association of School Administrators, Orlando, FL.

Kowalski, T. J., & Reitzug, U. C. (1993). *Contemporary school administration.* New York: Longman.

Larkin, R. (1973). Contextual influences on teacher leadership styles. *Sociology of Education, 46*(4), 471-479.

Lieberman, M. (1986). *Beyond public education.* New York: Praeger.

Little, J. W. (1993). Teachers' professional development in a climate of educational reform. *Educational Evaluation and Policy Analysis, 15*(2), 129-152.

Louis, K. S., & King, J. A. (1992). *Professional cultures and reforming schools: Does the myth of Sisyphus apply?* (ERIC Document Reproduction Service No. ED 349 693).

Lucas, S., Brown, G. C., & Markus, F. W. (1991). Principals' perceptions of site-based management and teacher empowerment. *NASSP Bulletin, 75*(537), 56-62.

Mertens, S., & Yarger, S. J. (1988). Teaching as a profession: Leadership, empowerment, and involvement. *Journal of Teacher Education, 39*(1), 32-37.

National Commission on Excellence in Education. (1983, April). *A nation at risk: The imperative of school reform.* Washington, DC: U.S. Government Printing Office.

Newman, J. W. (1990). *America's teachers.* New York: Longman.

Owens, R. G. (1991). *Organizational behavior in education* (4th ed.). Boston: Allyn & Bacon.

Prestine, N. A., & Bowen, C. (1993). Benchmarks of change: Assessing essential school restructuring efforts. *Educational Evaluation and Policy Analysis, 15*(3), 298-319.

Purkey, S. C., & Smith, M. S. (1985). School reform: The district policy implications of the effective schools research. *Elementary School Journal, 85,* 353-389.

Reitz, H. J. (1987). *Behavior in organizations* (3rd ed.). Homewood, IL: Irwin.

Robbins, S. P. (1986). *Organizational behavior: Concepts, controversies, and applications* (3rd ed.). Englewood Cliffs, NJ: Prentice-Hall.

Rosenholtz, S. J. (1989). *Teachers' workplace: The social organization of schools.* New York: Longman.

Schubert, W. H. (1986). *Curriculum: Perspectives, paradigms, and possibility.* New York: Macmillan.

Smylie, M. A., & Denny, J. W. (1990). Teacher leadership: Tensions and ambiguities in organizational perspective. *Educational Administration Quarterly, 26*(3), 235-259.

Spring, J. (1990). *The American school: 1642-1990* (2nd ed.). New York: Longman.

Stallings, J. A., & Kowalski, T. J. (1990). Research on professional development schools. In W. Houston (Ed.), *Handbook of research on teacher education* (pp. 251-263). New York: Macmillan.

Strike, K. A. (1993). Professionalism, democracy, and discursive communities: Normative reflections on restructuring. *American Educational Research Journal, 30*(2), 255-275.

Tyack, D. (1990). Restructuring in historical perspective: Tinkering toward utopia. *Teachers College Record, 92*(2), 170-191.

Wilson, M. (1993). The search for teacher leaders. *Educational Leadership, 50*(6), 24-27.

Zeichner, K. M. (1991). Contradictions and tensions in the professionalization of teaching and the democratization of schools. *Teachers College Record, 92*(3), 363-379.

Zeichner, K. M., & Gore, J. M. (1990). Teacher socialization. In W. Houston (Ed.), *Handbook of research on teacher education* (pp. 329-348). New York: Macmillan.

11 Introducing Prospective Teachers to Contemporary Views of Teaching and Learning Science: The Science and Youth Project

Richard Ponzio

Charles Fisher

Richard Ponzio is Director of the National Science and Youth (SAY) Project at the University of California, Davis. His research interests include development and assessment of science education and science literary programs in nonschool settings, development of critical thinking skills using science content and methodology, teacher education and teacher partnerships, and school reform issues.

Charles Fisher is Associate Professor and Director of the Center for Research on Teaching and Learning at the University of Northern Colorado. His research interests include classroom processes, formal and informal science education, and classroom discourse.

ABSTRACT

In this chapter, we describe an innovative plan for engaging prospective teachers in authentic early teaching and learning experiences. The Science and Youth (SAY) Project involves several hundred high school students in 10 urban areas who have indicated a strong interest in teaching as a career by enrolling in teaching academics within their schools. These prospective teachers are trained to work with 9- to 12-year-olds on a variety of "hands-on, heads-on" science activities that culminate with teams of high school "student teachers" and their pupils designing and implementing action-oriented community service projects by applying their newly acquired science knowledge to local situations. The curriculum for the SAY Project, developed for and widely used in informal education settings, incorporates constructivist learning and teaching principles. The prospective teachers, organized in teams, are coached by volunteer scientists and engineers from local businesses. Participation in the project is intended to provide early teaching experiences in authentic settings and opportunities for guided reflection on these experiences. Preliminary results of the project are described by drawing heavily on experiences at a site in Northern California.

Reform in Science Education

One need only pick up the daily newspaper to appreciate our society's demand for technological and scientific literacy. With increasing frequency, voters are asked to pass judgment on issues such as offshore oil drilling, the fate of endangered species, and the implications of genetic engineering. Consumers choose, on a daily basis, among products that vary widely in the energy and resource costs used to make, package, and deliver them, as well as their cost in dollars. Employers and employees alike are faced with decisions regarding environmental sensitivity in the workplace. How would increased scientific literacy affect the way these choices and decisions are made? What role does education, in the broad sense, play in increasing day-to-day science literacy of Americans? And, how do we educate prospective science teachers to help raise levels of scientific literacy among all segments of American youth?

To address this increasingly important demand, science educators have advocated widespread reform in elementary and secondary schools. Although calls for reform in science education are not new, the current wave can be distinguished from earlier reforms in several ways. Reforms in the 1970s and 1980s tended to focus on increasing the amount of time students spent on science in their schooling, with a corresponding increase in the amount of content to be learned. The emphasis was also on improving access to science education and science careers for female and minority students. The American Association for the Advancement of Science (AAAS, 1989, p. 14) concluded:

> The present science textbooks and methods of instruction, far from helping, often impede progress toward science literacy. They emphasize the learning of answers more than the exploration of questions, memory at the expense of critical thought, bits and pieces of information instead of understandings in context, recitation over argument, reading in lieu of doing. They fail to encourage students to work together, to share information and ideas freely with each other, or to use modern instruments to extend their intellectual capabilities. The present curricula in science and mathematics are overstuffed and undernourished.

Recent attention has been directed to reforming both the content and pedagogy of school science while maintaining the emphasis on improving access for all Americans to science education and science-based careers. Contemporary science education advocates the use of scientific thinking processes, reorganization of science content, and applications of the scientific principles being learned to social issues in the homes and communities of school-age students. These shifts have fostered new interest in "hands-on" and "heads-on" approaches to science teaching and learning.

Linking Learning and Service

Even as science education has been questioned, broad economic shifts have fueled criticism of traditional schooling practices in general. For example, Reich (1983, 1991) has suggested that the United States is no longer dominated by a production-line economy, but is rapidly moving toward a dynamic, entrepreneurial, global economy and that therefore our school system should provide experiences for learners that are dynamic and entrepreneurial by design. In part, this notion suggests that schooling should include more activities that allow students to work cooperatively on the heuristics of problem finding, problem framing, and problem solving.

Additional impetus for entrepreneurial applications of learning to real-world problem solving can be found in the renewed national interest in a community service ethic and rekindled interest in service learning, which is defined as the blending of service and learning in such a way that both occur and are enriched by the other. The support of the federal government for this trend toward the blending of learning and service can be seen in the Congressional reauthorization of the National and Community Service Trust Act of 1993, designed to place up to 25,000 participants in national service assignments that include service learning components.

Limitations of Traditional School Science

Current research on schools and schooling (AAAS, 1989; Goodlad, 1984) questions the inability of traditional school structures to provide students with even minimal opportunities for learning from hands-on community-based science experiences. In part, this lack of opportunity is based on the way schools are organized and what forms of student learning are assessed. Lagemann (1989), speaking of traditions of educational research, claims "one cannot understand the history of education in the United States during the twentieth century unless one realizes that Edward L. Thorndike won and John Dewey lost" (p. 185). Also, finding the money, time, or space in the regular school curriculum for increasing science instruction related to real life or careers in science has in general met with little success, and further, has separated science, scientific thinking processes, and the pursuit of science-based careers from students' aspirations:

> Those who seek the reform of science education see the prevailing science curriculum as isolated from the realities of our culture and the lives of citizens. The charge is that the 200-year-old science curriculum is largely irrelevant and should be replaced by modern concepts of science. . . . Much of scientific research done today is done by teams of scientists and technologists pooling their expertise and insights. . . . In this century, science and technology have become socialized. Research endeavors are now more socially than theory driven; witness the volume of research on finding ways of controlling the AIDS pandemic, improving agriculture, managing the natural environment, and maintaining a long and happy life. Science and technology today lie at the center of our culture and economy, thus fostering enculturation as a goal of science teaching. (Hurd, 1992, p. 36)

Each of these factors—changes in the content and pedagogy of science education, stronger linkages between learning and service, and dissatisfaction with traditional science education—has contributed to the current wave of reform in classroom science instruction and inevitably to calls for reform in training of science teachers. To bring about more hands-on, heads-on science learning in elementary school classrooms, the content and methods for teacher training must also change.

Changes in Training Experiences
for Science Teachers

From Transmitting Content
to Constructing Knowledge

There is considerable agreement about the need for reform in the education of science teachers, but it is less clear just which particular reforms to attempt. Some reformers view science content to be the primary concern and suggest revising primary and secondary school curricula. Other reformers argue that not only must content be changed, but also methods of teaching and the contexts in which learning takes place must undergo sweeping changes simultaneously. From this viewpoint, content and pedagogy are inextricably entwined.

Fundamentally, these views represent different assumptions about the nature of knowledge itself. A traditional view of science education that is now being viewed as inadequate proposes that knowledge is external, objective, static, and independent of the learner. From this perspective, changes in science content alone could be expected to benefit students. In this manner of thinking, knowledge is transmitted from those who know more (teachers) to those who know less (students). In this scenario, teaching is primarily an act of transmitting knowledge to students and correlative training of teachers is primarily centered on the content of science.

Recent reforms propose that knowledge is internal, subjective, dynamic, and dependent on the learner. From this perspective, more than the content must change to bring large numbers of students to higher levels of scientific literacy. In this way of thinking, students (and teachers) construct knowledge based on what they already know and what they do during the learning process. In the construction metaphor, teaching becomes not so much a matter of telling about content as co-constructing knowledge and understanding. Teaching in this latter sense is a more subtle undertaking for which content knowledge is necessary but not sufficient for high levels of performance. If science teachers are to implement more active hands-on, heads-on science activities that are authentically related to students' prior experiences and everyday lives, as well as learning activities that mirror the processes that practicing scientists engage in, then radically different training experiences are needed.

Learning to Teach

Recent research on learning to teach (Kagan, 1992; Reynolds, 1992; Richardson, 1990) suggests that preservice students' beliefs about teaching are basically not changed as a result of university courses. Further, the meaning that preservice students make of courses on teaching is reported to be quite different depending on their entering beliefs. The same body of research also suggests that preservice students, especially students who have not yet had extensive teaching experience in some context and who are not "mature students," have few distinctions about pupils that are useful for pedagogical purposes. Apparently a substantial number of preservice students explicitly or implicitly expect their pupils to be like they themselves were as youngsters. In addition, in elementary schools, where teachers are typically responsible for all subject areas, science instruction is sometimes a relatively low priority. In his national study on the state of schooling in the United States, Goodlad (1984) found that even when science was taught in the elementary grades, it often was little more than a reading lesson from a science text.

More and Different Early Experiences

With these issues in mind, at least three kinds of early experiences for prospective science teachers are advocated. First are *early experiences in teaching science*, especially for prospective elementary school teachers. The science education literature is replete with studies documenting elementary teachers' reticence to teach science due to lack of experience, background, and confidence. Too often actual experience in teaching science is delayed while novice teachers work in the basic skills areas. By the time teachers begin to develop their science teaching repertoire, their identities as teachers are already well established, relegating science teaching to peripheral status.

Second are *early experiences with contemporary teaching and learning theories and practices*, especially variations on the learning cycle and discourse patterns that are characteristic of learner-centered and problem-centered pedagogies. If teachers teach the way they were taught, then we must provide more variety in their early experiences so that their repertoires as mature teachers will be broader. Early positive experiences with constructivist teaching and learning frameworks will shape the personal teaching models that beginning teachers continue to use as professionals.

Third are *early experiences with learners.* Prospective teachers' stereotypes about learners, often overly narrow stereotypes, must be confronted early. All students are not the same and few interventions work well with most students most of the time. The sooner prospective teachers come face to face with real students with the intention of promoting learning, then the sooner perceptions about learners will be challenged, a process that appears to be a rite of passage on the path from novice to expert.

In the interest of encouraging innovative thinking about training experiences for prospective teachers of science, in the next section we describe a training model for early intervention and initial experiences with its implementation in one urban setting. In 1994-1997, 12 additional sites will implement variations on these themes in other major urban areas.

The Science and Youth Project

Overview of Project

The overarching goals of the Science and Youth (SAY) Project are (a) to provide early science teaching experiences for prospective teachers while they are still in high school, and (b) to introduce hands-on, heads-on science activities to large numbers of elementary school students. The participating teenagers, all of whom intend to teach science during their subsequent careers, receive practical training in informal science education. Following training, teams of teen leaders plan a sequence of lessons with a coach and then teach the lessons to elementary school students from their local area. The coaches, who are also specially trained, are practicing scientists and engineers who have been recruited from local industries to work with the teens. Each sequence of lessons culminates in a community service project that in one way or another uses the scientific principles that students have been learning about to address a local problem or issue. The community service projects are brainstormed, designed, developed, and implemented by the participants themselves. The activities that SAY Project participants engage in occur in out-of-school settings such as parks, day camps, city squares, shops, and industrial plants, as well as in school classrooms.

From this very brief overview, you can see that SAY gets groups of people together, for example, teenagers and elementary school students, or working scientists and teenagers, who do not typically work with one another, to talk about and do science. The activities take place in a variety of community settings, many of which are unusual places to find students during school hours. Most often teenagers are in charge, the activities are enjoyable as well as educational, and students have an opportunity to make authentic contributions to their communities. The SAY Project encourages the kind of group problem solving that goes on in the workplace rather than having students complete exercises in a formal environment controlled by adults. The elementary school students explore a variety of science content areas with physical objects to manipulate and apply their new knowledge to improve the community around their homes and schools.

For the teens, there are a number of benefits. They receive training in the content and pedagogy provided by the program and then are given responsibility for working with elementary school students. These responsibilities are real and provide both authentic motivation for preparing and doing the job well, and genuine satisfaction when the work is completed successfully. The teens also get to work with practicing scientists and engineers, often visit their places of work, and get a firsthand look at what a career in science could be. In that the teens typically work in teams both while planning and while implementing lessons, a large part of the program could be thought of as leadership development. Although all of these potential benefits to teens are important to the SAY Project, in the current context we focus somewhat more on the role of the project in teacher training. In this respect, SAY provides teenage prospective teachers with early experiences with teaching science, early experiences with constructivist and alternative models of teaching and learning, and early experiences with real learners. To broaden our description of the SAY Project, we will now consider several of the key components of the design more closely.

High School Teaching Academies

Many high schools throughout the country have special centers designed around vocations, performing arts, subject matter specialties, and so on. These programs operate like schools within a school and often have some of the characteristics of magnet schools in that they draw students from more than one attendance area. Magnet schools of one kind or another, beginning primarily as vehicles for desegregation in the 1970s, have continued to be an arena for educational innovation and change (Clinchy, 1993). Some high schools have programs of this type that are designed for students who are interested in exploring teaching as a career. These programs, referred to as teaching academies, provide clusters of classes that blend academic content with pedagogical considerations and serve cohorts of students who move through 4 years of high school together.

At the present time, there are approximately 20 teaching academies in the United States. In most cases, the teaching academy is housed at one high school in the district and draws students from throughout the district. A unique exception to this pattern is found in North Carolina, where there are 133 high schools, each of which has most of the components of a teaching academy. In addition to coursework, participants in the teaching academy programs typically engage in tutoring and provide other educational experiences for younger children. Each academy usually has some kind of partnership with one or more local teacher training institutions.

Thirteen of these teaching academies are participants in the SAY Project and, with some variation from academy to academy to account for local needs, are beginning to use SAY to structure early science teaching experiences for their members. Or alternatively, the SAY Project has introduced training and materials for more student-centered and problem-centered science activities into an innovative but stable existing structure within urban school systems. If the project is successful, not only will several hundred prospective science teachers get early experiences teaching science using constructivist teaching and learning methodologies and working with real students, but thousands of elementary school students will experience innovative science activities before they reach secondary schools.

These teaching academies, with their staffs' extensive knowledge and experience with prospective teachers and local communities, represent a unique opportunity for innovation in teacher education and are an important structural and political element of the SAY Project. If teaching academies are the context in which the SAY Project works and teams of high school students working with elementary school students are the primary actors, what kinds of science activities do they engage in?

Table 11.1   Curriculum Modules Used in the SAY Project

Curriculum Title	Topic Area
Beyond Duck, Cover, and Hold	Earthquake and disaster preparedness
Chemicals Are Us	What chemicals and chemical reactions are and how to use chemicals responsibly
Recycle, Reuse, Reduce	Natural cycles, ways to recycle and reuse materials, reduce amounts of materials discarded
What's Bugging You?	Pests and responsible pest management
Snailing and Sciencing	Learning to use seven scientific thinking processes
Oak Woodland Habitats	Environmental interdependence
It Came From Planted Earth	Agriculture, plant food, and fiber uses
From Ridges to Rivers	Watershed explorations

An Innovative Science Curriculum

The SAY Project uses an innovative hands-on science curriculum that engages pupils in science inquiry processes. When pupils are using these processes—that is, actively framing and solving problems, handling materials, and making observations—they participate in the very processes that constitute the heart of science.

The curriculum consists of eight topic-centered modules drawing on a wide variety of scientific phenomena and principles. The titles of the modules and the general topics they deal with are listed in Table 11.1. Groups of elementary school pupils, led by specially trained teenage leaders from a high school teaching academy, work together in a sequence of about six sessions per curriculum unit. Each session is approximately 1-2 hours in length and may take place in a regular school classroom or as part of a more informal educational experience, such as an after-school club or part of a parks and recreation program. As part of the group work, the teen leaders and elementary school pupils design and carry out a community service project related to the science topic and appropriate to local neighborhood needs. The science processes included in the curricula are commonly found in the guidelines of most state departments of education for elementary school science education. The consumable materials, such as baking soda, vinegar, and even backyard snails, are inexpensive and readily obtained, making it easy for pupils to continue science investigations on their own. Most modules are available in Spanish and English. Although the activities in the modules are inherently interesting, the cornerstone of the curriculum involves the manner in which the activities are carried out. Most of the activities are conducted in groups, with extensive interaction among pupils and often among the leaders. The program is characterized by a kind of playfulness that invites exploration, experimentation, and learning.

The curriculum materials were originally developed for informal science education by the National 4-H Science Experiences and Resources for Informal Education Settings (SERIES) Project. The SERIES Project has used the curriculum for several years with a wide range of youth groups, including groups that are consistently underrepresented in traditional science education. During 1993, SERIES estimated that more than 50,000 youngsters participated in its program in 32 states and Puerto Rico. The SERIES materials and training program were chosen as the pedagogical core of SAY because of the opportunity for prospective teachers to engage in meaningful early experiences integrating school goals with out-of-school learning experiences.

Theoretical Framework for Curriculum and Activities

The instructional activities in the SERIES curricula emphasize use of the scientific thinking processes included in virtually all school science texts used in the United States. These processes—observing, communicating, comparing, organizing, relating, inferring, and applying—are used by participants in each of the activities. The teen leaders thus have early experiences in using scientific thinking processes in the SERIES inquiry-based activities and in teaching the processes.

Each of the curricula is built on a model of instructional design known as the learning cycle (Karplus et al., 1967; Renner & Marek, 1988). This model, widely used in contemporary science education, has shown consistent learning gains in a variety of educational settings (Guzzetti, Snyder, & Glass, 1992).

The learning cycle suggests three distinct segments for an activity within a lesson. In the general formulation of the model, each activity begins with an exploration segment, during which pupils manipulate the materials, encounter some interesting phenomenon, and perhaps attempt to understand the phenomenon by changing something in the environment to see possible effects on the phenomenon itself. In the second segment, the pupils and their teen leader or leaders engage in a discussion of the events that occurred in the first segment. During this segment, one or more concepts relevant to the phenomenon are introduced and related to the students' prior knowledge. After key concepts are developed and articulated through discussion, in the third segment students apply the concept or concepts in some personally meaningful context. This general structure, exploration followed by concept introduction followed by concept application, is the primary template for the SERIES curricula used in the SAY Project.

In the SAY Project, the first two components of the learning cycle are embedded in the teen-led learning activities, and the third component is developed in the community service activities. The learning cycle structure is explicitly taught to the teen leaders as part of the training associated with the SAY Project.

Community Service Projects

The inclusion of community service projects as an integral part of the SERIES curricula used in the SAY Project is a crucial component of the program. The SAY Project draws on a collaborative working relationship with states' 4-H Youth Development Programs. Overall, 4-H is a National Youth Development Program under the auspices of the U.S. Department of Agriculture, administered through each state's land grant college or university system. The service learning component of the SAY Project uses the expertise of local paid academic staff and volunteer leaders to support youth in improving their neighborhoods and homes through community service projects.

There are at least four reasons for underscoring the importance of this component. First, as mentioned above, community service projects constitute the mechanism for completing the third segment of the learning cycle. These service projects provide a structured opportunity for students to apply what they have learned in a personally meaningful way. This does not imply that learning would not be applied by students if there were no community service project (or other mechanism to accomplish the concept application segment of the learning cycle), only that a substantially larger proportion of students are likely to successfully apply learning in the context of a community service project than would be the case if no such supporting structure were offered.

Second, the community service project represents a learning activity that is expressly initiated by the learners to address a perceived need. So much of traditional education runs one way, in the sense that the transactions flow primarily from the teacher to the students. In this admittedly stereotypic view, the teacher is the source of knowledge, talk, and tasks in the classroom whereas students are passive receivers and compliant doers. In contrast, contemporary teaching and learning frameworks are based on a dialogic process, a two-way process, where there is the presence of, if not equity between, both teacher and student voices. Because the community service projects are identified and initiated by the teens and younger participants, these projects provide a context within which the student voice is given more expression than is usually the case.

Third, community service projects afford an opportunity for elementary and high school students to make an authentic contribution to their communities. There seem to be fewer avenues for young people to make legitimate contributions to communities than there were even a few decades ago. The extension of formal schooling to what is now essentially a 16-year process may exacerbate the situation. Community service projects, like other types of service learning, create a context for students to identify an issue and do something about it.

Fourth, community service projects illustrate how scientific knowledge and processes can be used for social purposes. In the course of inventing and carrying out projects in their communities, students negotiate, make agreements, and depend on one another and members of the community at large. This action orientation encourages the development of leadership and civic responsibility.

Although the rationales for community service projects are appealing, it is difficult to describe the impact of participating in them in simple terms. To indicate the kinds of projects that teen leaders and 9- to 13-year-olds generate, here are several examples from 4-H SERIES programs in California:

In Santa Barbara County, two groups of youths cooperated in a beach debris comparison project as a culmination of work on the Recycle, Reuse, Reduce curriculum. First, group members went to Santa Cruz Island to visit a beach that on an annual basis had very few visitors. The group, in one day's effort, collected 600 pounds of debris over a one-mile strip of the beach. On analysis, the debris varied from old tires to fish traps to propane tanks, but the most prevalent items were plastic and Styrofoam. Using the data from this island beach as a point of comparison, each group subsequently took responsibility for monitoring debris on separate onshore beaches near their homes. Each group cleaned a designated one-mile strip of beach and recorded the results once a month. The debris was disposed of in a responsible manner, most of it recycled, and data on the local beaches were reported to county authorities. Other examples of projects include distribution of earthquake preparedness information and strapping of water heaters in earthquake-prone communities, and production of clothing for homeless people.

Teen Training Program

Teen leaders entering the SAY Project receive training on the curriculum early in the school year. The training sequence is itself a variation on the learning cycle. Training begins with a trainer leading an activity from the curriculum while the teen leaders take the roles of learners. When the group completes the activity, the trainer introduces pedagogical concepts as part of a discussion. In this segment, the design features of the curriculum are emphasized. The trainer provides explicit examples and explains the science processes, learning cycle components, and cooperative learning elements included in the demonstration activity. In subsequent activities, teen leaders take turns leading while the trainer coaches their performance. This latter training activity corresponds to the third segment of the learning cycle. The application segment is extended when teen leaders prepare for and work with elementary school students later in the program.

This training sequence provides teens with knowledge and firsthand experience with the science content included in the curriculum as well as information on how to teach the concepts. In the guided, learn-by-doing environment of SAY, teen leaders learn to carry out program activities by performing them and then reflecting on their performances with trainers.

The training of teen leaders and the subsequent work of teens teaching elementary school students is designed to emphasize the value of social interactions for improving learning. In both of these instances there are numerous opportunities for youngsters to learn science from each other, as teens interact with younger learners to solve problems, record data, make inferences, and so on. Perhaps because of reduced age and status differences, teen leaders and elementary school students interact easily, enthusiastically, and frequently. For elementary school students, participation in SAY means learning and applying both the processes and concepts of science; in short, it means doing science. The cross-age instructional strategy, coupled with the opportunity to see the usefulness of what they are learning, should encourage many youngsters to participate in other science-based recreational learning such as visiting science museums and participating in science fairs and other school science programs.

Mentoring of Teen Leaders by Adult Volunteer Scientists

The SAY Project recruits scientists and engineers from local businesses as volunteers to work with the teen leaders in the teaching academy. Volunteers receive training on coaching and mentoring from the SAY staff. Ideally, the volunteers also join the teen leaders during training on the curriculum. When the teen leaders complete their training and begin to plan for their work with elementary school students, one or two volunteer scientists are assigned to each team of teens, attend some of their planning meetings, and attend a portion of the actual teaching sessions. This arrangement provides a unique opportunity for engineers and scientists to provide guidance for the teen leaders' presentations of science activities, thereby influencing both the teen leaders' and younger participants' views of science and science-related careers. Although teens are responsible for instruction, volunteers take on responsibilities similar to those of an athletic coach. They serving as mentors for the teen leaders who in turn serve as instructors to younger learners. The relationships that develop between teen leaders and volunteer scientists can increase the prospective teachers' awareness of applications of scientific problem solving and the daily pursuits of working scientists.

The National Society of Women Engineers features SAY as a program for its members to help increase scientific literacy among U.S. youth and to encourage women and minorities to pursue careers in science and mathematics.

Reflective Practice

In recent years, the notion that reflection provides an avenue for teacher development has increasingly influenced the design of teacher education programs. Seminal work by Schön (1983, 1987) has been extended to teacher education (Clift, Houston, & Pugach, 1990; Grimmett & Erickson, 1988; Zeichner & Liston, 1987) and science education (Russell, 1993; Russell & Munby, 1990). In the SAY Project, prospective teachers are encouraged to reflect on teaching and learning experiences. Two mechanisms are provided to support this activity. Volunteer scientists invite the teens to reflect on actions as a regular part of the mentoring relationship. This arrangement allows each teen to talk with an interested, knowledgeable adult about science content, teaching issues, or career aspirations over the course of the school year. Because the volunteer scientists, unlike teaching academy staff, have no role that calls for evaluation of the teens, the likelihood of catalyzing reflection within this relationship is increased.

A second mechanism for supporting reflection occurs in the development and presentation of a project portfolio. Teen leaders, in collaboration with volunteer scientists, develop portfolios demonstrating the contents and processes of their instructional and community service accomplishments. Portfolios include personal journals documenting the development of the teens' work with their teaching team and elementary school students. Additional materials, such as photos, interview data, newspaper articles, samples of pupils' work, parent testimonials, and other artifacts indicating the results of the educational activities and community service projects are also included in these portfolios. By providing a partial record of thoughts and actions, portfolios not only support reflection during the project but also constitute an early baseline against which to consider later career developments.

The design of the SAY Project brings together the structure of teaching academies within high schools, SERIES curricula built on the learning cycle and cooperative learning models, service learning through community service projects, mentoring by practicing scientists, and reflective practice through relationships with volunteers and portfolio development. The practical training and experience in informal science education provided by SAY are intended to equip future teachers to make the changes demanded by current education reform movements in science education. At the same time, large numbers of elementary school students learn science process skills and concepts and then apply their new learning to finding, framing, and solving issues related to science in their homes and local communities. Having outlined the SAY model and its components, we now turn to a description of the project in action.

Implementation of the SAY Model
in Northern California

The Teaching Academy at Alpha High School

Alpha High School in the San Francisco Bay Area serves more than 3,000 students in an urban setting. The school has an attractive, expansive campus in a primarily residential neighborhood. Eighty percent of the students come from ethnic minority groups, groups that are underrepresented in both the teaching and scientific professions. Many of the students are bilingual or have limited proficiency in English.

Alpha High has supported a teaching academy for several years. Like many other teaching academies, the program operates as a school-within-a-school providing a differentiated curriculum for about 200 students each year who have indicated a strong interest in teaching as a career. The program consists of a core academic curriculum and a supplemental program that gives participants a variety of experiences related to teaching. They learn instructional skills and serve as tutors to students in elementary and middle school classes. Many graduates of the program enter teacher training programs at the nearby state university. For the past two years, Alpha Teaching Academy has experimented with SERIES curriculum materials and techniques for science instruction with youngsters in school-based and out-of-school, community-based learning settings.

The Formal Beginning

In the fall semester 1992, Alpha Teaching Academy formally began using the SAY model to guide a substantial part of its program. Approximately 50 teens were trained by the SERIES staff. Following training, the teens divided themselves into four-person teams, were assigned a mentor from engineers and scientists who volunteered for the program, and began a series of planning sessions to prepare lessons to be taught to elementary school students.

With the local county office of the Division of Agriculture and Natural Resources at the University of California as a partner, Alpha Teaching Academy arranged for a cadre of fourth- and fifth-grade classes in four elementary schools near the Alpha High to participate in the project. Beginning in January, teams of teens visited the elementary schools for approximately one hour per week to lead fourth- and fifth-graders in hands-on science activities. A given team returned to the same class four to six times, implementing a sequence of lessons related to one curriculum topic area (see Table 11.1). When the sequence was completed, that team of teens moved to another class and taught the lessons to a new group of elementary school students. On some occasions, the team of teens stayed with the same group of students and began work with a new curriculum unit. Scientist volunteers often accompanied teams to the elementary school sites. The teams met regularly during the week at Alpha High to discuss their experiences and refine plans for subsequent visits.

During the year, both teens and elementary school students made several field trips to local science attractions and to a number of industrial and research sites. The latter were usually visits to the workplaces of volunteer scientists and engineers.

Liaison With the Community

This implementation of SAY also had a substantial community awareness and education component. With the help of a SAY Project staff member, parent groups were formed at each of the elementary schools. These groups met approximately once a month to discuss the project and to learn about the science activities that their children were doing in the project. Through its community liaison work, the project also arranges and sponsors occasional community events. During the first year of the project, a community day to raise awareness of the project attracted 800 people.

The Participants in Action

The following paragraphs provide a snapshot from the point of view of the teen leaders of some of the key activities that took place. The descriptions are taken from real events that occurred in the first 18 months of the project. There is considerable variation from one work session to another, depending on the curriculum unit and a number of local setting considerations, but the example conveys the general outline of the process in action.

Planning an Activity. A team of four teen leaders, having completed the curriculum unit It Came From Planted Earth, continued working with the same fifth-grade youngsters on a second unit, Recycle, Reuse, Reduce. The teen leaders, with their adult coaches, a scientist from a nearby computer equipment research facility, and a teaching academy faculty member, met to plan the sequence of upcoming sessions. They reviewed a section in the curriculum guide, "Advance Preparation and Materials You Will Need," for the "paper-making" activity. They planned to do this activity during their first session with the elementary school students and worked out exactly what each of the team members would do. The coaches reviewed the science concepts and processes that would be introduced by the teens and shared with them some teaching tips to make an accurate presentation. With plans finalized, the group set out to obtain the necessary supplies and materials to carry out the paper-making activity.

A Teen-Led Classroom Activity. When the teen leaders arrived by bus at the elementary school site, they prepared the room for making paper. Tables were covered with newspapers and supplies set out. As fifth graders entered the room, they were organized in groups of five or six members with one teen leader per group. Each group surrounded a table and began the activity. The teens led discussions of cycles involved in paper, seasons, water, aluminum, air, and food. They then explored a cycle by working with paper as an example. Then they made planter cups from recycled newspapers. Group members tore up old newspapers and put them into a bucket of hot water. They began to blend the mixture into a paper pulp.

The teen leaders asked "sciencing" questions, capitalizing on the sense of inquiry that emerged in the group: Describe what you are observing. What does this paper pulp look like? How does it feel? What does it smell like? Do you know what is happening? Have you ever done anything like this before? What other materials can be recycled?

A Community Service Project. The group molded their paper pulp into drinking cups and set them out to dry. They then made plans for their next steps. What could they do with these recycled newspaper cups? How could they share these with their community? The group decided they would plant seeds in their recycled paper cups and take the seedlings to a nearby convalescent home for senior citizens. They discussed the possible arrangements that would have to take place.

Over the course of the next few weeks, while waiting for their seeds to sprout, the group continued meeting and teens led the participants through other hands-on Recycle, Reuse, Reduce activities. When the seedlings were ready, the entire group walked to the convalescent home and met with the seniors. The students each adopted a senior and the pairs spent time together. The youngsters discussed gardening and plants with the seniors and explained what they had learned while working on the project. They spoke of what they had learned about seeds, soil, water, and food while working on It Came From Planted Earth. They discussed cycles, diversity, adaptation, and the environmental effects of an oil spill, from the Recycle, Reuse, Reduce curriculum. Then they asked their senior partners to help plant and care for the seedlings they had brought. Each team of student and senior worked the soil and planted the seedlings. Each student asked his or her senior partner to care for the seedling and promised to return to visit. The garden of seedlings grew. The seniors spent time each day caring for the plants and looked forward to sharing each plant's progress with the returning youngsters.

Results of First-Year Experience

The implementation of the SAY Project in Northern California is ambitious in its intentions both to create an innovative program of early experiences for prospective teachers and to change the amount and kinds of science experiences available to primary and secondary school students. The project also has a complex organization in that it involved two school districts, the University of California Division of Agriculture and Natural Resources, several scientific and engineering professional agencies such as the Society of Women Engineers and the Society of Hispanic Engineers, and several community agencies. Practically every activity required cooperative coordinated action among two or more of these agencies, most often without any formal or binding agreements. Given the number of agencies involved and the fact that the project leaders also had time-consuming commitments to other high-priority activities, the project made remarkable progress during its first year. Although there was progress in every area of the project, some areas made greater strides than others. The project's primary program goals were accomplished, and the necessary support mechanisms to expand and improve project performance were put in place.

From examination of project documents and information collected during a one-week site visit by interviews with staff, teachers, teens, elementary school students, parents, and volunteer scientists; classroom and field observations; and tests of attitudes toward science, several aspects of the project were identified as strengths. Cross-age teaching as implemented in the project appeared to fully engage both teen leaders and elementary school students. Elementary school teachers reported lower rates of absenteeism among their students when teen leaders were scheduled to work with their classes, and both teens and elementary school students reported that the cross-age teaching was both challenging and exciting.

A second aspect of the project that was often mentioned as a strength was the organization of teens into cooperative teams to work on and implement the hands-on science experiences. Teen leaders reported learning from each other and being supported by other team members both when work was going well and especially when individual team members either lost focus or motivation to complete their contributions to the team's work.

The curriculum tasks and activities were very well received by the elementary school students. Regardless of setting, active engagement with hands-on tasks had a strong appeal for students.

Potential concerns about the appropriateness of the curriculum tasks for elementary school children came from two sources. First, would the tasks be interesting and engaging for the students, engaging enough so that elementary school students would cooperate in acting on them? Second, there was concern initially whether the tasks would fit the science curriculum in the district and state sufficiently well to garner support from school faculty members. Although most of the elementary school teachers viewed the tasks as appropriate for their students, they also suggested that the units were shorter than they would typically design themselves for use in school classrooms. This response seemed to be motivated, at least in part, by a desire on the part of the teachers to extend the activities into additional sessions with their students between the occasions when teens worked in their classes.

During the first year of the project, teen leaders visited their elementary school classes on Wednesday afternoons. As a result, elementary school students worked intermittently on, say, earthquakes once a week for about 6 weeks. If the classroom teacher initiated science instruction during this 6-week period, it was not clear whether this instruction should extend the project curriculum or be completely independent of it. This potential conflict between teen-led science activities and ongoing teacher-led activities is being addressed during the second year of the project.

During the first year, there was considerable variability in how scientist volunteers participated in the project. A substantial number of volunteers were identified and recruited by the project. Volunteers came from two sources, those recruited through contacts in the Society of Women Engineers and other professional organizations, and those recruited from a nearby research institute. Although an orientation to the project and opportunities for the scientist volunteers to meet and talk with teen leaders took place, relatively few volunteers were able to attend. As a result, some volunteers began working with teams of teens after having training in the curriculum content and pedagogy and an orientation to their roles, whereas others did not have these prior experiences. During the first year, volunteer scientists were most successful when they kept in consistent communication with their teams of teens by telephone as well as attending face-to-face sessions.

Teen Leaders' Comments on Learning to Teach

The teens who participated in the first year of the SAY Project were very positive about their experiences. They generally described the project as an authentic intervention in the science programs of elementary school students rather than as an exercise of the Alpha Teaching Academy. They spoke about it with enthusiasm, leaving the interviewers with no doubt that the experience had had a strong effect on the teens. Excerpts from interviews with teens are included here, in the teens' own words, as another way of describing the project (Fisher, 1993). When asked to describe the project, teen leaders suggested:

The project is more where the SERIES Program and the [Alpha] Teaching Academy joined together and formed a small organization of our own allowing the Teaching Academy sophomores to go into elementary schools and teach interesting science lessons that make . . . science learning interesting to the students.

Like a project to help get the kids involved and to get them excited about science.

We go into elementary school and teach science projects and make it more exciting for them to want to learn about science instead of just sitting there just doing lectures—and to listen to you but have fun at the same time and doing a project afterwards.

From these comments, it appears that teen leaders saw the active hands-on science activities and their own potential as motivators to be the primary thrusts of the program. None of the teen leaders perceived the project primarily as a practice teaching situation where the teens were getting field experience with elementary school students. Although this may have been considered too obvious by the teen leaders, it may also be evidence of the authenticity of the teaching task as experienced by the teens. They were being real teachers.

When asked about what they actually did in the project, teen leaders focused primarily on teaching.

> Okay, I was the group leader for my group. Like there was five of us and what we did basically is every Wednesday we went out to, well my school was [school name] but we were all at different schools. So they'd take two different fifth-grade classes and we were there for five weeks and we went every Wednesday. And we taught them about science. My subject was chemicals. We had them do a lot of activities, we tried to make them so that the kids would learn everything.
>
> Let's see, other than going to the classrooms and teaching them the science lesson. And most of the lesson, you know we revised them and try to teach them different ways and we've also gone into, like for the community project, besides going in, like the days that they had community projects so the kids could show their parents what they were learning. I'd go in and help the kids set up, you know help them show their parents what they were learning with the snails.

Most teen leaders found their actual interactions with the elementary students to be rewarding, but several also commented on their training experiences and the preteaching planning activities. Many teen leaders commented on the interactions among teens while preparing to teach. These planning activities were usually carried out by a four-member group. Although this group work was not often mentioned by teens as something that they liked best about the project (there was probably too much conflict in the groups for that), all of the teens mentioned this aspect of their work in other portions of the interview. As one might expect, work was not always evenly distributed among team members, and this created a potent context for the teens to test each others' limits. This was also a context in which teens could struggle with and practice elements of leadership. In some cases, team leaders arose who went to considerable lengths to get participation from other team members. Some teams developed phone trees to keep communication flowing regarding meetings and team tasks. This is also a context within which some of the volunteer scientists demonstrated their maturity, interpersonal skills, and high levels of commitment to the teens. Although the teens valued the suggestions of their volunteer scientists about science content, it was the mentors who facilitated their group interaction and spent time talking with them on the telephone who seemed to earn greatest respect among the teens.

When asked what they had learned about teaching as a result of their participation in the project, teens were almost unanimous in stating that teaching is more difficult than they had thought.

> I learned that it's not easy. I didn't know that a teacher's lesson plan had to be planned minute by minute and getting all the materials together and it's not easy but it's fun once you do it.

> Teaching is a lot harder than I thought it was. . . . There are lots of things that you have to do, you can't get real mad at the kids because a lot of them ask stupid questions and you want to say, you know if you just think about it, you know use your common sense, but you've got to explain it to them.

> I learned that it's hard, because sometimes there's days like "Oh my goodness, get me out of here" because it's stressing. But you know it's very stressful getting the things together and all of that. . . . Teaching is one of the top three [careers] that I want to do. I want to teach, I think I want to teach high school.

> Well what I've learned was it's been real helpful— depending on my other group mates and everything—all our ideas together, more of a team teaching effort, and the lessons went good. I think generally for teaching I've learned to take more time and plan the lessons instead of just keeping them right out of the book and reading and answering questions. You know that's what I thought at first, that's all there was [to teaching]. Then after awhile, you know once with the project and everything, it's like it's a lot more fun when you get to get the kids to do a lot more and everything.

> And I just learned more about like how, like how teachers need to change their—like how some teachers—you have to be different than like—you don't have to change your personality but you have to adjust to what class you have. Because I mean, I—we had two classes and I acted different. I had to be more strict and more mean like in the second class than my first class because we had the GATE class and I was like more open. I was really nice to the kids but the second class was like really out of hand and we had to be mean to them. And like, you know be really strict. I just learned about the kid's personalities.

That kids can know when you're nervous. That, you know when you're nervous . . . they can tell right off the bat. And they can usually get to you. But if you're outgoing and you make it fun, they'll respect you and they'll work for you. But I have a lot of fun doing it [teaching]. I don't know if I'd want to do it as a career; it seems very stressful, but it seems very rewarding.

It's not very easy. Well we had taught a lot of times but not as much and it just helps me realize what things you can work on, what things you can improve, what things you need to cut out of your curriculum and stuff like that. It just really helps you find out what they like and what they don't and things like that. . . . Yeah I think I'm probably going to be teaching—before I hadn't really. Yeah I'm thinking about it—and really having more experience with the kids and it's helped me do more hands-on with kids and I think it made me realize how much they really need someone to teach them all that stuff.

Oh the first one [lesson] that I ever did we were so nervous, we were like "Oh my goodness what are we going to do," what are we going to do, but we went in there and I think that was our best one. We did so good the first one. I couldn't believe it because I didn't think we would. We went up there like "Oh we're not going to do good," and everything like that, but we did really good.

These statements give an indication of what teens learned about teaching, about working with others, and about themselves. These very real experiences are likely to change the way that these teens approach teacher education programs should they follow through with career intentions. One might also expect that experiences in the project might have an impact on how the teens see themselves as high school students. When asked about this, they commented on several aspects of their behavior.

I myself felt that I changed a lot, so did my teachers. I respect them a lot more. It's not that I didn't respect them before, but I respect them a lot more now. And I feel that like if I don't do my homework or something, you know I feel real bad. I feel that if I'm going to tell the kids to do their homework or something like that and they wouldn't do it—that I would think gosh, now I feel like "Oh shoot I want to do my homework."

Kind of, yeah. I'm not so afraid to talk [in high school classes] anymore. Yeah, because you know I feel if I can get in front of a bunch of fifth graders and tell them what to do I should be able to get in front of a bunch of high schoolers and talk about things. . . . Let's see, well I think a little bit more about what I say. Because, you know when you're around fifth graders you can't really talk like you do around here—because they get really shocked when you slip—they really get shocked. So I start thinking a little bit more about what I'm going to say.

But it's just inspired me to want to go out [to teach in elementary schools] by myself. I was even considering some time in June returning to [school name] with more of an additional recycling demonstration for them and stuff. And then on the 25th of May I'm taking an earthquake lesson to [school name] which is in the [name] school district. It was my school when I was young.

Yeah, it's kind of helped me more to realize, it's helped me be a better student I think, I don't know. It's given me—it didn't give me more time but since it took more time, more of my energy, it helps me put, you know more of my energy, you know into school with the project and it helped me to be a better student. But I put the same energy, I've kind of thought about putting the energy I put into the project into school. . . . Probably because the Project, it's fun, it's so much fun but it takes a lot of time planning all the lessons and stuff and you don't realize how much time it takes until you're there doing it and how much time it takes to get all the materials and plan all the lessons. So that does take a lot of time.

Yeah, I've become a much better student. But at the beginning of the year my grades were dropping, but then I started doing better. [Interviewer: Why do you think you changed?] Probably because if I want to be a teacher I have to get good grades and go to college and slacking off won't help.

Teen leaders had a strong positive response to their participation in the project. They seemed to see themselves as being involved in real teaching as opposed to an exercise. They liked working with the elementary school students and their overall experiences in the project provided striking insights about the nature of teaching and insights about themselves as teachers, students, and leaders.

Summary

The SAY Project engages future teachers in using an educationally sound set of science learning experiences with elementary school students. The goal of the project is to develop and strengthen an understanding of the applications of scientific problem solving for both the teen and youth participants. SAY was developed to involve U.S. youth directly in learning about scientific concepts and processes, and to support them in using those concepts and processes to solve real-world problems in their homes and communities. But the project is also an innovative way to provide prospective teachers with early experiences with teaching science, using contemporary methods of teaching and learning, and getting to know real students. The SAY Project emphasizes that these early experiences include an expanded vision of education, a vision beyond the classroom walls, and beyond the classroom bells. Project participants have opportunities to see students work in explicit and implicit problem-solving situations, and to experience their ability to help children learn. Project SAY encourages prospective teachers to dabble, to work cooperatively with others, to share their thoughts and questions, and to receive support from teaching professionals. These experiences could have a strong influence on the effects of teacher training programs on beginning teachers and provide the youngsters with whom the teens work with more and better opportunities to learn science in authentic and meaningful contexts. The SAY Project promises to improve the science literacy of both the prospective teachers and the students they teach.

References

American Association for the Advancement of Science. (1989). *Project 2061: Science for all Americans.* Washington, DC: AAAS Publications.

Clift, R., Houston, R., & Pugach, M. (Eds.). (1990). *Encouraging reflective practice in education: An analysis of issues and programs.* New York: Teachers College Press.

Clinchy, E. (1993, December 8). Magnet schools matter: Why are we ignoring our one sure, proven path to successful reform? *Education Week,* pp. 28-31.

Fisher, C. (1993, December). *Project Excel: An assessment of year 1.* Unpublished manuscript, Boulder, CO.

Goodlad, J. I. (1984). *A place called school.* New York: McGraw-Hill.

Grimmett, P., & Erickson, G. (Eds.). (1988). *Reflection in teacher education.* New York: Teachers College Press.

Guzzetti, B., Snyder, T., & Glass, G. (1992). Promoting conceptual change in science: Can texts be used effectively? *Journal of Reading, 35,* 542-649.

Hurd, P. (1992, September 16). "First in the world by 2000": What does it mean? *Education Week,* p. 36.

Kagan, D. (1992). Professional growth among preservice and beginning teachers. *Review of Educational Research, 62*(2), 129-169.

Karplus, R., Lawson, A., Wollman, W., Appel, M., Bernoff, R., Howe, A., & Thier, H. (1967). *A new way to look at elementary school science.* Chicago: Rand McNally.

Lagemann, E. (1989). The plural worlds of educational research. *History of Education Quarterly, 29,* 185-214.

Reich, R. B. (1983). *The next American frontier: A provocative program for economic renewal.* New York: Penguin.

Reich, R. B. (1991). *The work of nations: Preparing ourselves for 21st century capitalism.* New York: Knopf.

Renner, J., & Marek, E. (1988). *The learning cycle and elementary school science teaching.* Portsmouth, NH: Heinemann.

Reynolds, A. (1992). What is competent beginning teaching? A review of the literature. *Review of Educational Research, 62*(1), 1-35.

Richardson, V. (1990). Significant and worthwhile change in teaching practice. *Educational Researcher, 19*(7), 10-18.

Russell, T. (1993). Reflection-in-action and the development of professional expertise. *Teacher Education Quarterly, 20*(1), 51-62.

Russell, T., & Munby, H. (1990). Science as a discipline, science as seen by students and teachers' professional knowledge. In R. Miller (Ed.), *Doing science: Images of science in science education* (pp. 107-125). London: Falmer.

Schön, D. (1983). *The reflective practitioner: How professionals think in action.* New York: Basic Books.

Schön, D. (1987). *Educating the reflective practitioner: Toward a new design for teaching and learning in the professions.* San Francisco: Jossey-Bass.

Zeichner, K., & Liston, D. (1987). Teaching student teachers to reflect. *Harvard Educational Review, 57,* 1-22.

12 Preparing Teachers for the 21st Century

Robert Alley

Burga Jung

Robert Alley is Professor in the Department of Curriculum and Instruction at Wichita State University. His research interests in teacher education include the future of education, teacher efficacy, and instructional strategies involving motivation and classroom discipline.

Burga Jung is Assistant Professor in the Department of Curriculum and Instruction at Texas Tech University. Her research interests incorporate qualitative methods to study curriculum decision making in professional development schools, curriculum development courses, and student teaching.

ABSTRACT

Preservice teachers completing their programs in the coming years will serve virtually all of their careers in the 21st century. Yet, teacher education programs continue to emphasize a foundations program that ignores changes teachers will face in the next century. A futurist component is needed in the knowledge base for teacher education. This chapter (a) delineates seven trends that futurists have identified as likely to effect major change upon our society in the 21st century; (b) indicates effects these trends will likely have upon our educational systems; and

(c) suggests that in teacher education curricula, students
should acquire a knowledge base about the future.

As educators consider the base of knowledge and practice that they
believe must underlie teacher education, psychological, philosophical,
cultural, and social foundations are quickly identified as keys to the
background that teachers must possess as professionals. Teacher education curricula are, of course, developed with those foundational areas in
mind; they encompass a considerable portion of the teacher education
curriculum, often well over half of the required credit hours. Although
these foundational areas of study are essential background for a professional educator, they are insufficient.

One additional foundational area should be a part of every teacher
education curriculum. *Futurism*, or the study of the future, is crucial if
future teachers are to adapt to an ever-changing, dynamic society. The
central argument is not so much that futurism must be studied as a
separate and distinct discipline (although it could be), but that systematic
study of the future, largely missing from today's teacher education programs, should be made an integral part of every teacher education curriculum.

In this chapter, we (a) delineate a series of trends that futurists have
identified as likely to effect major change in our society in the 21st century,
(b) indicate the effects the trends will likely have upon our educational
systems, and (c) suggest that in teacher education curricula, students
should acquire a knowledge base about the future.

The Trends

Futurists have identified numerous trends that will impact our society. Here we discuss seven important trends that are expected to especially
influence educational systems.

TREND #1: *We are participants in a revolution, the change from an industrial to an information or communications society.* Theobald (1976) first suggested the emergence of a new era based upon improved communications;
all futurists now accept the notion that such a fundamental change in our
society is under way. It has come to be described as a "communications
revolution." Toffler (1980), in his book *The Third Wave*, described the

emergence of a new world order, or "third wave," equivalent in impact to the agricultural revolution and the industrial revolution. As Toffler (1980) pointed out, the dawn of this Third Wave (emergence of a new civilization) "is an event as profound as that First Wave of change unleashed ten thousand years ago by the invention of agriculture, or the earthshaking Second Wave of change touched off by the industrial revolution" (p. 25).

In *PowerShift*, Toffler (1990) attempts to make sense of the astonishing changes propelling us into the 21st century. He describes the importance of information from a business executive's perspective. Quoting the California financier Robert I. Weingarten, he states, "Nowadays the ability to make a deal happen very often depends more on knowledge than on the dollars you bring to the table. At a certain level it's easier to obtain the money than the relevant know-how. Knowledge is the real power lever."

Others have written of the same changes under such different terms as information age, space age, electronic era, postindustrial society, or global village. Pelton (1990) described these communication changes as "telepower," but Naisbitt (1982) really popularized the communications concept by describing a "high-tech" society.

By whatever name it is called, this combined scientific, economic, and social communications revolution can easily be observed in our everyday lives through contemporary communications systems that utilize the telephone, the television, the computer, or some combination of the three (O'Hair, O'Rourke, & O'Hair, in press). It can also be observed through changes such as the establishment of neighborhood computer and video stores that have replaced corner gasoline stations and neighborhood grocery stores of earlier eras as major influences in our communities and our daily lives.

This fundamental trend, the communications revolution, has so changed the nature of our economy that as early as the 1970s only 5% of *new* jobs in our society were in manufacturing, whereas 90% were in the information, knowledge, or service sectors of the economy (Birch, 1981). Further, although currently about 12% of our workforce is engaged in manufacturing, by 2020 it is expected that as few as 3% of our population will be employed in blue-collar, manufacturing jobs. Cetron and Gayle (1990) estimate that by the year 2000 as many as 43% of available new jobs will be in knowledge (information) fields. Clearly, a shift in the nature of jobs created in the society continues to occur. As pointed out, these new jobs will require more education and technical skills than presently provided to public school students and will be with small companies (Birch, 1987; Cetron & Gayle, 1990; Coates, Jarratt, & Mahaffie, 1991).

Those seeking the available jobs will need more education and training or retraining opportunities than are currently available in public schools to enable them to compete well with others for the jobs. Educators and business leaders will collaborate and integrate workplace competencies into academic subjects. In this way, not only will academic subjects, such as mathematics, science, and English, acquire career relevance for students, but students will also be alerted early to changes in the business and professional worlds and enabled to make better career choices.

The communications revolution has resulted in the emergence of a practice described as the electronic cottage (Wolfgram, 1984). In our society a computer can be available, along with the television set, in virtually every home. A linking of the two to the telephone system permits instantaneous communications by voice, printed word, and picture throughout the society. Electronic mail systems, now a reality among corporations and public agencies and rapidly entering elementary and secondary schools, are one further example. As schools and teachers become habituated to the usefulness of computers in classroom activities, subject content, and instructional strategies, they will add complementary instructional vehicles such as E-mail.

Gradually, the E-mail concept is also being adapted for the home, making for a true electronic cottage. Anyone with a home computer can subscribe to an information service to receive specific information or receive communications from other persons throughout the world. Presently, stock quotations, catalog ordering, personal messages, and sports news can be acquired without ever leaving the home. The electronic cottage also enables countless people to conduct business operations from their home, traveling to an office in a separate location only sporadically (Cunningham & Porter, 1992). Library services are now commonly provided through a similar process. Although E-mail is not yet evident in most schools, it is sure to come (Pesanelli, 1993). And not far behind will be the technologies of teleconferencing, multimedia applications, and Internet.

TREND #2: *Change is occurring ever more rapidly.* Over two decades ago Toffler (1970) talked about a concept he called future shock. Second only to the communications revolution in its importance, the phenomenon he described, rapid change, continues to be evident. Some examples of rapid change include: One third of the shelf items in the local supermarket were not there 10 years ago; approximately 1,000 new books are published each day; nearly 250,000 of our present complement of 450,000 words in the

English language were unknown to Shakespeare; and 50% of today's factual, scientific knowledge will be obsolete 10 years from now.

This rapidity of change is further exaggerated by a phenomenon known as the telescoping effect. To illustrate, people who have reached the age of one average lifetime (62 years) have seen as much change in their lives as did all the generations that lived during the previous 800 lifetimes (Toffler, 1970). Further, it is expected that the next 10 years will bring as much change as did the last 40 years. Compression of change into shorter and shorter time spans is expected to continue to a time when the amount of change to which we must adapt will double every 3-5 years.

The enormity of this change process can be easily understood by many older teachers who literally have lived in both the horse-and-buggy era and the space age. However, all teachers must consider changes that best serve educational purposes in schools and then incorporate and adapt changes to enhance subject content areas and instructional strategies.

TREND #3: *Personalization and self-reliance will be essential amid technological changes.* Naisbitt (1982) articulated an important concept, "high tech," which received a great deal of attention both from the press and the public. Of special importance to educators, but often lost in the attention given to the high-tech concept, was a corollary, "high touch." High touch focuses on a counterdemand for more personalization of services by people in response to the demands that technology places upon their lives.

Evidence of self-reliance within institutions is found in the increasing emphasis on self-reliance in our schools and in the business world. Managers as well as secretaries are expected to be computer literate. School principals and teachers are expected to access computer programs as easily as computer science instructors. Evidence of self-reliance also can be seen on a more individualized scale as has been pointed out elsewhere. Cottage industries are thriving. The home schooling movement points not only to dissatisfaction with public schools but also to a desire by university-educated parents to increase reliance on their own resources.

Decentralization of power is further evidence of self-reliance. Confidence in government has declined (Fields, 1993; Toffler & Toffler, 1993). As a result there has been a decided move to decentralize and democratize government in this country (Naisbitt, 1982). Power and decision making are being transferred from Washington to state capitals and from state capitals to local communities. Within the local community the trend has been extended to neighborhood groups that have received increased attention and power.

A parallel in education can be seen in the movement to site-based school management. As states reassert their power over education vis-à-vis Washington, local education agencies (LEAs) are implementing state-approved, site-based management practices. Some LEAs are seeking autonomy from their state education agency. School-based management teams include not only teachers and administrators but also parents, students, business leaders, and health service professionals. For the remainder of the decade and into the 21st century, moving the control of education more directly to the local level, especially through forms of parental choice, may well become the watchword for education. Teachers are no longer expected to stay behind closed classroom doors. They are expected to engage in collaborative decision making over school curricula (Jung, 1991, 1993) and other school concerns, such as budgets.

TREND #4: *Demographic shifts are under way that parallel the decline of the industrial society and the development of the communications society.* First, a well-documented population shift from the industrialized Northeast to the Sunbelt has taken place over the past several decades. What is less well understood is that our population shift has been largely to specific areas: the Southwest, the West Coast, and Florida. In these ways, both cities and whole states are experiencing a pattern of rapid growth, especially among their younger populations.

Second, the "aging" of the United States, a social change of monumental proportions, is described quite graphically by Dychtwald and Flower (1989) in *Age Wave.* Our population, in spite of the recent baby boom, is an increasingly older one. In the United States we have more people over 60 than under 18 (Mirga, 1986). Many of these senior citizens are retiring from one career to seek a second (or even a third).

Third, we are nearing the time when a majority of the population in many states will be from minority cultures. Indeed, certain cities in the southwestern United States and one state, California, already find that to be true among their school-age population (Cetron, Soriano, & Gayle, 1985). Increased numbers of Hispanic and Asian immigrants and differential birth rates among various ethnic groups are the principal reasons for the present minority growth pattern.

Fourth, teacher education programs are beginning to be inundated with postbaccalaureate students who wish to become certified to teach. Some have just completed their undergraduate education whereas many others (such as retiring military personnel) are entering a second career. Most are willing to relocate to find teaching positions.

TREND #5: *We no longer live in an either/or society; we now live in a both/and society.* Sometimes referred to as the Baskin and Robbins Society (Naisbitt, 1982) because everything seems to come in 31 flavors, our society has developed into a "multioption" society. The educational equivalent to the Baskin and Robbins Society can be found in the emergence of thousands of alternative schools, magnet schools, independent schools, denominational schools, and home schools across the country, intended to give parents and students a choice about the type of school they will attend. In addition, entire school districts are adopting restructuring models such as Professional Development Schools, Essential Schools, Accelerated Schools, and Coalition Schools. Large school districts include many of these alternative schools to expand parental choice beyond the neighborhood school and to specialized schools offering foci such as foreign languages, fine arts, computer technology, science, mathematics, and health careers. Many school districts are also developing schools within schools in an attempt to both support neighborhood schools and include specialized programs.

TREND #6: *Changing lifestyles are evident.* A majority of children in the United States live in homes where both parents, or the only parent, work away from home (Cetron, 1994). Only 4% of our family units fit the supposed traditional pattern of homemaking mother, working father, and two children (Cetron & Gayle, 1990; Mirga, 1986). However, as recently as 1980, 11% of the families in the United States fit that pattern, providing evidence of a radical lifestyle change in the 1980s. As a result, as many as 10 million children are home alone most of each afternoon, or for longer periods, most weekdays ("Hello? I'm home alone," 1993). Further, Coates, Jarratt, and Mahaffie (1990) point out that the number of children under 6 needing supervision during the day will increase by 50% by the turn of the century.

Schools, though, continue to organize their daily, weekly, and yearly schedules and programs as if traditional family units were in the majority. Students are dismissed daily by mid-afternoon, hours before working parents return home. Few after-school programs can be found to coincide with parents' working hours. Teachers continue to expect parental supervision of students' homework assignments, parental attendance on day-long field trips and at school assemblies, and volunteer work at bake sales and in classrooms.

Other changes of an even more revolutionary nature may influence our future lifestyles. Millions in our population will shift roles and become self-employed entrepreneurs in one- or two-person cottage industry businesses (Cetron & Gayle, 1990; Wolfgram, 1984). For example, persons developing computer software for sale to others can develop, copy, package, and distribute those programs at home. Such persons are excellent examples of the combining of the cottage industry concept of the past with the communications revolution of the present into a new form of employment for the future through the electronic cottage. By the year 2000, it is estimated as much as 22% of the labor force will work at home (Cetron & Gayle, 1990). As a result of these changes, increasing numbers of adult citizens are expected to seek further education or training to make career changes.

TREND #7: *Increasingly we acknowledge that we live in a culturally pluralistic society.* A diversity of cultures exists in the United States (Carlson & Goldman, 1991). U.S. culture, though dominant (and notoriously difficult to define), is only one culture among many in this society. Other cultures exist in every major city as well as in most towns and are celebrated through parades, memorials, fiestas, and the like.

Teachers who have learned to honor the diverse cultures of their students will usually celebrate cultural diversity through emphasis on foods, clothing, and music. Though these cultural components are important, they are not necessarily substantive. Understanding cultural beliefs, valuing contributions from diverse cultures, and applying appropriate communication and social skills are examples of learning outcomes difficult to measure but essential to life in a culturally pluralistic society such as ours. Examples of ways in which schools include students' cultures are units of instruction in social studies on Native Americans, African American History Month, Mexican American Cinco de Mayo festivities, and Chinese New Year observances. Perhaps, assimilation is making way for accommodation (Nieto, 1992).

Implications for Teachers

To understand the future, classroom practitioners and preservice teachers must accept one axiom: The future is determined by the choices made today. Teachers have the choice to sit back, let the trends become pervasive, and then respond to them or to take an active role in shaping the future. And although society's responses to some of the enumerated trends are not yet well developed, it is clear that certain fundamental decisions in response to these trends must be made by education professionals if they are to shape their own destiny and develop a measure of control over their own lives (Dill, 1990; Longstreet & Shane, 1993). Critical changes in our educational system will be precipitated by the trends we have described here, mandating teacher responses to these changes (Alley, 1992-1993, 1993).

Our first response to this revolution, as it is to all trends, must be one of values. We must know our values (Barrow & Woods, 1988; Chambers, 1983; Fitzgibbons, 1981; Pratte, 1992; Reagan, 1983) and ask whether the society and we, as teachers, want the changes brought on by the trends. If so, for whom? For example, if as some have suggested only 10%-15% of our population will be working in for-pay jobs by the year 2020, who will have those jobs? Will holding those jobs be viewed as privilege or punishment? These are examples of fundamental questions that must be answered by society and most surely by teachers. Who benefits from tracking in schools? Who is eligible to attend specialized schools? Which resources are made available to which students? Who is counseled into college preparatory courses? These questions elicit answers and provoke implications about which teachers must be willing to deliberate and act (Goodlad, 1984; Goodlad, Soder, & Sirotnik, 1990; Kozol, 1991; Oakes, 1985).

Those persons in our society who oppose value-oriented curricula in schools are destined to fight a losing battle. Curricula are always value laden. If teachers want to help students formulate their own values, then teachers will have to prepare themselves for this task (Goodlad et al., 1990). Students deserve the opportunity to make intelligent decisions concerning their futures.

Teaching will become much more high touch. Schools can ill afford to continue to impart only knowledge to students (hoping students will remember it long enough for a test) whether through technology or didactic instructional practices. Humanization and personalization of our responses to technology, as suggested by Naisbitt's "high-touch" concept, will become increasingly important. In the 21st century the excellence movement will be tempered by an emphasis on socialization skills and a pedagogy of caring. Teachers are beginning to establish classrooms to meet two major goals: (a) a social environment where problem solving and thinking are group functions, and (b) a warm, human-oriented place to which students may return to fulfill their need for high touch as they interact with high tech in other areas of their lives.

The first goal can be addressed by thoughtfully planned heterogenous grouping, attention to the development of students' critical thinking skills, and cooperative learning strategies (Cohen, 1986; Johnson, Johnson, & Holubec, 1990; Little, 1980; Slavin, 1990). However, most teachers are not themselves cooperative learners, and thus rarely do preservice teachers experience cooperative learning before entering a teacher education program. Equally of concern, many teachers show little evidence of critical thinking in their daily schooling practices (Goodlad, 1984).

Teacher educators must find ways of introducing the social, pedagogical, and academic values and skills of cooperative learning and critical thinking. In addition, they must find ways of consistently modeling these values and skills, reinforcing them through their own instructional practices.

Given the diverse classroom most teachers will encounter, a pedagogy of caring is particularly timely (Nieto, 1992; Noddings, 1984; Stephens, Blackhurst, & Magliocca, 1988). Preservice teachers must believe that caring for each student is critical to students' educational welfare. They also must learn how to practice caring in the classroom through a pedagogy of caring for *all* students. In these ways, students will be encouraged to show caring for each other (Des Dixon, 1994; Noddings, 1984).

A fresh look at motivation will become increasingly important. A decreased emphasis upon the work ethic and a corresponding rise in hedonism resulting from the decline of for-pay jobs, reaction to change, and other factors, is a possibility society and its teachers must consider. In their planning efforts, teachers will be forced by changes in society to give motivation renewed attention. In particular, new forms of motivation other than today's common ones, such as job-related privileges, monetary rewards, or the acquisition of tangible possessions, will be required. The current emphasis on traditional behaviorism should be reexamined.

In the school of the future, self-reliance and self-motivation will be the classroom norm (Des Dixon, 1994). Teachers will be expected to use motivational strategies more appropriate to the interests and needs of children and youth who will live in the 21st century. Though the relationship of self-motivation and interests is a long-standing one (Dewey, 1956, 1938/1963), few teachers have taken this relationship seriously in their daily curriculum plans. One way teachers can attend to students' interests and needs is to develop instructional strategies based upon high touch concepts (such as cooperative learning), the socialization process, and the inclusion of students in curriculum planning. Teachers must also be more attentive to student diversity as special education students are mainstreamed (Stephens et al., 1988). Preservice teachers must be shown ways of adapting curricula and collaborating effectively with classroom aides and parents to ensure learning opportunities for all students in the inclusive classroom.

Teachers must be prepared to teach culturally different children. Cultural diversity is both a given and an asset in U.S. society (Alba, 1990). Teachers must come to recognize that fact and to value cultural diversity by affirming it (Nieto, 1992). Curricula that proactively include multicultural components will become increasingly important in a society in which demographic minorities are the majority in metropolitan areas and even entire states (Lomotey, 1990; McCarthy, 1990; Nieto, 1992). Teachers will be expected to accommodate students from diverse cultures (Nieto, 1992).

But curricula with multicultural components are also important in schools serving mainly majority students (Banks, 1992). In fact, all teachers will be responsible for incorporating the elements of a culturally diverse society into their curricula regardless of where in the United States they teach. For example, teachers in rural communities cannot assume that their students will return to the monocultural communities from which they came; most will live in culturally diverse areas of the society.

Education will be a lifelong pursuit. With society experiencing a combination of increased life span, the decline of for-pay jobs, an increasingly older population, multiple career changes, and rapidly increasing minority and immigrant populations, an educational system that serves the needs of all segments of society is a necessity. Our current practice of thinking of education as schooling for ages 5 to 18 is clearly outmoded and must be replaced with a new system wherein individuals can find the education and training needed for a productive life in a democratic society. For example, the communications revolution will demand an educated, well-trained, and periodically retrained populace. To support a populace prepared to make use of these rapidly changing and highly technological careers, teachers must themselves be willing to continue developing professionally (Clift, Houston, & Pugach, 1990; Connelly & Clandinin, 1988) and even take on entirely new leadership or support roles (Fosnot, 1989; Henderson, 1992; Jung, 1991, 1993). Many school districts are asking teachers to become involved in making schoolwide decisions rather than instructional decisions affecting only their own classrooms.

In addition to sharing decision making, many teachers are asked to become curriculum specialists, computer educators, and mentor teachers in their schools. In addition, teachers will be called upon to provide education and training for a wide range of ages, preschool to older adult, as more and more school districts are encouraging community use of public school facilities. For example, schools' computer facilities will be made available to the larger community. Also, teachers may be called upon to provide parents with necessary skills to effectively reinforce teachers' efforts with their own children at home. In essence, teachers may become consultants to parents and other adults in their community. Opportunities for teaching new and different populations will continue to expand well into the 21st century.

New forms of education and schooling may emerge. Some have suggested that nothing short of burning down the old school will enable us to restructure public education to meet future needs of the society (Illich, 1971). Such radical suggestions are, however, likely to give way to more gradual processes whereby new environments (such as community services), institutions (e.g., businesses, hospitals), and strategies (e.g., accessing Internet) make education more responsive to the needs of 21st century society. Teachers, in concert with leaders of other professions, may generate wholly new approaches to teaching and learning.

Schooling designed to meet the needs of an agrarian or industrial society will give way to other alternatives as citizens continue to demand options. Rigid daily and weekly scheduling of classes, an August/September through May/June school year, and school as a set of isolated classrooms in a building are examples of agrarian and industrial vestiges.

These outdated and now unproductive administrative practices can be replaced by practices that are developmentally appropriate for students, driven by learner interests and goals, facilitated by teachers and principals, community based, and real-life oriented. Meeting individual student needs is a major responsibility for teachers and will continue to be so in the 21st century.

As the electronic cottage with its computer and interactive video systems, options for teleconferences, and other electronic media become more common, it will also become imperative that teachers recognize that education is more than those experiences that fit a school-based design. Educational opportunities can be literally everywhere in our communities. With such an educational system teachers will be forced to redesign their curricula around these enormous changes and to be ever more flexible and adaptable (Ben-Peretz, 1990; Longstreet & Shane, 1993; Male, 1994). Teachers must think in terms of education taking place anywhere, at any time, rather than just in a school building. Clearly, the teacher's role must change under such a revolutionary system. Although school buildings may well continue to house some educational activities and resources, Illich's (1971) community-based public education will receive much more support than heretofore.

The central teaching function may change dramatically. Teachers will have to learn to concentrate on higher-level cognitive skills and applications of the knowledge along with the affective learning so critical to the high-touch need for the future. Again, teachers will be forced by such changes to rethink and redefine their role.

Teachers must adjust their role to accommodate increased technologically based teaching materials (Hawisher & LeBlanc, 1992), the need for high-touch experiences, and other changes. These obvious changes in teaching imply a fundamental change in the teaching function and consequently in the teacher's role. Preservice teachers must learn to become flexible facilitators of students' learning experiences and supportive coaches as students practice a variety of relevant skills. Preservice teachers are *flexible* facilitators insofar as they attend to students' daily interests and needs. Continuous changes in subject matter knowledge will require teachers to remain current (Dill, 1990), as they must be knowledgeable resources for their students (Ben-Peretz, 1990; Stodolsky, 1988) as well as facilitators of learning opportunities.

Finally, the dual concepts, change and futurism, will become curriculum content. Curriculum material and teaching specialties related to the dual concepts of change and futurism may be as important to 21st-century education as social studies or sciences are to today's curriculum (Longstreet & Shane, 1993). The concepts may be taught as free-standing units or courses of study or integrated into existing curricula. But clearly they will be taught. Such materials and curricula have been developed and are currently being implemented in school systems scattered about the country. More will follow as preservice teachers are educated to enact curriculum practices that accommodate student diversity, the habits of a reflective practitioner, and a fuller understanding of the teacher's changing role.

Summary

With the nation addressing the health care issue in the latter half of the current decade, education will be the major public agenda item as the 21st century begins. It seems likely that the public will increasingly turn its attention to "solving the education problem." The structure of the system, delivery modes, and the learning process, among other facets of the education system, are all likely to undergo fundamental restructuring. As a consequence of such profound changes, classroom practitioners will find the changes to which they must adjust to be staggering.

As the nation focuses upon educational changes, teachers would do well to remind themselves from time to time that the education profession can be nothing if it is not a reflection of the educational needs of the society. Teachers can view these projected changes as opportunities for self-renewal or as problems that they must confront. Perhaps they will be a bit of both. Teacher educators can play a decisive role in promoting "change for the better" by preparing preservice teachers to acknowledge these desirable changes as also necessary and to work for their implementation. Preservice teachers can also help to introduce schools to new instructional strategies (such as cooperative learning), up-to-date subject matter knowledge, and a pedagogy of caring as they practice their newly acquired teaching skills.

Whether teachers seize the opportunity to shape their own future or through inaction permit others to do so is their decision to make. The decisions teachers make now—or fail to make—will establish the nature of the educational system of the next century.

References

Alba, R. (1990). *Ethnic identity: The transformation of white America.* New Haven, CT: Yale University Press.

Alley, R. D. (1992-1993). Teacher education in the 21st century: Challenges for the new South. *SRATE Journal, 2*(1), 10-14.

Alley, R. D. (1993). *Teacher education in the twenty-first century: Challenges for America.* Paper presented at the annual meeting of the Association of Teacher Educators, Los Angeles.

Banks, J. A. (1992). Multicultural education: For freedom's sake. *Educational Leadership, 49*(4), 32-36.

Barrow, R., & Woods, R. (1988). *An introduction to philosophy of education.* London: Routledge.

Ben-Peretz, M. (1990). *The teacher-curriculum encounter: Freeing teachers from the tyranny of text.* Albany: State University of New York Press.

Birch, D. L. (1981). Who creates jobs? *Public Interest, 65,* 3-14.

Birch, D. L. (1987). *Job creation in America.* New York: Free Press.

Carlson, R., & Goldman, B. (1991). *2020 visions: Long view of a changing world.* Stanford, CA: Stanford Alumni Association.

Cetron, M. J. (1994). The American renaissance in the year 2000: 74 trends that will affect America's future—and yours. *Futurist, 28*(2), 27-37.

Cetron, M. J., & Gayle, M. E. (1990). Educational renaissance: 43 trends for U.S. schools. *Futurist, 24*(5), 33-40.

Cetron, M. J., Soriano, B., & Gayle, M. (1985). Schools of the future. *Futurist, 19*(4), 8-23.

Chambers, J. H. (1983). *The achievement of education: An examination of key concepts in educational practice.* New York: Harper & Row.

Clift, R. T., Houston, W. R., & Pugach, M. C. (Eds.). (1990). *Encouraging reflective practice in education: An analysis of issues and programs.* New York: Teachers College Press.

Coates, J. F., Jarratt, J., & Mahaffie, J. B. (1990). *Future work.* San Francisco: Jossey-Bass.

Coates, J. F., Jarratt, J., & Mahaffie, J. B. (1991). Future work. *Futurist, 25*(3), 9-19.

Cohen, E. G. (1986). *Designing groupwork: Strategies for the heterogeneous classroom.* New York: Teachers College Press.

Connelly, F. M., & Clandinin, D. J. (1988). *Teachers as curriculum planners: Narratives of experience.* New York: Teachers College Press.

Cunningham, S., & Porter, A. L. (1992). Communication networks. *Futurist, 26*(1), 19-22.

Des Dixon, R. G. (1994). Future schools—and how to get there from here. *Phi Delta Kappan, 75*(5), 360-365.

Dewey, J. (1956). *The child and the curriculum.* Chicago: University of Chicago Press.

Dewey, J. (1963). *Experience and education.* New York: Macmillan. (Originally published 1938)

Dill, D. D. (1990). *What teachers need to know: The knowledge, skills, and values essential to good teaching.* San Francisco: Jossey-Bass.

Dychtwald, K., & Flower, J. (1989). *Age wave: Challenges and opportunities of an aging America.* Los Angeles: J. P. Tarcher.

Fields, D. M. (1993). Institutions for the 21st century. *Futurist, 27*(1), 33-34.

Fitzgibbons, R. E. (1981). *Making educational decisions: An introduction to philosophy of education.* New York: Harcourt Brace Jovanovich.

Fosnot, C. T. (1989). *Enquiring teachers, enquiring learners: A constructivist approach for teaching.* New York: Teachers College Press.

Goodlad, J. I. (1984). *A place called school: Prospects for the future.* New York: McGraw-Hill.

Goodlad, J. I., Soder, R., & Sirotnik, K. (Eds.). (1990). *The moral dimensions of teaching.* San Francisco: Jossey-Bass.

Hawisher, G. E., & LeBlanc, P. (1992). *Re-imagining computers and composition: Teaching and research in the virtual age.* Portsmouth, NH: Boynton/Cook.

Hello? I'm home alone. (1993, March 1). *Time,* pp. 46-47.

Henderson, J. G. (1992). *Reflective teaching: Becoming an inquiring educator.* New York: Macmillan.

Illich, I. (1971). *Deschooling society.* New York: Harper & Row.

Johnson, D. W., Johnson, R. T., & Holubec, E. J. (1990). *Circles of learning: Cooperation in the classroom.* Edina, MN: Interaction Book Company.

Jung, B. (1991). *Stakeholder interests in curriculum decision making: A case study.* Paper presented at the Conference on Curriculum Theory and Practice, Dayton, OH.

Jung, B. (1993). Curriculum development: Teacher empowering and professional. In M. J. O'Hair & S. J. Odell (Eds.), *Diversity and teaching: Teacher education yearbook I* (pp. 285-299). Fort Worth, TX: Harcourt Brace Jovanovich.

Kozol, J. (1991). *Savage inequalities: Children in America's schools.* New York: Crown.

Little, J. F. (1980). *Critical thinking and decision making.* Toronto: Butterworths.

Lomotey, K. (1990). *Going to school: The African-American experience.* Albany: State University of New York Press.

Longstreet, W. S., & Shane, H. G. (1993). *Curriculum for a new millennium.* Boston: Allyn & Bacon.

Male, M. (1994). *Technology for inclusion: Meeting the special needs of all students.* Boston: Allyn & Bacon.

McCarthy, C. (1990). *Race and curriculum: Social inequality and the theories and politics of difference in contemporary research on schooling.* Philadelphia, PA: Falmer.

Mirga, T. (1986, May 14). Traditional families—a dying breed? *Education Week,* p. 22.

Naisbitt, J. (1982). *Megatrends.* New York: Warner.

Nieto, S. (1992). *Affirming diversity: The sociopolitical context of multicultural education.* New York: Longman.

Noddings, N. (1984). *Caring: A feminine approach to ethics and moral education.* Berkeley: University of California Press.

Oakes, J. (1985). *Keeping track: How schools structure inequality.* New Haven, CT: Yale University Press.

O'Hair, D., O'Rourke, J., & O'Hair, M. J. (in press). *HarperCollins business communications handbook.* New York: HarperCollins.

Pelton, J. N. (1990). *Future talk: Global life in the age of telepower.* Boulder, CO: Cross Communications.

Pesanelli, D. (1993). The plug-in school. *Futurist, 27*(5), 29-32.

Pratte, R. (1992). *Philosophy of education: Two traditions.* Springfield, IL: Charles C Thomas.

Reagan, G. M. (1983). Applied ethics for educators: Philosophy of education as something else? In *Proceedings of the thirty-ninth annual meeting of the philosophy of education society.* Normal, IL: Philosophy of Education Society.

Slavin, R. E. (1990). *Cooperative learning: Theory, research, and practice.* Boston: Allyn & Bacon.

Stephens, T. M., Blackhurst, A. E., & Magliocca, L. A. (1988). *Teaching mainstreamed students.* New York: Pergamon.

Stodolsky, S. S. (1988). *The subject matters: Classroom activity in math and social studies.* Chicago: University of Chicago Press.

Theobald, R. (1976). *Beyond despair.* Washington, DC: New Republic Book.

Toffler, A. (1970). *Future shock.* New York: Random House.

Toffler, A. (1980). *The third wave.* New York: William Morrow.

Toffler, A. (1990). *PowerShift.* New York: Bantam.

Toffler, A., & Toffler, H. (1993, October 31). Societies at hyperspeed. *New York Times,* p. 17.

Wolfgram, T. H. (1984). Working at home. *Futurist, 18*(3), 31-34.

Curriculum:
Reflections and Implications

Kenneth A. Sirotnik

As promised, the preceding authors presented very different takes on curricula for educating teachers for leadership and change. Combining the perspectives of these three chapters yields a portion of a leadership and change curriculum. Following some reflections on issues raised by the authors, I conclude with implications for curriculum that build on their work and begin to flesh out the issues raised in my introduction to these chapters.

Reflections

Kowalski, in Chapter 10, notes in regard to the occupation of teaching that "the road to true professionalism is strewn with countless obstructions." He goes on to direct deserved attention to such features of schools and the work life of teachers as (a) the obdurate character of the organizational structure and culture, and the difficulties of changing substantially the ordinary day-to-day routines, roles, and expectations; (b) the powerful and conservative effect of socializing new teachers into old traditions; (c) the dilemmas and tensions between centralization and decentralization, control and autonomy, costs and benefits, professionals and patrons, and professionalism and unionism, among others; and (d) the debate around the existence, absence, or even the conceptual viability of a professional knowledge base.

In the main, I agree with Kowalski's analysis and his recommendation for a leadership curriculum that confronts these obstacles to "true professionalism." But there is at least one other major obstacle that must be noted: Perhaps the greatest obstruction on the "road to true professionalism" is the trip itself—at least according to the conventional itinerary. Although never explicitly defined by Kowalski, the elements of professionalism can be inferred and are generally consistent with traditional criteria of autonomy and self-regulation, knowledge and expertise, altruism, and social status. Comparisons to the "established professions" such as medicine, law, architecture and the like are made.

As argued persuasively by Soder (1990), however, claims to professionalism or attempts to professionalize the occupation of teaching based on mimicking criteria for professions such as medicine will inevitably fail. Following Johnson's (1972) penetrating sociological analysis of professionalism in terms of power relations, Soder (1990) notes that "doctors managed to gain privileges, power, higher incomes, and social status not solely through their own internal efforts but because their own efforts at consolidation and control were congruent—fortuitously, from the doctors' point of view—with external societal interests and values" (p. 62). This is not likely to happen for schoolteachers or administrators, regardless of appeals to "knowledge bases," "board certification examinations," and the like. Arguing more generally, Johnson (1972) puts the point this way: "A profession is not, then, an occupation, but a means of controlling an occupation. Likewise, professionalization is a historically specific process which some occupations have undergone at a particular time, rather than a process which certain occupations may always be expected to undergo because of their 'essential' qualities" (p. 45).

A leadership curriculum that deals with professionalism and professionalization, therefore, must challenge conventional notions of these concepts and raise the possibility of a new "professionalization rhetoric" that argues from definition of the occupation, has a moral basis, and "derives from a collective sense of the moral praise worthiness of that occupation" (Soder, 1990, p. 72).

A very different cut on these issues is offered by Ponzio and Fisher, in Chapter 11. In their analysis, an important part of the warrant for claims to leadership come from epistemological and pedagogical assumptions about the nature of knowledge and knowing and of teaching and learning. Although their focus is on science, their examples and discussion could be applied to teaching and learning more broadly.

Using contemporary terminology, Ponzio and Fisher would be described as constructivists. They see their discipline not as a corpus of content and information that can be packaged and delivered to students, but as a way of organizing and producing knowledge that requires the active engagement of teachers, students, and their experiential contexts. Consequently, they see teaching not as dissemination but as mentoring; teachers not as conduits of content but as knowledgeable guides through the disciplined ways of knowing. Moreover, they see learning not as receiving but as interacting; students not as passive recipients but as active agents in constructing their own understandings.

Wouldn't it be nice if teachers could approach their own work in these same ways? Constructivist views, of course, are quite compatible with the ideas of reflective practice (Schön, 1983) and of developing habits of critical thinking and reflection in future teachers (Zeichner & Liston, 1987), and with the general notion of schools as centers of inquiry and change (Schaefer, 1967; Sirotnik, 1989). To begin to realize these possibilities, Ponzio and Fisher attempt to break through the less than desirable training most all of us get to become classroom teachers—13 years of conventional, classroom education. They describe a novel high school curriculum for interested teens designed to intervene well before their formal teacher education (should they ever seek it).

Why not extrapolate the argument to its logical conclusion? Why not begin to see all formal education as preparation for teaching? I know no better way to teach powerful concepts than to engage learners with them in ways that they could then engage others. Teaching to learn, in this view, is learning to teach. Imagine a kindergarten through baccalaureate experience of this kind of teaching and learning—even harder, imagine it extending through graduate school! Formal teacher education programs, then, would continue to model appropriate concepts and practices; they would not have to spend valuable time trying to undo the bad habits acquired during K-16 apprenticeships; and they would not have their work undone once students were back in schools on the job.

This is a dream worth thinking about and trying to approximate. In the meantime, there are important points of intervention along the way, and Ponzio and Fisher illustrate one of them. It is important to remember, however, that fostering more reflective and constructivist teaching and learning—laying the foundation for instructional (or better, *pedagogical*) leadership—is not sufficient; it must be combined with a working awareness of the complexities of schools as cultural and sociopolitical organizations, and with the moral agency and responsibility that goes with accepting work in these places.

So far, our discussion of a leadership curriculum has attended to empirical observations about the problems of leadership, organizational change, and school improvement; perspectives on teaching and learning; and normative arguments about how public schooling in a democracy should be organized and conducted. Our discussion has not paid attention to predictions about the future and their likely impact on our present aspirations.

Futurists are inclined to remind us that if we aren't careful, we will be expending much time and effort trying to do a better job of preparing educational leaders for the schools and society we won't have. Thus, Alley and Jung, in Chapter 12, suggest that a curriculum for teacher leadership and change must pay attention to what the futurists have to tell us about societal trends, projections, and the like.

I do not think that futurism, or the study of the future, is a discipline (as suggested by the authors). Rather, it is a fairly generalized set of high-level inferences drawn from multidisciplinary analyses of the past and present. In fact, the main sources of argument used by Alley and Jung are nearly 15 years old. This does not mean necessarily that the trends they suggest are inaccurate; it just means that the "future" has been with us for some time.

By taking a critical stance with respect to futurism, I am not suggesting ostrichlike behavior with respect to best guesses about what is yet to come. I am suggesting that notwithstanding these best guesses, educators ought to be just as inclined to participate in producing as well as predicting the future. There are at least two related reasons for this. First, there are important problems with the accuracy and longevity of predictions, especially at levels specific enough for contemporary decision making. Alley and Jung note that "50% of today's factual, scientific knowledge will be obsolete 10 years from now." One wonders which half that statement or any other futuristic account falls into.

Second, these kind of high-inference guesses provide little in the way of prescription for the present. Nor does moral justification for present work necessarily derive from what the future might hold in store. Based upon current trends, for example, we might predict that our future schools, especially in urban areas, will be more violent and dangerous places to work in, and even more prisonlike in form and function. Should programs for preparing future teachers and educational leaders include combat training, use of various types of weaponry, disarming techniques, and self-defense? One trend, according to the authors, is that we live in an increasingly culturally pluralistic society. Do concerns for and with multiculturalism and diversity stem from the predictions of demographers, or should these concerns have surfaced the moment this country was taken from those who were here first and then reconstructed on the backs of people imported from elsewhere?

My point is simply this: We do not need to reify the "future" in order to ask fundamentally important questions about schools, schooling, and society. Alley and Jung seem to contradict certain aspects of futurism by noting that "the future is determined by the choices made today" and that "the decisions teachers [and I would add other public and private sector persons of influence] make now—or fail to make—will establish the nature of the educational system of the next century." Although these claims may be overstated, they are important in that they draw attention to the impact of the will and intentions of those alive today. Let's hope that futurism will serve to inform us about what *we* can do for the future. And let's take some degree of comfort in what Dean Acheson apparently once said: "The best thing about the future is that it comes one day at a time."

Implications

A recurring theme in my remarks has been to underscore the moral content of stewardship that is inherent in the nature of the work of educators, whether leaders in classrooms, teams, departments, schools, school districts, or state houses. As Goodlad (1990) argues, "the most compelling moral imperatives for [educators] pertain to their necessary vigilance in ensuring that their school fulfills its designated functions well and equitably and to the nature of the unique relationship between the teacher and the taught" (p. 53).

It is not easy to work through the philosophical grounding of these issues, as our book *The Moral Dimensions of Teaching* (Goodlad, Soder, & Sirotnik, 1990) unintentionally illustrates. Yet it is a lot easier to talk about moral matters than it is to figure out their specific implications in the day-to-day work of educators in schools. For example, in my chapter (Sirotnik, 1990), I struggle through what I hope is a reasonable argument for moral commitments to the ideas of inquiry, knowledge, competence, caring, and social justice—ideas that should form the core of the relationship between teachers and learners and that should give warrant to the work of educators as a profession. Yet these ideas are abstractions—critically important abstractions—that must be constructed and reconstructed in the context of experience (Cherryholmes, 1988).

This interpretive struggle is central to the curriculum for educating teachers for leadership and change. There are countless texts and articles that could be useful in this regard in addition to the one above and others already cited. To illustrate the variety of additional readings that could be useful in promoting critical and reflective discourse, consider this eclectic mixture: Bellah, Madsen, Sullivan, Swidler, and Tipton (1985); Dewey (1916); Giroux (1988); Gutmann (1987); Kotlowitz (1991); Noddings (1984); Sergiovanni (1992); Sockett (1993); Tom (1984); and Tyack (1974). Whatever materials they use, cohorts of teachers (or teachers-to-be) will need to be actively involved through the use of reflective seminars, problem-based learning approaches, and case study methods relying on hypothetical and real-life ethical and moral dilemmas encountered in schools.[1]

One interesting set of readings using case study materials that bridges the gap between the moral and pedagogical dimensions of teaching and leadership is the Thinking About Education Series (Feinberg & Soltis, 1992; Fenstermacher & Soltis, 1992; Phillips & Soltis, 1992; Strike & Soltis, 1992; Walker & Soltis, 1992). In effect, this series attempts to link arguments about the moral purposes of public schooling in democratic society with curriculum deliberation, debates on appropriate methods of teaching and learning, and considerations of ethics and moral dilemmas. Missing from this series, but readily found in many other sources (examples already cited above), is the link to organizational theory and improvement, and the principles and practices of schools as centers of inquiry and change.

Finally, there is a plethora of literature on organizational leadership generally (just look over a recent Jossey-Bass flier, for example) and a rapidly growing literature on teacher leadership and decision making more specifically (for example, see the reviews by Conley, 1991, and Smylie, 1994; the many edited volumes of readings such as Astuto, 1993, Lieberman & Miller, 1991, and Little & McLaughlin, 1993; and the thematic issues of popular journals such as *Educational Leadership*, 1993, the *Journal of Teacher Education*, 1988, and *Phi Delta Kappan*, 1993.)

In conclusion, I should note that I have not paid much attention to whether the curriculum for educating teachers for leadership and change should be one for preservice or inservice programs. This is probably because the essential features of the curriculum belong in both domains. Although content and pedagogy will likely be adjusted in line with learners' experiences, withholding a leadership curriculum when educating beginning teachers, for example, will prove to be counterproductive and will only reinforce existing conventions and stereotypes. Exercising significant and responsible influence demands a curriculum for lifelong learning.

Note

1. Our work in creating an alternative program for preparing school principals provides one possible approach for developing, organizing and conducting this kind of leadership curriculum (see Mueller, 1993; Sirotnik & Mueller, 1993).

References

Astuto, T. A. (Ed.). (1993). *When teachers lead.* University Park, PA: University Council for Educational Administration.

Bellah, R. N., Madsen, R., Sullivan, W. M., Swidler, A., & Tipton, S. M. (1985). *Habits of the heart: Individualism and commitment in American life.* New York: Harper & Row.

Cherryholmes, C. H. (1988). *Power and criticism: Poststructural investigations in education.* New York: Teachers College Press.

Conley, S. (1991). Review of research on teacher participation in school decision making. In G. Grant (Ed.), *Review of research in education, 17*, 225-266.

Dewey, J. (1916). *Democracy and education.* New York: Macmillan.

Educational Leadership. (1993). *51*(2).

Feinberg, W., & Soltis, J. F. (1992). *School and society.* New York: Teachers College Press.

Fenstermacher, G. D., & Soltis, J. F. (1992). *Approaches to teaching.* New York: Teachers College Press.

Giroux, H. A. (1988). *Schooling and the struggle for public life: Critical pedagogy in the modern age.* Minneapolis: University of Minnesota Press.

Goodlad, J. I. (1990). *Teachers for our nation's schools.* San Francisco: Jossey-Bass.

Goodlad, J. I., Soder, R., & Sirotnik, K. A. (Eds.). (1990). *The moral dimensions of teaching.* San Francisco: Jossey-Bass.

Gutmann, A. (1987). *Democratic education.* Princeton, NJ: Princeton University Press.

Johnson, T. J. (1972). *Professions and power.* London: Macmillan.

Journal of Teacher Education. (1988). *39*(1).

Kotlowitz, A. (1991). *There are no children here.* New York: Anchor.

Lieberman, A., & Miller, L. (Eds.). (1991). *Staff development for education in the '90s: New demands, new realities, new perspectives.* New York: Teachers College Press.

Little, J. W., & McLaughlin, M. W. (Eds.). (1993). *Teachers' work: Individuals, colleagues and contexts.* New York: Teachers College Press.

Mueller, K. K. (1993). *A five-year evaluative case study of an innovative program for the preparation of school principals.* Unpublished doctoral dissertation, University of Washington, Seattle.

Noddings, N. (1984). *Caring: A feminine approach to ethics and moral education.* Berkeley: University of California Press.

Phi Delta Kappan. (1993). *75*(3).

Phillips, D. C., & Soltis, J. F. (1992). *Perspectives on learning.* New York: Teachers College Press.

Schaefer, R. J. (1967). *The school as a center of inquiry.* New York: Harper & Row.

Schön, D. A. (1983). *The reflective practitioner: How professionals think in action.* New York: Basic Books.

Sergiovanni, T. J. (1992). *Moral leadership.* San Francisco: Jossey-Bass.

Sirotnik, K. A. (1989). The school as the center of change. In T. J. Sergiovanni & J. H. Moore (Eds.), *Schooling for tomorrow: Directing reforms to issues that count* (pp. 89-113). Boston: Allyn & Bacon.

Sirotnik, K. A. (1990). Society, schooling, teaching, and preparing to teach. In J. I. Goodlad, R. Soder, & K. A. Sirotnik (Eds.), *The moral dimensions of teaching* (pp. 296-327). San Francisco: Jossey-Bass.

Sirotnik, K. A., & Mueller, K. K. (1993). Challenging the wisdom of conventional principal preparation programs and getting away with it (so far). In J. Murphy (Ed.), *Preparing tomorrow's school leaders: Alternative designs* (pp. 57-83). University Park, PA: University Council on Educational Administration.

Smylie, M. A. (1994). Redesigning teachers' work: Connections to the classroom. In L. Darling-Hammond (Ed.), *Review of Educational Research, 20,* 129-177.

Sockett, H. (1993). *The moral base for teacher professionalism.* New York: Teachers College Press.

Soder, R. (1990). The rhetoric of teacher professionalization. In J. I. Goodlad, R. Soder, & K. A. Sirotnik (Eds.), *The moral dimensions of teaching* (pp. 35-86). San Francisco: Jossey-Bass.

Strike, K. A., & Soltis, J. F. (1992). *The ethics of teaching.* New York: Teachers College Press.

Tom, A. E. (1984). *Teaching as a moral craft.* White Plains, NY: Longman.

Tyack, D. (1974). *The one best system: The history of American urban education.* Cambridge, MA: Harvard University Press.

Walker, D. F., & Soltis, J. F. (1992). *Curriculum and its aims.* New York: Teachers College Press.

Zeichner, K., & Liston, D. (1987). Teaching student teachers to reflect. *Harvard Educational Review, 57,* 23-48.

13 Changing Role of the Teacher

Joseph Murphy

Joseph Murphy is Professor and Chair, Department of Educational Leadership, Peabody College of Vanderbilt University. His work focuses on school improvement with particular interest in the role that school leaders can play in the process. Recent books include *The Landscape of Educational Leadership: Reframing the Education of School Administrators* (1992), *Restructuring Schools: Capturing and Assessing the Phenomena* (1991), and *Understanding the Principalship: Metaphorical Themes 1920 to 1990* (with Lynn G. Beck, 1993).

Throughout this volume, a number of important themes emerge. Perhaps the three most important are reflected in the title of the yearbook itself: (a) change is on the agenda for schools; (b) teachers need to be key actors in helping define and shape that change (see Jacobs, Chapter 7); and (c) if teachers are to assume this more proactive role, the education they receive will need to change as well. In this chapter, the focus is on the first two themes. I begin with an analysis of the forces that appear to be propelling change efforts in our system of education for children and young adults. I then turn to the responses of the education industry to these forces. In the final section, I examine how the changing nature of schooling is redefining the role of teachers.

Forces Reshaping Education

As has been true throughout the history of education reform, recent demands have originated outside the education profession. They are grounded primarily in social and economic concerns. In particular, three interrelated forces have combined to form a powerful platform for a fundamental restructuring of U.S. public education—a perceived crisis in the economy, the evolution toward a postindustrial world, and our changing social fabric.

Crisis in the Economy

At the base of proposed reforms in education is the belief that the United States is losing, and perhaps has already lost, its foremost position in the world economy—that its "once unchallenged preeminence in commerce, industry, science, and technological innovation" (National Commission on Excellence in Education, 1983, p. 5) has taken a terrible battering. Evidence of this belief is omnipresent in the reform documents that have fueled the educational reform movements of the 1980s and 1990s. Reformers then proceed to draw connections between the state of the economy and the health of our nation's schools: "The 1980's will be remembered for two developments: the beginning of a sweeping reassessment of the basis of the nation's economic strength and an outpouring of concern for the quality of American education. The connection between these two streams of thought is strong and growing" (Carnegie Forum on Education and the Economy, 1986, p. 11). The development of this causal linkage between schooling and the economy allows reformers both to document the failure of the educational enterprise and to establish a rationale for that failure. To complete the cycle, critics return to the very institutions they blame for these failures and ask them to remedy the economic ills plaguing society.

The Evolution to a Postindustrial World

In this period of economic upheaval and demographic changes, most organizations are being forced to examine their fundamental structural assumptions. Bureaucracy—the basic infrastructure of organizations in the industrial world—is ill suited to the demands of our demographically diverse information society of the 21st century. Bureaucratic tenets not only are being viewed as less than useful, but in many instances are actually considered to be harmful (see Kowalski, Chapter 10). Hierarchy of authority is viewed as detrimental to the cultivation of commitment and creativity in the workplace. Impersonality is found to be incompatible with cooperative work efforts. And specialization and division of labor coupled with the separation of labor and management seem to be both ineffective and inefficient strategies.

Whatever label one chooses to describe postindustrial organizations, it is clear that methods of performing work therein will look considerably different from those in hierarchically based ones. There is little use for the core correlates of bureaucracy. Also coming into focus is the understanding that schools are and will continue to be increasingly shaped by the need to organize collective efforts consistent with the evolution of organizational structures in the larger environment. Just as schools have mirrored the industrial age's bureaucratic model during the 20th century, so must they adopt a more heterarchical model as society moves into the information age. Further, just as new language is being developed to describe these inchoate structures, so too will new roles evolve to describe the work of the men and women who teach in them.

The Changing Social Fabric

As Gmelch and Parkay (Chapter 3) and Alley and Jung (Chapter 12) document, the fabric of our society is changing. It is being rewoven in some places and is unraveling in others, resulting in conditions that have powerful implications for schools. At the heart of these revisions are demographic shifts that often appear to overwhelm the ability of society and schools to respond. Minority enrollments in schools are increasing. A quarter century hence, nearly half of all U.S. students will be nonwhite. The country is experiencing rapid growth in the number of students whose primary language is other than English. More and more children come from single-parent homes (25% of all families are headed by a single parent) or from families in which both parents work outside the home.

At the same time that these new threads are being woven into the fabric of U.S. society, other parts of that fabric are unraveling. The number of social ills confronting society appears to be expanding geometrically. Ever-increasing numbers of families are falling into poverty. Children are disproportionately represented among the ranks of the poor, and the number of children in poverty—currently one in five— continues to grow. Concomitantly, we are bombarded with news of alarming increases in measures of dysfunctions and ill health among youth and their families: unemployment, unwanted pregnancies, alcohol and drug abuse, and violence. A particularly troublesome aspect of this situation is the fact that these are the students—low-income, minority, and disadvantaged young-sters—with whom schools have historically been least successful. To continue to operate schools as we have in the past is a recipe for failure.

The Changing Nature of Schooling

Responses to the three forces described above—jumpstarting the economy, moving schooling into the information age, and tackling the needs of a rapidly changing society—are leading to important changes in schooling, changes that in turn carry important implications for the role of teachers. In this section, I attempt to capture the most important alterations to the infrastructure of schooling under the following three headings— the marketization of schooling, the development of schools as communities, and the infusion of constructivist views of learning.[1]

Marketization

One direction in which these external forces are pushing education is toward the marketization of U.S. public education. Three interconnected movements—the privatization of schooling, the inculcation of market principles in schools, and deregulation—define the marketization theme.

Privatization. Buttressed by data suggesting that private schools out-perform public ones as well as by a renewed interest in the benefits of competition, plans to privatize schooling are quickly rising to the forefront of the reform agenda. On the more radical end of the privatization contin-uum are efforts to redefine public education to include private schools. The reemergence of voucher proposals that allow tax dollars to flow to any school, private or public, as well as some of the more comprehensive choice programs fall within this category. Such proposals in effect take public schools into the private sector.

A second strategy encompasses efforts to expand the availability of alternative schools. The development of an alternative private system of schooling—possibly vying with public institutions for tuition dollars—is a good example of this strategy.

The charter school movement that allows (and sometimes encourages) schools to opt out of district control—thus turning education into a cottage industry—is a third method being used to privatize schooling. Controlled choice plans are the least radical of the privatization schemes. These plans generally unfold within existing district structures and thus by definition, choice is limited to traditionally defined public schools. Within this constraint, however, efforts are undertaken to use parental choice—and accompanying market forces—as leverage to instill greater sensitivity and responsiveness to client needs and interests.

The benefits of these privatization schemes are open to question, and similar ideas mean different things in different states and different school systems, but there is little doubt that these schemes are designed to introduce into schools the underpinnings of the market philosophy, especially market-sensitive measures of accountability.

Market Principles. Market principles are also increasingly finding their way into the routines of transformed schools. At the district level, school systems are finding it desirable to contract out for services rather than to provide everything in-house, a movement paralleling trends in the corporate world. As the district-level monopoly on providing services is dismantled through school deregulation, individual schools in turn are purchasing services from whomever they believe offers the best product at the best price. In a practice unheard of only a quarter century ago, and even more recently limited to such peripheral sectors of school operations as transportation and food services, schools and school districts are increasingly turning to private contractors for a wide array of goods and services, including in the most radical cases the total management of the school district by for-profit firms. Concomitantly, schools are being treated more like private enterprises. Demands for accountability are being accompanied by additional degrees of freedom at the site level. Individual schools are widening the extent to which they control their goals, budgets, organizational structures, core technology, and staff. In return, they are being asked to adopt operating routines that are more consistent with those found in competitive enterprises.

Deregulation. On a more indirect front, efforts are afoot to extricate schools from a confining web of governmental regulations. This deregulation thrust includes efforts to disentangle schools from federal, state, and district guidelines and policies. It is occurring on a broad front employing three different strategies: full deregulation, enhanced flexibility, and waivers. Under the most radical deregulation model, the entire regulatory structure is pulled back. Schools are given goals (or in some cases asked to provide their own) and are held accountable for results. Considerable autonomy in the methods and procedures used to achieve those goals is granted to schools. Under the enhanced flexibility strategy, the regulatory framework remains in place but is pared back to eliminate excessive and overly confining directives. The waiver approach allows schools to seek permission to override regulations that they believe interfere with the development of locally sensitive improvement programs. Originally the most widely employed deregulation option, waivers are giving way to more radical measures to pull schools out of the web of government directives, policies, guidelines, and rules.

Schools as Communities

As Bredeson (in Chapter 2) and others in this volume reveal, in the still-forming image of schools for the 21st century, the hierarchical bureaucratic organizational structures that have defined schooling since the onslaught of scientific management give way to systems that are more organic, more decentralized, and more professionally controlled. The basic shift is from a *"power over* approach . . . to a *power to* approach" (Sergiovanni, 1991, p. 57).

In these redesigned, postindustrial school organizations, traditional patterns of relationships are altered. Authority flows are less hierarchical; for example, traditional distinctions between administrators and teachers begin to blur. Role definitions are both more general and more flexible—specialization is no longer viewed as a strength. Leadership is dispersed and connected to competence for needed tasks rather than to formal position. Independence and isolation are replaced by cooperative work. Further, the traditional structural orientation in schools is overshadowed by a focus on the human element. The operant goal is no longer the maintenance of the organizational infrastructure but rather the development of human resources. Developing learning climates and organizational adaptivity replaces the more traditional emphasis on uncovering and applying the one best model of performance. A premium is placed on organizational flexibility. The metaphors being developed for this new design for schools—for example, from "teacher as worker" to "teacher as leader"—nicely portray these fundamental changes.

Constructivist Views of Learning

Preliminary sketches of redesigned schools suggest that we may be on the threshold of significant changes in the core technology of schooling. A more robust understanding of the education production function is beginning to be translated into new ways of thinking about learning and teaching. The strongest theoretical and disciplinary influence on education—behavioral psychology—is being pushed off center stage by constructivist psychology and newer sociological perspectives on learning. This shift toward "research on cognition as a basis for understanding how people learn casts an entirely different perspective on how the schooling process should be redesigned" (Hutchins, 1988, p. 47). Underlying this change are radically different ways of thinking about the educability of children. Those who are at the forefront of transforming schools that were historically organized to produce results consistent with the normal curve, to sort youth into the various strata needed to fuel the economy, see education being transformed to ensure equal opportunity for all learners. This transformation has a significant impact on classroom activity.

At the center of this newly forming vision about schooling for tomorrow are fairly radical changes in assumptions about intelligence and knowledge (Ponzio & Fisher, Chapter 11). The alpha paradigm of knowledge—the view that "knowledge can be assumed to be an external entity existing independently of human thought and action, and hence, something about which one can be objective" (Fisher, 1990, p. 82)—"dominant for so long in classroom practice, has begun to be critically examined in a new way" (p. 84). A new view, one that holds that knowledge is internal and subjective, that it "depends on the values of the persons working with it and the context within which that work is conducted" (p. 82), is receiving serious consideration. Thus, the new educational design considers "knowledge not as somehow in the possession of the teacher, waiting to be transmitted to the student or to be used to treat the students' problems, but as mutually constructed by teacher and student in order to make sense of human experience" (Petrie, 1990, pp. 17-18). Learning is seen as a social phenomenon and considerable attention is devoted to the social origins of cognition.

New views about what is worth learning characterize emerging perspectives on schooling for the 21st century. The traditional emphasis on acquiring information is being replaced by a focus on learning to learn and on the ability to use knowledge. New perspectives on the context of learning are also being developed, directing attention to active learning. A century-old concern for independent work and competition—a focus on the individual dimension of human existence, especially on individual ability—is slowly receding in favor of more cooperative learning relationships—a focus on the social dimensions of human existence.

New ways of thinking about learning are also emerging in postindustrial organizations. Vigorous attacks on the practice of tracking are accompanied by calls for a core curriculum for all students. Reformers involved in the redesign of education are also tackling the traditional emphasis in schools on content coverage, rote learning of basic skills, and reliance on textbooks as the primary source of knowledge. They promulgate an alternative image of a core technology that (a) reflects an interdisciplinary vision, (b) features a curriculum that is more vertical and less horizontal—that covers fewer topics in more depth, (c) highlights higher-order thinking skills for all students, (d) spotlights the use of technology and original source documents in lieu of textbooks, (e) underscores the use of a broadened evaluation system that highlights authentic measures of assessment, and (f) pushes service learning to center stage (see Ponzio & Fisher, Chapter 11).[2]

In schools of the postindustrial era, a learner-centered pedagogy replaces the more traditional model of teacher-centered instruction. The model of the teacher as sage on a stage, in which instructors are viewed as content specialists who possess relevant knowledge that they transmit to students through telling, is replaced by an approach in which teaching is more of a guiding function. The student becomes the primary actor. Substantive conversation replaces conventional classroom talk and didactic instruction. Analysts believe that in the 21st century, schools will be conceived of as "knowledge work" organizations (Schlechty, 1990, p. 42), learning will be seen as the construction of understanding, and teaching will be viewed as facilitating this development. Students are seen as "producers of knowledge" and teachers "as managers of learning experiences" (Hawley, 1989, p. 23). The focus is on learning, not on the delivery system.

The Changing Role of Teachers

As new understandings of the roles, rules, relationships, and responsibilities that govern the daily work educational professionals are forged, it is critical that we understand the implications of these changes for teachers. (Bredeson, Chapter 2)

If schools are changing along the dimensions described above, what does this mean for the teaching role? It is in answering this question that insights about reforming teacher education take shape. It seems to me that what transformational change spotlights is what Rallis (1990) calls "an elevated conception of teaching" (p. 193). Teachers are considered more as professionals and less as semiskilled laborers, employees, and technicians. Freed from the technocratic metaphor that currently describes their work, teachers will be more concerned with developing the purposes of schooling than with implementing predetermined goals. They will also exercise considerably more control throughout the school over the core technology—instructional strategies, curriculum, and assessment. At the same time, they will as a collective wield significantly more influence than they have in the past over the resources that support learning and teaching.

One way to envision these changes is to think metaphorically about the evolving role of teachers in schools undergoing transformational reform. Conceptualizing teaching as a set of roles that unfolds at three levels—the classroom, the school, and the larger school community—the following roles appear likely to define tomorrow's teachers: teacher as guide, teacher as decision maker, teacher as leader, teacher as colleague, teacher as learner, and teacher as student advocate (see McCarthey & Peterson, 1989; Murphy, 1991).

Teacher as Guide

At the classroom level, constructivist perspectives of learning exercise important influences over the activities of teachers. Teachers are no longer in the knowledge transmission business but act as guides and coaches who help students construct their own understandings of the world. The role of the teacher is one of empowering students. Educating for insight (Perkins, 1991) and teaching for meaningful understanding (Murphy, 1991) replace teaching as telling as the dominant instructional metaphor. In the definition of this new role for teachers, the limitations of reductionist views of instruction embedded in technical conceptions of teaching are confronted. The complexity of teaching is acknowledged. Instruction becomes less generic and more personalized. Developmentally appropriate instruction moves to center stage. Teachers are less concerned with finding the most effective instructional strategy than they are with expanding the variety of approaches needed to tailor classroom experiences to the needs of individual children.

Teacher as Decision Maker

Teachers in restructuring schools are assuming control over decisions that traditionally have been the province of school administrators. At its core, this redefinition means that teachers historically organized to carry out instructional designs and to implement curricular materials developed from afar begin to exercise considerably more influence over their profession and the routines of the workplace. As noted above, analysts see this reorganization playing out in a variety of ways at the school level. Teachers have a much more active voice in developing the goals and purposes of schooling—goals that act to delimit or expand the conception of teaching itself. They also have a good deal more to say about the curricular structures and pedagogical approaches employed in their schools—how time is used, how students are organized for learning, what materials are to be used, and so forth.

Teacher as Leader

The notion of teacher as leader plays out at both the classroom and school levels. At the classroom level, the constructivist perspective on learning we described earlier moves teachers out of—and students into—the central role of worker, of knowledge builder. The teaching role becomes much less one of performing and much more of helping others—students in this case—to act. Concomitantly, much of what teachers do as decision makers and colleagues pulls them into leadership roles at the school level. This, as Sykes and Elmore (1989) remind us, entails "acknowledging and institutionalizing the central managerial role of teachers" (p. 85).

Teacher as Colleague

Analysts who connect teaching and the types of changes unfolding in schools discussed above believe that restructuring will lead to a teaching profession that is much more collegial than it has been in the past. In conventional practice, teachers are entrepreneurs of their own classrooms. They orchestrate their own operations nearly independently of their peers and engage in few leadership or decision-making activities outside their own cubicles. They are viewed as pedagogical specialists whose function it is to deliver educational services to their young charges. Little time and energy are available for or devoted to self-renewal and professional growth with colleagues. In restructuring schools, as Ponticell, Olson, and Charlier (Chapter 5) so nicely show, the isolation that is so deeply ingrained in the structure and culture of the profession gives way to more collaborative efforts among teachers. At the macro level, teachers are redefining their roles to include collaborative management of the profession, especially providing direction for professional standards. At a more micro level, new organizational structures are being created to allow teachers to plan and teach together and to make important decisions about the nature of their roles.

Teacher as Learner

Central to the behavioral view of learning and the hierarchical model of schooling that undergird education today is the notion of the teacher as the fount of knowledge. In contrast, constructivist conceptions of learning and nonorganizationally grounded views of schooling ask teachers to become members of a community of learners. As Carter and Larke (Chapter 4) help us see, teaching and learning form a seamless web of activity for teachers in restructuring schools.

Teacher as Student Advocate

It appears likely that teachers in restructuring schools will be much more active than they have been heretofore at the interface of the school and the community—in the past the purview of formal school leaders, that is, school administrators. Gmelch and Parkay (Chapter 3) are correct in concluding that "in their new leadership roles, teachers are being called upon to form new partnerships with business and industry; institutions of higher education; social service agencies; professional associations; and local, state, and federal government agencies." As teachers assume more fully their new roles as leaders and decision makers, it is likely that they will be much more active in fostering links between schools and a wide variety of external agencies.

Notes

1. The material in this section is taken from Murphy (1992, 1993) and is used with the permission of the publisher, Corwin Press. J. Murphy, *The Landscape of Leadership Preparation: Reframing the Education of School Admin-*

istrators (pp. 115-121). Newbury Park, CA © 1992; and J. Murphy, Restructuring: In Search of a Movement. In J. Murphy & P. Hallinger (Eds.), *Restructuring Schooling: Learning From Ongoing Efforts* (pp. 9-11). Newbury Park, CA © 1993.

2. It is important to reinforce the message of Glickman, Lunsford, and Szuminski (Chapter 1) that even these "desirable interventions" can miss the mark if they are not grounded in a common mission of education.

References

Carnegie Forum on Education and the Economy. (1986). *A nation prepared: Teachers for the 21st century.* Washington, DC: Author.

Fisher, C.W. (1990). The research agenda project as prologue. *Journal of Research in Mathematics Education, 21*(1), 81-89.

Hawley, W. D. (1989). Looking backward at education reform. *Education Week, 9*(9), 23, 35.

Hutchins, C.L. (1988). Design as the missing piece in education. In Far West Laboratory for Educational Research and Development, *The redesign of education: A collection of papers concerned with comprehensive educational reform* (Vol. 1, pp. 47-49). San Francisco: Far West Laboratory.

McCarthey, S.J., & Peterson, P.L. (1989, March). *Teacher roles: Weaving new patterns in classroom practice and school organization.* Paper presented at the annual meeting of the American Educational Research Association, San Francisco.

Murphy, J. (1991). *Restructuring schools: Capturing and assessing the phenomena.* New York: Teachers College Press.

Murphy, J. (1992). *The landscape of leadership preparation: Reframing the education of school administrators.* Newbury Park, CA: Corwin.

Murphy, J. (1993). Restructuring: In search of a movement. In J. Murphy & P. Hallinger (Eds.), *Restructuring schooling: Learning from ongoing efforts* (pp. 1-31). Newbury Park, CA: Corwin.

National Commission on Excellence in Education. (1983, April). *A nation at risk: The imperative of educational reform.* Washington, DC: U.S. Government Printing Office.

Perkins, D. N. (1991, October). Educating for insight. *Educational Leadership, 49*(2), 4-8.

Petrie, H. G. (1990). Reflecting on the second wave of reform: Restructuring the teaching profession. In S. L. Jacobson & J. A. Conway

(Eds.), *Educational leadership in an age of reform* (pp. 14-29). New York: Longman.

Rallis, S. F. (1990). Professional teachers and restructured schools: Leadership challenges. In B. Mitchell & L. L. Cunningham (Eds.), *Educational leadership and changing contexts of families, communities, and schools* (89th NSSE yearbook, pp. 184-209). Chicago: University of Chicago Press.

Schlechty, P. C. (1990). *Schools for the 21st century: Leadership imperatives for educational reform*. San Francisco: Jossey-Bass.

Sergiovanni, T. J. (1991). *The principalship: A reflective practice perspective* (2nd ed.). Boston: Allyn & Bacon.

Sykes, G., & Elmore, R. F. (1989). Making schools manageable: Policy and administration for tomorrow's schools. In J. Hannaway & R. Crowson (Eds.), *The politics of reforming school administration* (pp. 77-94). New York: Falmer.

Challenge for Teacher Educators

Educating teachers for leadership and change requires that teacher educators commit firmly to working collaboratively with colleagues in schools, educational leadership, human services, businesses, and communities in order to establish connections between internal and external forces of change. *Teacher Education Yearbook III* challenges teacher educators to examine critically themselves and the programs they represent. Specifically, the themes listed on the next page may serve as a guide for self and programmatic reflection.

If you wish to become involved in the conceptualization and development of the National Teacher Leadership Forum designed to promote teacher leadership and school change, contact:

Mary John O'Hair
Department of Educational Leadership and Policy Studies
University of Oklahoma
Norman, OK 73019-0260
(405) 325-4202
mjohair@aardvark.ucs.uoknor.edu

Democratic Schools	Constructivist Teaching and Learning	Complex Cultural and Sociopolitical Organizations	Moral and Ethical Guidance
Understand the purpose of public education.	View teaching not as dissemination but as mentoring.	Respect and celebrate diversity.	Understand that one cannot act on the basis of knowledge alone.
Avoid distractions that weaken original purpose.	See teachers not as content providers but as knowledgeable guides.	Examine social reconstruction and schooling.	Articulate a set of values and beliefs to guide actions.
Help guide students in identifying, analyzing, and solving problems facing their local communities.	Consider learning not as receiving but as interacting.	Advocate a broader social reconstruction along with school change and teacher leadership.	Engage in ethical inquiry designed to prepare the *person* rather than to prepare the person for a *role*.
Model democratic governance.	Model constructivist teaching and learning.	Develop collaborative work cultures with community.	Emphasize concern for values or role of values in teacher education programs.
Debate "big" issues involving the teaching and learning.	View students not as passive recipients but active agents in constructing their own understandings.	Focus on the inclusion of all community groups in school decision making.	Avoid behavior in the absence of values and beliefs.

Index